ESSAYS

IN

HONOR

OF

EDWARD

FARLEY

THEOLOGY AND THE INTERHUMAN

ESSAYS
IN
HONOR
OF
EDWARD
FARLEY

THEOLOGY AND THE INTERHUMAN

EDITED BY
Robert R. Williams

TRINITY PRESS INTERNATIONAL
Valley Forge, Pennsylvania

The essay "Issues of *Good and Evil*" by Walter Lowe originally appeared in *Religious Studies Review,* July 1995, and is used with permission.

Trinity Press International, P.O. Box 851, Valley Forge, PA 19482–0851

Library of Congress Cataloging-in-Publication Data
Theology and the interhuman : essays in honor of Edward Farley /
  edited by Robert R. Williams. — 1st ed.
    p. cm.
  Includes bibliographical references and index.
  ISBN 1-56338-126-5 (cloth : alk. paper). — ISBN 1-56338-127-3
(pbk. : alk. paper)
    1. Theology. 2. Farley, Edward, 1929- . 3. Farley, Edward,
1929- Good and evil. 4. Farley, Edward, 1929- Theologia.
I. Farley, Edward, 1929- . II. Williams, Robert R.
BR50.T434 1995
230–dc20   95-23845
                                                      CIP
Printed in the United States of America

95   96   97   98   99   10   9   8   7   6   5   4   3   2   1

EDWARD FARLEY

Contents

Part Three
ESSAYS ON PRACTICAL THEOLOGY

Part Four
REPLY BY EDWARD FARLEY

Preface

The essays prepared for this volume are intended to recognize, honor, and respond to the multifaceted theological thought of Edward Farley. Farley's constructive theology was inaugurated in his theological prolegomena, *Ecclesial Man* (1975), that appropriated not only Husserl's phenomenological method for theology but also Husserl's concept of the life-world (*Lebenswelt*). The life-world, as the concrete historical a priori underlying theoretical thought, is an interhuman domain that is also the locus of faith and ethics. In a sequel volume, *Ecclesial Reflection* (1982), Farley offered an extensive critique of the "House of Authority" that prepared the way for his historicist reformulation of theological method and inquiry, that retrieves the tradition demolished in its first part. The practical implications of Farley's theological prolegomena were developed in *Theologia* (1983), hailed as a landmark in the history of North American theological education. Farley's constructive theology proper appeared in *Good and Evil* (1990), which is a theological anthropology rivaling Reinhold Niebuhr's *Nature and Destiny of Man* and Paul Tillich's *Courage to Be* in its scope and depth. However, for those familiar with Schleiermacher's discussion of the three forms of theological propositions — namely, statements about human self-consciousness (to wit, life-world ecclesial community), statements about world (cosmology), and statements about God (rational metaphysical theology) — *Good and Evil* may also be regarded as a theology of the first form of proposition. It is a controversial work, its reflective ontology of human existence appearing to be too close to Schleiermacher for some and its account of being-founded too close to Barth for others, quite possibly because Farley's theological portraiture and concept of determinate theological universality are heavily influenced by Ernst Troeltsch.

The title we have chosen for this volume, *Theology and the Interhuman*, articulates both a central theme carefully and technically developed in Farley's constructive theology and a broad connection between theology and other concerns: reflective ontology and deconstruction, intersubjectivity, ethics, and social-political criticism of advanced industrial society. The essays chosen for the volume are unified by the title in this latter broad sense. As a result, many voices and concerns are in play, from the philosophical to the practical and socio-political. These different voices and levels of concern reflect the diverse, multifaceted character of Farley's work.

Some of the essays in this volume concentrate on Farley's historicist philosophical theology, focusing on or responding to *Ecclesial Man, Ecclesial Reflection,* and *Good and Evil* as well as work currently in progress. Others respond to his analysis of theological education (*Theologia, Fragility of Knowledge*). Still others deal with or extend his work into various areas of practical theology. Many of the essays are critical and continue conversations that have been going on for some time.

This project began with the intention of recognizing and honoring Edward Farley. But a recognition that is one-sided falls short of its full reality and threatens to turn its recipient into an object or an icon. Owing to a happy set of contingencies, the project has turned into a dialogue between its contributors and Edward Farley, who will have the last word, at least as far as this volume is concerned.

I wish to thank the contributors for their enthusiastic support for the project, for the seriousness with which they took their assignments, and for the quality of their work. Thanks also go to Hal Rast of Trinity Press International for his interest and support. Finally, I want to thank Edward Farley for accepting a surprise invitation to join this train as it was arriving at the station and thereby making what will probably prove to be for many the most important contribution to the volume.

ROBERT R. WILLIAMS

Contributors

DAVID BUTTRICK is Professor of Homiletics and Liturgics at Vanderbilt University Divinity School. Among his books are *Homiletic* (1987), *Preaching Jesus Christ* (1988), *The Mystery and the Passion* (1992), and *A Captive Voice: The Liberation of Preaching* (1994).

JOHN B. COBB, JR., is Professor Emeritus of the School of Theology at Claremont and continues limited teaching at Claremont Graduate School. He is a co-director of the Center for Process Studies. Among his books are *The Structure of Christian Existence, Christ in a Pluralistic Age,* and *Can Christ Become Good News Again?*

JAMES O. DUKE is Professor of the History of Christianity and Historical Theology at Brite Divinity School, Texas Christian University. He is author of *Horace Bushnell: On the Vitality of Biblical Language* and editor and translator of three Schleiermacher texts: *Hermeneutics; On the "Glaubenslehre": Two Letters to Dr. Lücke;* and *Christian Caring: Selections from "The Practical Theology."*

WENDY FARLEY (Edward Farley's daughter) is associate professor in the college and chair of Theological Studies in the Graduate School of Religion at Emory University. She is the author of *Tragic Vision and Divine Compassion: A Contemporary Theodicy* and has just completed a manuscript, *Eros for the Other: An Essay on Truth,* which will be published by Penn State Press.

JACK FORSTMAN is Finney Professor of Historical Theology at Vanderbilt University Divinity School and Graduate Department of Religion. He is author of *Word and Spirit: Calvin's Doctrine of Biblical Authority* (1962), *Christian Faith and the Church* (1964), *A Romantic Triangle: Schleiermacher and Early German Romanticism* (1977), and *Christian Faith in Dark Times: Theological Conflicts in the Shadow of Hitler* (1992), and is co-translator with James Duke of *Friedrich Schleiermacher's Hermeneutics* (1977).

MARY MCCLINTOCK FULKERSON teaches feminist theology at Duke University Divinity School. One of Edward Farley's graduate students in the late 1970s, she gives him credit for bringing her into the modern world theologically (for good or ill). Her book *Changing the Subject: Women's Discourses and Feminist Theology* is forthcoming from Fortress Press.

PETER C. HODGSON is Professor of Theology and chair of the Graduate Department of Religion at Vanderbilt. His most recent books are *God in History: Shapes of Freedom* (1989) and *Winds of the Spirit: A Constructive Christian Theology* (1994). He is currently completing an anthology of Hegel texts on religion for Fortress Press entitled *G. W. F. Hegel: Theologian of the Spirit*. He is editor and translator of the critical edition of Hegel's *Lectures on the Philosophy of Religion* (1984–87). He has been a colleague of Farley since he went to Vanderbilt in 1969.

DAVID H. KELSEY is Weigle Professor of Theology at Yale Divinity School. He is the author of *The Uses of Scripture in Christian Theology*, *The Fabric of Paul Tillich's Theology*, *To Understand God Truly: What's Theological about a Theological School*, and *Between Athens and Berlin: The Theological Education Debate*.

WALTER J. LOWE is Professor of Theology at Candler School of Theology at Emory University. A former student of Farley's, he is author of *Mystery and the Unconscious, Evil and the Unconscious*, and *Theology and Difference: The Wound of Reason*.

NANCY J. RAMSAY is Professor of Pastoral Theology at Louisville Presbyterian Theological Seminary. She received her Ph.D. from Vanderbilt University. An ordained minister in the Presbyterian Church (USA), she is a member and former chair of the Society for Pastoral Theology and a member in the American Association of Pastoral Counselors and the American Academy of Religion. Her book *Pastoral Diagnosis* is forthcoming from Fortress Press. She is author of "Sexual Abuse and Shame: The Travail of Recovery," in *Women in Travail and Transition: A New Pastoral Care*.

CHARLES E. SCOTT is Edwin Erle Sparks Professor of Philosophy at Pennsylvania State University. Previously he was Professor of Philosophy at Vanderbilt University. He has been executive director of the Society for Phenomenology and Existential Philosophy. Among his books are *The Language of Difference, The Question of Ethics*, and *On The Advantages and Disadvantages of Ethics and Politics*.

SHARON D. WELCH is Associate Professor of Religious Studies and Women Studies at the University of Missouri–Columbia. She graduated from Vanderbilt University Divinity School and has taught at Rhodes College and Harvard Divinity School. She is author of *Communities of Resistance and Solidarity* (1985) and *A Feminist Ethic of Risk* (1990).

BARBARA G. WHEELER is president of Auburn Theological Seminary and director of its Center for the Study of Theological Education. She has edited several volumes of essays on theological education, including, with Edward Farley, *Shifting Boundaries: Contextual Approaches to the Structure of Theological Education*. She has published articles on theological education and on congregations and American Protestantism.

ROBERT R. WILLIAMS is Professor of Philosophy at Hiram College. He is one of Farley's undergraduate students, for whom Farley also served as dissertation advisor in correspondence. He is author of *Schleiermacher the Theologian: The Construction of the Doctrine of God* (1978) and *Recognition: Fichte and Hegel on the Other* (1992) and is editor and translator of *I. A. Dorner: Divine Immutability Reconsidered* (1994). He is currently working on a monograph, *Hegel's Ethics of Recognition*, and translating Hegel's *Lectures on the Philosophy of Subjective Spirit 1827–28*.

PART ONE

Essays on
Philosophical Theology

➤ 1 ◄

Good and Evil in Process Perspective

JOHN B. COBB, JR.

I. Farley's Accomplishment

In *Good and Evil* Edward Farley has set a standard for theological work that few can match.[1] The book is encyclopedic in the scope and variety of the literature from which it draws. It references primarily the continental tradition of the past two centuries, but it shows familiarity also with Anglo-American literature. Far from being a synopsis of the work of others, however, it embodies control over the ideas and uses them for Farley's own original contribution. It is insightful, comprehensive, and wise. Every formulation is careful, precise, and well-supported. It is professional work of a sort that makes most of what has been written by theologians on anthropology appear amateurish.

The book is theological in that it deals with questions of central theological importance and is informed in its treatment by long study of the Jewish and Christian traditions. It is certainly not theological if that entails appealing to any one tradition as decisively authoritative. Every argument stands on its own merits in the context of public discourse.

Farley brings to the task long experience in phenomenological work. But the book is not narrowly or rigorously phenomenological. It describes a human condition with whatever tools commend themselves to Farley. The phenomenological method shows up especially in the care and objectivity with which phenomena are described.

Farley's objectivity is particularly impressive in Part One. This is his account of a human condition, drawing on scientific and philosophical sources. One would expect it to be written with the theological ideas of Part Two in mind in such a way that it would select from the vast body of literature that which lent itself best to this use. Instead, it seems simply to follow the most convincing arguments and descriptions. Farley makes no claim to avoid the universal human conditionedness, nor does he deny that his own work expresses a particular perspective. But his

3

training and temperament equip him to come as close to objectivity as is reasonably to be hoped.

The book provides an "ontology."[2] Farley is keenly sensitive to the bias against ontology in the contemporary literature that claims to be at the cutting edge. Hence he knows that his enterprise as a whole and as such seems to be out of step with current trends. His response is to survey the critical literature with great care, thoroughness, and even appreciation. He shows that much of what is objected to in most received ontological work is rightly subject to criticism. But he also shows that if this criticism is interpreted as a total rejection of ontology as such, it is self-contradictory. Even those who are most forceful in their criticism make continuous appeals to their own ontology in the process.

One major criticism is that ontological thinking neglects the radically historical character of all thought and reality. It describes what is as if it were necessarily that way. It supports essentialism and thus privileges some aspects of what is over others.

A second major criticism is that ontology distracts attention from issues that are immediate and urgent. These demand attention to the specific features of the situation rather than to the general. The ontological approach tends to support the status quo rather than to promote the needed changes.

Farley takes these criticisms seriously. But they do not call for total abandonment of the task of ontology. They call instead for replacement of inadequate ontologies with better ones, more sensitive to the dangers of misuse. Farley's ontology affirms the historicity of thought and reality and supports the goal of liberation.

Farley's defense of ontological thinking is remarkable for its lack of defensiveness. It expresses his irenic spirit and readiness to learn from others. It would be easy to drive home the inconsistencies and self-contradictions in the arguments used against ontology, but Farley does not press the advantage. Instead he listens for the valid point that is too often couched in exaggerated language. He affirms the critic for the valid point rather than attacking him or her for the inexact formulation of that point.

It would be quite possible to continue the adulation of this book. But that would not be the sort of honor Farley deserves. Even one who admires the accomplishment inevitably brings to the work a perspective different from that of the author. The ongoing task of further thinking is advanced when that difference is expressed and allowed to play its role.

I entitled this essay "*Good and Evil* in Process Perspective." By "process perspective" I refer to my own point of view as that has been shaped by years of immersion in process thought. From that point of view Farley's book offers very definite gifts, and I want to explain how this is so. Also from that point of view, the project is slightly skewed, and I want to explain why, if I had the equipment to pursue a similar project (which I do not), I would do it in a somewhat different way.

Process thought, like Farley's, is ontological. But the nature of the ontology differs in the two cases. Farley provides what phenomenologists once called a "regional ontology." He takes as his subject matter a widespread human condition and describes its structure. Process thought aims toward a general ontology or a metaphysics. It seeks and develops the implications of the structure of whatever is.

Despite this difference, Farley's defense of ontology applies to process ontology as well as to his own. His thorough survey of the arguments against ontology together with his convincing reply are a service for which process thinkers can only be grateful. But this does not mean that the differences are unimportant. In Section II I will comment on the weakness of process thought because of the extreme generality of its model and the important ways in which it can learn from Farley's work. In the following sections I will note the criticism that can be brought to bear on Farley's work from the perspective of this very general model.

II. The Contribution of *Good and Evil* to Process Theology

Process thought tends to move from the universal, that is, from what is true everywhere and for everything, to the very specific. This is not simply its expression of the tendency of metaphysicians generally. It is also an expression of the specific metaphysical assertions of process philosophy. These include the emphasis that no two entities are, or could possibly be, the same. Each is the product of its history or its past, and this cannot be the same in any two instances. Furthermore, exactly what any event will be is not decided until it occurs.

Given this emphasis on the radical historicity and contingency of events, process thinkers are leery of any attempt to describe such things as human nature. There is no essence embodied in all human beings and absent in all other creatures. Individual human beings are not to be understood by subsumption to what we know is true of all human beings. Each is what he or she has been constituted to be by his or her history and decision.

In general, from the process perspective, "laws" are statistical generalizations about the behavior of sets of entities. They do not "govern" the behavior of these entities. Successive generations of this type of entity, although profoundly influenced by their predecessors, may yet change their behavior. This means that laws also change.

I continue to subscribe to these views. Nevertheless, I also recognize the valid criticism repeatedly raised both without and within the community of process thinkers that this strong emphasis on the meta-physically universal and the concrete particular has prevented us from dealing helpfully and wisely with the vast structure of patterns that in fact mediates between these.[3] Much of what is most important for our lives consists of commonalities that are by no means metaphysically universal. Merely to point out that these commonalities change over time hardly suffices as a guide to life in the meantime, while they prevail.

Process thinkers have, of course, had to adopt many ideas about this intermediate level of generalizations that are not universal or static. We have been guided in doing so by the double question of whether the ideas are consistent with the process model of reality and whether they seem insightful and illuminating. Obviously, we have not all adopted the same ideas, but our common commitments and similar contexts often express themselves in attraction to the same or similar thinkers.

An example will help to clarify how this has worked. I select for this purpose the doctrine of sin. Whitehead's model of the ultimate unit of actuality, the actual occasion, includes the function of God as lure. That is, each occasion is called to some quite specific response to the actual world that informs and forms it, but whether it responds as called or resists that call and constitutes itself somewhat differently is decided by the actual occasion itself. At the human level this suggests a straight-forward doctrine of sin as, in New Testament language, *hamartia,* or missing the mark. To sin is to fail to actualize fully the ideal possibility given by God in and for that moment.

I find that understanding of sin satisfactory as far as it goes. But it does not go very far. The serious question is why we resist God's gift and call and how, in general, our resistance expresses itself. The relation of sin to the body, to society, to culture, to evil, to tragedy, and to redemption all remain to be examined and studied. The metaphysical analysis is not invalidated by these further investigations, but answers to them cannot be derived from the metaphysics and may not be especially advanced by it. In other words, the metaphysics does not help us directly with widespread historical and existential problems. Indeed, the impossibility of deriving from the metaphysics any conclusions about the contingent is part of what the metaphysics affirms.

Among my generation of process theologians, most turned to Reinhold Niebuhr for their doctrine of sin. Niebuhr developed his doctrine from the evidence with no authoritarian appeal. His analysis was congenial to Whiteheadian metaphysics and seemed intrinsically convincing. Along with his broader interpretation of history and of contemporary affairs, it provided a basis for relating process theology to the world in which we found ourselves. We might occasionally modify some of his formulations in light of our metaphysics,[4] but in general we relied on his authority.

It was not possible for us to establish a very positive relation with Karl Barth and his followers. This was both because their arguments presupposed a starting point in faith that seemed to us fideistic and also because what they drew from this source often seemed discordant with our basic view of reality. But with Bultmann this was much less true. Schubert Ogden claimed Bultmann's own authority for freeing him from the last vestige of fideism, combined his anthropology and kerygmatic proclamation with a process doctrine of God, and affirmed the whole as the needed synthesis. Other process thinkers turned for help to Heidegger and Sartre. The analysis of human existence in all these thinkers resonated with aspects of the metaphysical model derived from Whitehead, emphasizing radical contingency and decision. Of course, we were critical of some features of what we found. But none of us undertook for ourselves the arduous task of constructing an anthropology out of our own examination of the phenomena and guided by the metaphysical model that we cherished.

That model should have warned us that we had allied ourselves with anthropologies that were far too individualistic and separated humanity far too much from the natural world. And looking back one can see that a few were sensitive to these matters. But on the whole we failed to relate these features of our model to anthropology until the inadequacy of existentialism was pointed out by others: especially political theologians, feminists, and other liberationists.

The realization that we have been insufficiently creative or critical has not invalidated for us the goal of learning from others and appropriating their work in a way that makes for a larger coherence and adequacy. It would be foolish pride to suppose that those few who operate consciously from the process model could carry out all the many tasks that confront us. Our view is that many are thinking much more profoundly than we about many matters. Our task in most fields is to identify the most creative thought that is compatible (or can be rendered compatible) with our own and bring it into fruitful relationship with other thought. In this way a coherent vision can be developed over against the fragmentary one emerging from the university or the nihilistic tendencies so widespread among the intelligentsia. But though we have not abandoned this enterprise, we have been chastened by the recognition of our failures.

I recite this history of weakness to show the importance for us of Farley's accomplishment. He offers a rich and important theory from which process thinkers can appropriate extensively. He clarifies the distinction between human evil (his preferred identification of sin) and psychological disturbance on the one side and the tragic element in the human situation on the other. He identifies the primary sin as idolatry and shows in brilliant detail how this affects all aspects of human life. He goes on to distinguish human evil in the sphere of agency from evil in the spheres of the interhuman and society. He clarifies the possibilities of overcoming evil and the limits of that overcoming in a way that is realistic but does not lead to hopelessness.

Most of Farley's descriptions and analyses are quite congenial to process thinkers, and they carry the authority of intense and clearheaded thinking. Because his theory is integrative of the work of so many others, it already accomplishes much at which we aim. It shows that a theologian can build on the work of philosophers and scientists and advance it. Thus it both inspires and informs.

In sum, process thought is weak at just that level at which Farley is so strong. Its emphasis on radical historicity and contingency has deterred it from developing the regional ontologies so important for the guidance of thought and life. Farley's brilliant proposal tempts process thinkers simply to appropriate his offering as many of them appropriated Niebuhr, Bultmann, Heidegger, Sartre, and others in the past.

III. Critique of *Good and Evil* from the Process Perspective

I have explained the reasons for the neglect of regional ontologies by process thinkers both so that our weakness may be acknowledged and also so that our suspicion of the work of those who do engage in this work can be understood. We fear that too much is likely to be claimed for these regional ontologies. My own suspicions were honed in relation to Martin Heidegger's *Being and Time*.

Although at one point, in passing, Heidegger recognizes that his analysis of the structure of *Dasein* may not apply to our remote human ancestors, the overwhelming impression left by the book is that he is dealing with human beings universally, or that any exceptions are trivial. Before I became critical of Heidegger because of his individualism and his separation of *Dasein* from nature, I was troubled by his apparent claims to transcultural universality.

On the one side, I found a great overlap in Heidegger's analysis of *Dasein* and Whitehead's description of the actual occasion. I appreciated the much greater richness of Heidegger's account as it dealt with the specifically human rather than with what is universal. But I also came to the conclusion that much of the rich analysis applied to some cultures and not to others. In the end, it seemed to me that Heidegger was describing post-Christian North Atlantic society rather than humanity in general. I wrote a book, *The Structure of Christian Existence*, in which I emphasized the diversity of structures of existence shaped in different cultures and the ways they changed over time.[5] I bring that perspective with me as I read Farley's regional ontology.

Farley is far more sensitive to this problem than was the Heidegger of *Being and Time*. His subtitle, "Interpreting a Human Condition," makes explicit that he is describing the structure of *a* human condition. He is far clearer than Heidegger that not all of his analysis will apply to every member of the human species. He explicitly leaves "the issue of their historical reach to rest with their power to evoke recognition."[6]

Despite these careful qualifications on Farley's part, my suspicion is not entirely allayed. The whole account is shaped by the work of North Atlantic writers of the past century or two. They are describing the human condition they know. Their description as interpreted, advanced, and systematized by Farley is brilliantly illuminating of that condition. But is it equally illuminating of the condition of people in any other culture?

I am not suggesting that Farley's analysis would be irrelevant to the human condition of any other culture, that it would evoke no recognition at all. I *am* suggesting that what it would highlight in other cultures might not be the most central features of their human condition. Applying this analysis to others might prove to be another case of bringing Western categories to bear on phenomena that are better understood in the categories of the cultures in which they occur.

An example may help to sharpen the issue. Farley distinguishes three spheres of human reality: the interhuman, the social, and the agential. Agency is without doubt an extremely important category for understanding ourselves in the West, and understandably this sphere gets most of the attention in the treatment of good and evil in Part Two. Furthermore, according to my process metaphysics, every actual occasion whatsoever, human or not, has agency. Hence I am not at all interested in dismissing its relevance in the account of the human condition in non-Western cultures.

Nevertheless, it is striking that agency is not thematized in most other cultures. To avoid exaggerated generalizations, I will limit myself to Buddhist culture. There the deepest analysis of the human condition is in terms of *pratitya samutpada,* often translated as "dependent origination." The human condition in each moment is understood to be the coming together of all else that is. Of course, what happens there will be part of the "all else" that comes together in others, and thus there is some testimony to what in the West we would call agency. But the sense of time and of personal identity that comes to expression in the Buddhist account is so different from ours that the use of the Western categories does seem an inappropriate imposition.

This topic is very complex. One could say that agency is clearly present in Buddhist cultures and is that which one strives to overcome.

Or one could say that true agency emerges for the first time through Enlightenment. But these multiple possibilities witness to the difficulty of
taking the account shaped in the West as the normative one and then
trying to fit the Buddhist condition into it.

For Farley agency is closely related to personal existence. In the West
this is taken to be both a given and a norm. For Buddhists, however,
much that is meant by "person" belongs to the category of the illusory
that is to be seen through rather than to the given and normative. This
may not invalidate much of the description Farley offers, but that description seems to presuppose a kind of self-identity through time that is
denied by both Buddhists and Western process thinkers. Although much
of what Farley says does not presuppose this form of self-identity, there
can be little doubt that his assumptions shape his formulations.

One might argue that in fact the majority of people in Buddhist lands
have by now been so influenced by the West that Farley's interpretation
of a human condition applies to them. There is surely some truth to
that. But if *Good and Evil* is a regional ontology of Western existence
as it is now becoming global, that is somewhat different from its self-
presentation.

Again, it is important to recognize that Farley is open to restricting
the range of application of his ontology as much as evidence requires.
For that reason this is not a severe criticism of his work. Nevertheless, for those of us for whom the global, multicultural perspective on
such matters is primary, the delimitation of the relevance of analyses
based on Western experience seems very important. Indeed, it is especially important that after centuries in which others have been forced to
give expression to their experience in our categories on pain of exclusion from the common discourse, we emphasize the importance of our
hearing them on their own terms. This book does not take this step.

A second danger of regional ontology is that by neglecting the historical character of what it describes, it fails to understand it fully. Again,
this criticism does not apply to Farley as much as to many, but I state it
anyway. It does have some application.

From a process point of view, a thing *is* its history. It is precisely for
this reason that there are the massive continuities that make regional
ontology possible. But it is also for this reason that an ontological approach that ignores how things came into being is not exhaustive of
the real phenomena. Farley is aware of this importance of history. But I
would argue more radically than he that the larger structures, and even
the three spheres, are what they are because of the way they have become. To separate the present form of the sphere from the history of
how it became what it is reduces our understanding.

For example, Farley points out that the distinction of sin from the
tragic condition and psychological problems is possible because we have

inherited insights from Israel. Thus he is fully aware that different features of the human situation come to be understood in diverse cultural contexts. But he leaves the impression that this understanding affects only the understanding of the human condition, not the condition itself. My view is that there is a dialectical relation between the human condition in a culture and its way of understanding itself. Something about the total condition in Israel enabled this insight to arise. With the rise of the insight the human condition became different. In cultures where this insight does not arise but others do, the human condition takes a different form. The division into the three spheres selected by Farley reflects the way in which the human condition has developed in the West. It is not the most appropriate way to describe the human condition in other cultures.

More broadly, Farley's account of the three spheres tends to hypostasize them. In Whitehead's language, he commits "the fallacy of misplaced concreteness." If he had examined how the spheres came historically to be as separate as they are in the West, if he had located them thus in the ongoing flow of history, there would have been less tendency to reify them in their distinctions.

Since the analysis of the human reality into three spheres organizes the book as a whole, my questioning of what he does here is my major criticism. But before launching on this critique, I should make several points. First, in my own view no one way of dividing up reality for analysis is *the* true one. Reality is almost infinitely complex and is susceptible of analysis in an almost infinite number of ways. Various analyses are to be judged by their fruitfulness. Farley's way of identifying the three spheres and his use of this approach are extremely fruitful. Although I believe a slightly different way might prove more fruitful, I have certainly not shown it. Hence my criticism is not against his use of this three-sphere pattern. It is only against those expressions that seem to imply that these three spheres exist in overlapping separateness and constitute *the* way in which a human condition is truly describable. My own judgment is that this particular analysis is the outcome of the way the Western university has organized its research and writing rather than being written into the nature of the human condition.

Second, even if I am correct, this does not invalidate the numerous detailed discussions organized under this threefold rubric. I have no doubt about their general accuracy or the rich insight they afford. Occasionally, I find that the three-sphere organization leads to some distortions, and I will note some of these below. But the book remains an overwhelmingly reliable guide to the human condition as I experience it.

Third, my critical reflections are entirely dependent on his achievement. In no way do I wish to suggest that I could have done a better job (or one half as good). To be able to detect flaws in a masterwork does not imply that one can produce a masterwork oneself.

The model of all reality with which I approach Farley is that of each unitary event as a coming together of the many into a new one. The many include all the events that have occurred in the past and also the relevant possibilities for how the new one could constitute itself in response to them. There is finally a decision among these relevant possibilities.

My purpose now is to question the sharp distinction of the spheres and their exhaustiveness. I will focus on the distinction of the inter-human and the social and their exhaustiveness of the many whose becoming-one constitutes each moment of human existence. Farley be-gins with the interhuman, the sphere of personal relations. These are an important part of the way in which each occasion of human existence is initiated. But by abstracting these relations from the whole matrix of relations, something is also lost. It is implied that the way we relate to some other humans is fundamentally different from the way we re-late to animals of other species, to our bodies, and to the rest of the physical world. It is also implied that these interhuman relations are sharply different from the relation to society. None of these assumptions is acceptable from the process perspective.

This is not to say that Farley omits reference to relations with other creatures or with the body. He asserts that the norms derived from "the face" should be extended to our treatment of all other creatures. And he devotes an entire chapter to "the biological aspect of personal being" and another to "corruption and freedom of bodily life." Nevertheless, the natural world does not constitute a sphere alongside the interhuman, the social, and the agential. What is said about it has to be fitted in under these other headings.

From a process perspective this is a misreading of the human condi-tion. The relation to the body, the wider world, and the living things within it is as primal and important as the relation to human beings. In the origins of experience they all come together. The sorting out, and the special importance of the interhuman, comes later. It occurs differently in diverse cultures.

I have not distinguished in the above between the interhuman and the social. For Farley this is a fundamental distinction. Our immersion in the social sphere shapes the human condition in a quite different way from interhuman relations. And there can be no question that making this distinction illumines much about our human condition.

Nevertheless, it may obscure other features. Once the spheres are separated, every feature of the human condition must be assigned to one or another. In Farley's case, community is treated under the sphere of the social, whereas communion is redemption in the sphere of the interhuman. But are not communion and community closely related?

This is not a serious criticism of Farley, since he recognizes that however distinct the spheres are they also overlap. In his climactic chapter he shows how they are to be brought into closer relations with one another. The question, therefore, is only whether they are best treated as radically distinct in the first place before they are brought together.

This is a pragmatic question. Much is gained by Farley's organization of the material. I am arguing only that something is also lost, namely, a profounder understanding of the extent to which the spheres are convenient ways of ordering the complexity of the data rather than existing realities. My view is that the interhuman provides the basis for the social, that indeed the social is a complex derivative from the interhuman. It would be better to see them from the first in this sort of relation.

To do so, the discussion of the interhuman would need some revision. As I see it, role and status play a role in the interhuman. When this is neglected we are dealing with a limiting case of the interhuman that separates it maximally from the social. The infant very early experiences the parent not only in terms of alterity, intersubjectivity, and the interpersonal, but also as authority and power. Even siblings and playmates have role and status. Role and status constitute much of what we mean by society.

It is certainly possible to abstract from these actual interhuman relations those elements that lead toward the communion of two persons from those that lead toward the more complex structures of communities. As these communities are subordinated to larger, more impersonal societies, the differences become much greater. It is important to recognize these differences and to analyze the emergent phenomena in their differences rather than in terms of categories that have their primary application elsewhere. Hence, again, I do not object to the distinction of the interhuman and the social. My objection is only to the reification of the spheres.

If we avoided such reification, we could introduce more distinctions. For example, we could distinguish the interhuman, the communal, and the social. Of course, Farley does so. But his basic commitment to the independent reality of three, and only three, spheres requires that he locate the communal under one of the other two. This is one practical solution. Another, equally practical one, would be to treat it as distinct from both the others. This would have the advantage of showing the artificial element present in every imposition of structure on the infinite complexity of the phenomena. It would show the continuities between spheres as well as their differences. For example, it is clear that when interhuman relations are not limited to the dyadic ones, they merge into communities. It is also clear that as role, status, and power assume more importance in communities and as their size causes them to lose most of their personal elements, societies emerge. It is clear also that there are intermediate phenomena between a group of playmates and a community and between a small community and a fully developed modern society. One can avoid essentialist tendencies in defining any of these.

IV. The Issue of Global Salvation

The fact that none of the three spheres directly involves the relation of human beings to their natural environment, combined with the reification of society as a given, has many consequences that, from my process perspective, are unfortunate. The present human condition, globally, is one of pressing on, or beyond, the carrying capacity of the planet. Farley is aware of this problem, but it does not affect his basic analysis. On the other hand, the threat of a global catastrophe that is already expressing itself in local ones dominates my sense of the evil from which we need redemption. When I seek redemption today, even more important than the topics Farley treats so brilliantly is the salvation of the human race from self-destruction through destruction of its natural support system.

I am not suggesting that Farley is ignorant of these aspects of the human condition or indifferent to them. Indeed, he explicitly indicates that he is open to the natural as well as the human horizon. I am suggesting, however, that his primary dependence on the philosophical, theological, and scientific writings on anthropology coming from Europe during the past century has led to structuring his thought about a human condition in a way that virtually excludes from consideration what I take to be the most important feature of the human condition today.

This criticism, of course, does not single Farley out from the great body of theological writing. Most theologians deal with that range of issues that came to prominence in central Europe in the nineteenth and twentieth centuries. The intellectual work of that period was of almost unparalleled genius. The issues posed are of absorbing interest. It is easily understandable that most of the finest theological minds are captured by this way of describing our condition.

Unfortunately, this whole tradition has been anthropocentric to the core. Indeed, the term "anthropocentric" is not strong enough. The human reality became the only reality to be considered. Both God and nature disappeared except as human ideas about them might be considered. The result is that, when one treats the issues that have been central in the finest theological discourse for two centuries, and when one is informed by the categories of that discourse, one cannot even consider what human beings are doing to the natural world or the drastic changes they are inflicting on fellow humans as a result.

Even if we limit ourselves to the effects on human beings, the categories derived from the dominant tradition, such as injustice and social oppression, are only tangentially useful. The evil that is now growing in many parts of the world is of a different type and magnitude, obscured more than illumined by use of terms of this sort.

I have been writing this essay shortly after being shocked by an article by Robert D. Kaplan entitled "The Coming Anarchy."[7] It is subtitled "How scarcity, crime, overpopulation, tribalism, and disease are rapidly destroying the social fabric of our planet." In short, it describes an emerging situation in which the sphere of the social (including the communal) is virtually gone.

Of course, projections of the future are to be understood more as warnings of what can happen than as predictions of what will happen. However, in part, the article is a description of what has already happened, especially in West Africa. It depicts there the emergence of a kind of evil for which it is hard to envisage any redemption. For many of the people of West Africa the discussion of redemption in Farley's book seems almost irrelevant.

The situation in West Africa is the product of centuries of exploitation. Colonization in the nineteenth century forced Africans to work on plantations whose function was to export to Europe for the profit of the colonizers. This weakened the capacity of the people to support themselves in their own land. However, the situation has grown much worse with independence and neocolonialism. Sierra Leone was 60 percent forested in 1961, when it became independent. Today forest cover has been reduced to only 6 percent. The remaining forest is still being cut. The loss of forest cover has led to erosion of farmland as well, so that traditional sources of economic life have largely been destroyed. Meanwhile population has grown rapidly. As a result, a large and increasing portion of the population lives in urban slums. Several armies operate in the country. The official government maintains a precarious order in the major urban centers by day, none by night.

Disease is rampant. The loss of forest cover has brought swamps into being where malarial mosquitoes breed unchecked. Virtually everyone in the interior has some form of malaria, and the situation in the cities is not much better. The traditional medication to control malaria is no longer effective. European visitors can still protect themselves with a new drug, mefloquine, but its side effects are very unpleasant. Furthermore, a strain of cerebral malaria is now developing that is resistant to this drug. As a result few outsiders visit this part of the world if they can help it. Tuberculosis and AIDS also ravage the population.

Since there are few natural resources left of interest to the rest of the world, West Africa now suffers from benign neglect. This neglect is exacerbated by the end of the Cold War, which means that neither

Russia nor the United States has a strategic interest in the region. For practical purposes it has been written off internationally.

West Africa's population of ninety million will probably soon begin to decline despite the continuing high birthrate. Disease seems to be the most likely agent of this decline. It is hard to imagine what salvation is possible for a large percentage of this population.

Kaplan points out that many of the same forces of neocolonialism and economic exploitation are generating similar conditions in many parts of the world. The global population that not long ago was predominantly rural is now predominantly urban. The great growth of urban population is in slums that do not have even the minimal facilities that "society" is expected to provide. Government plays little role in many of these slums. On the other hand, their populations will play a much larger role than we now anticipate in shaping the global future.

The point of this excursus is not to say that theologians should abandon all discussions of regional ontology and focus on the salvation of the world from imminent threats. It is to say that we need to challenge the hegemony of a type of thinking that makes theology seem irrelevant to the most terrible evils rampant in the world. It is also to say that it is important to see the extent to which a regional ontology tends to assume forms of human life that are themselves threatened by the economic forces that reign almost unchecked.

As with so many of my concerns and criticisms, Farley shows awareness of the problems. He notices that one reason it is so difficult to imagine social redemption today is that economic power is dominant over other forms and seems peculiarly impervious to their influence.[8] My complaint is that this very important point about the global human situation does not affect his basic account of "a human condition." In this account he describes the economic as a subsystem of the social, this being the relatively self-sufficient one.[9]

Even during the nineteenth century this way of relating the economic and the social made sense only for the North Atlantic countries. It did not apply to their colonies. It would have been impossible to think of the colony in the way Farley describes a society. Colonies were not at all self-sufficient. And the "subsystems" were not related as Farley describes. Their economies were perhaps subsystems of those of the colonizing powers. Perhaps the "society" as defined by Farley would be the colonizing power plus all its colonies, but this, too, would be a poor fit.

My point here again is that the North Atlantic origin of the categories and analyses is manifest. And again there is a tendency to suppose that the patterns found there are more universal than they are, both in space and time. Since Farley is correct that the economic has ceased to function as a subsystem of societies, the account is no longer applicable even to the North Atlantic societies. Indeed, societies with their subsystems are ceasing to exist anywhere, although today China, Tanzania, and Cuba may still be exceptions.

Farley rightly points out that we cannot attain redemption in all spheres by achieving it in one. For example, the healing of the inter-human through communion may not in itself effect redemption in society, and social redemption can leave the personal or agential disrupted. Farley is also concerned that the conditions for redemption not be neglected. My emphasis here is on the latter. As societies deteriorate or cease to exist through the exploitation of natural resources and cheap labor, the conditions for any form of redemption grow less promising. Reversing this trend would not assure us of any form of redemption, but it would restore a situation in which the forms of redemption that Farley describes could become relevant to more people.

V. The Ontological Issue

In Section II I affirmed the value of regional ontologies and deplored the weakness of process thought in developing them. In Section III, on the other hand, I offered a variety of criticisms of Farley's work based on my judgment that he succumbed too much to the tendency to ignore variety and change, a tendency endemic to regional ontologies.

In this concluding section I will comment on the more technical ways in which ideally, in my opinion, regional ontologies should be informed by a general ontology. The general ontology I commend for consideration is one in which entities are understood to be constituted primarily by their relations. That is, the entity does not exist apart from relations and then enter into relations. This presupposes that the entities in question are events.

Farley does not oppose this ontology, and he certainly does not explicitly affirm its major competitor, substance metaphysics. Nevertheless, like most of those who do not thematize a general ontology, his thinking expresses a commonsense substance perspective. This underlies the tendency to reify the three spheres.

This becomes clearest in the account of the sphere of the inter-human.[10] The interhuman is, for Farley, a distinct sphere because it focuses on relations that cannot be located within the persons related. It is important for Farley that violating a relation is distinct from violating a person or agent. In making this case, he clearly reifies the relation as the "between."

From the point of view of process thought Farley's emphasis on relations is one of the great strengths of the book. Also, the image of the "between" has proven to be a fruitful and illuminating one. Nevertheless, the reification of relations is a weakness. In the preceding section I noted how it led to a focus on the human in a way that, despite Farley's intentions, tended once again to render the natural environment (apart from the human body) invisible. Here I am pursuing the more strictly ontological issue of the status and locus of relations.

In process perspective, the ontological realities involved in the examples of the interhuman offered by Farley are the occasions of human experience. The occasion of experience of person A includes and is in significant degree constituted by a relation to person B, and the occasion of experience of person B includes and is in significant degree constituted by a relation to person A. Furthermore, both occasions of experience are also significantly constituted by their inclusion of previous experiences making up their personal past in which this relation to the other person was important. Perhaps we should add that the relation includes an awareness of the importance of oneself to the other person.

I believe this account includes the main elements emphasized by Farley. If not, I am convinced it can be so enriched as to do so. But what it excludes is the idea that persons A and B exist as agents who are not constituted by these relations and that the relation between them is not located in their respective experiences. Farley may object that this analysis implies that the relation of A to B is distinguished from the relation of B to A. That is correct. But is not that a more accurate reading of what actually occurs? The relation does not have exactly the same meaning for A and for B. Even as the violation of a relation is described by Farley, it becomes clear that the relation of the violator to the violated is not the same as the relation of the violated to the violator. Once we have understood that the occasions of experience that make up the life of a person are constituted by relations, we do not have to posit relations as existing outside of the people involved. We do not need to hypostasize the relations in order to take them with utmost seriousness.

A similar hypostasization occurs with the sphere of the social, although this is not as explicit as with interhuman relations. Perhaps it is most evident in the language of sedimentation. A society functions as it does because of the sedimentation of values, meanings, beliefs, structures of authority, and so forth. It is this accumulated sedimentation that provides it with objectivity over against agents and distinguishes it from interhuman relations.

There is no question but that the rhetoric of "sedimentation" is suggestive in very useful ways, just as is the rhetoric of the "between." But the criticisms in Section III have implied that societies do not have quite the ontological status that Farley suggests. The very existence of a society is contingent on particular historical circumstances. The rhetoric of "sedimentation" does not lead one to look for these circumstances or to expect the degree of fragility that is actually present.

Whitehead's analysis gives great prominence to societies, but, as would be expected, the notion of society is a very broad and inclusive one. Any group of occasions in which later occasions derive some common characteristic from earlier ones constitutes a society. The human societies described by Farley with their relative self-sufficiency and stable subsystems are societies by Whitehead's definition, but they are only one example of social order. A single human being is normally a member of many human societies, some of which are more important than others. One is also a member of many societies that include both human and non-human members.

There is nothing wrong with singling out the society Farley emphasizes, basically the nation state, for special attention. The nation has been the basic social unit for several centuries in the North Atlantic countries. Hence, this selection is quite appropriate in developing a regional ontology if one is careful to recognize that the applicability of the analysis depends on particular historical situations.

Furthermore, sedimentation is a fruitful image to describe the increasing number of inherited characteristics in many types of society, including the nation, as long as certain preconditions remain. Institutions are created to insure that this "sedimentation" is transmitted to later generations. Most of Farley's analysis is entirely compatible with this perspective.

I would close with a re-emphasis on the limitations of the general ontology with which I am operating and from whose perspective I am criticizing Farley. From this perspective the most fully accurate account of what occurs in complex societies and their institutions is in terms of what happens in all the individual occasions that make them up and relate to them. This awareness serves to check tendencies to committing the fallacy of misplaced concreteness. Unfortunately, it also discourages the extremely important work of describing what is occurring in particular types of societies in terms of categories that are appropriate to just those societies and no others. The individual occasions are constituted by their participation in just these societies. When we explain what happens in terms of the individual occasions, we are in danger of ignoring the fact that these individuals are already social beings. The particular societies to which they belong must be understood in terms of characteristics that obtain only in societies and not in individuals. Farley is engaged in analysis of just the sort that is needed by process thinkers and yet so rarely adequately pursued by us.

It seems almost inevitable that when one interacts with the work of another a predominant emphasis is on the differences and perceived limitations of the other's work. I have fallen into this trap. I have spent far less time rehearsing the many features of Farley's work that I admire, appreciate, and learn from than identifying features that I cannot accept in their present form. This distorts my actual reaction to the book.

Perhaps, nevertheless, there is value in describing how one who is shaped primarily by process thought views the work of one who is shaped primarily by phenomenology. My deepest judgment is that the two approaches are complementary rather than in opposition. But it is also clear that, in order for complementarity to be realized, each requires change and adaptation to the other. I am deeply grateful to Farley for providing me the occasion to reflect anew on these matters in relation to the work of one who has already considered many of the concerns that are central for me and who has already been engaged in so modifying the phenomenological tradition that many of these concerns are largely met.

NOTES

1. Edward Farley, *Good and Evil* (Minneapolis: Augsburg Fortress, 1990). (All further references to Farley are to this book.)
2. Ibid., 1–26.
3. Mary Elizabeth Moore, *Teaching from the Heart* (Minneapolis: Fortress, 1991).
4. See Daniel Day Williams, *The Spirit and the Forms of Love* (New York: Harper & Row, 1968).
5. John B. Cobb, Jr., *The Structure of Christian Existence* (Philadelphia: Westminster Press, 1967).
6. Farley, *Good and Evil*, 9.
7. Robert Kaplan, "The Coming Anarchy," *Atlantic Monthly* (February 1994): 44–76.
8. Farley, *Good and Evil*, 279–80.
9. Ibid., 55–56.
10. See especially 232ff.

⇒ 2 ⇐

Eros and the Truth

Feminist Theory and the Claims of Reality

WENDY FARLEY

Two themes circulate through Edward Farley's work, though not always thematized: two submerged marine mammals swimming through his thought, occasionally breaching. The first is the centrality of truth, or reality, for theology.[1] Although he will offer a nuanced interpretation of the historical, located, pluralistic, and incomplete character of truth, his work may be understood in part as a comprehensive resistance to relativistic implications of historicism and pluralism.[2] The second is the centrality of passion, or eros, to human consciousness, knowledge, and relationship.[3] It is the thesis of this essay that these two themes taken together may be of particular significance for feminist theology and ethics.

Various other particular analyses could be important to feminist reflection: Farley's account of authority or his phenomenology of oppression, for example.[4] But there is a deeper resonance between the passions that guide Farley's work and those of feminist thought. Both struggle to understand theology, society, and history in light of the ubiquity and sorrowfulness of suffering. Attentiveness to the reality of suffering challenges the temptations toward relativism so characteristic of the current intellectual mood. Vulnerability to suffering itself is testimony against claims that social construction "goes all the way down."[5] That persons and environments can be predictably harmed or destroyed by identifiable practices (violence, humiliation, toxic wastes) suggests that beings (human and otherwise) are not infinitely malleable or constructable. The reality of other beings has a certain objectivity about it: it can be harmed, misunderstood, and it evokes obligation.[6]

The realism presupposed in the recognition of suffering might, according to the fictions of oppositional logic, be understood as a reactionary reassertion of the worst of modern philosophy: the transparency of being to thought, the unseemly lust for premature and false unities

21

and totalities. But such a characterization of either Farley's thought or feminist realism would obscure the intimacy between truth and justice that attentiveness to suffering reveals. The radicality of this kind of realism lies in its ability to challenge assumptions at work in modern and, to a certain extent, postmodern thought. We inhabit a cultural world that renders the concrete and complex existence of beings invisible and evacuates reality of ethical and aesthetic dimensions. The invisibility to which a late industrial society condemns all features of reality that are indigestible by the profit system is only reinforced by theologies and philosophies that cannot find a language for the integrity, beauty, and vulnerability of persons and all beings. Ethical realism, by contrast, raises the question whether it is really true that beings — persons, other animals, plants, deserts, oceans, ecosystems — are value-neutral quiddities to be interpreted by the methods of science and exploited by the ambitions of capitalism or empty, passive nubs receiving their identity from systems of power.

The realism that is at work in Farley's theology and is at least tacitly present in most feminist writings is attentive to the sufferings of beings. It is therefore drawn into the concrete, plural, multidimensional, and historical character of existence. Awareness of suffering and its causes produces suspicion about ideologies and institutions that preserve unjust and destructive relationships. This brand of realism is therefore not naively opposed to the discoveries of the historical and politically constructed character of human society. Rather, it seeks ways of employing these discoveries for the work of justice. In embracing this kind of realism, feminism deepens its resistance to oppression by challenging not only particular institutions, practices, and theologies that are overtly oppressive of women but also the more general logic at work in our society that makes oppression both natural and largely inarticulate.

This essay will suggest how an analysis of eros provides a path toward a distinctively feminist understanding of the nature and importance of truth, one that simultaneously rejects absolutism and relativism. The first part of the essay argues that retaining some version of the category of truth is an important act of feminist resistance, particularly in the context of late industrial society. The second part of the essay analyzes eros and its role in feminist ethics. The indebtedness of this writer to Farley's work will be expressed less in exegesis or critical dialogue than in an appropriation that moves themes from his own work into an area where he himself could not go, that of constructive feminist thought.[7]

Truth and Feminist Ethics:
Why "God-terms" are Important

Farley employs Philip Rieff's expression "god-term" to refer to those words or concepts through which a culture expresses its "deep convictions of value" and according to which it calls its "own corruptions to account."[8] In most cultures such words are associated with the sacred, "the deep mystery of things, interpreted in Hebraic and Christian traditions as God.... [Words like] authority, obligation, love, nature, person, and tradition are both imperatives and forbiddings."[9] They provide the general vocabulary and conceptuality through which a culture struggles with evil, meaning, human destiny, and responsibility. These are words of power both in their prophetic and idolatrous forms. Like everything else under the sun, god-terms are subject to corruption, decay, and trivialization. Because of their enduring power, god-terms are particularly potent vehicles of corruption.[10] A god-term like "obligation" in the hands of patriarchal religion condemns women to a life of servitude by conflating subjugation with the servanthood of Christ. Likewise, "charity" comes to name a paternalism that controls the poor while resisting social changes demanded by justice. "Authority" and "tradition" become forms of domination that justify the first two corruptions. The capacity of god-terms to illuminate and challenge human existence is matched by their vulnerability to distortion. They always stand in need of correction and purgation. And yet they remain god-terms because they provide ways of speaking of dimensions of experience that demand expression.

God-terms become a theme in Farley's work not only because they are in a general way the stuff on which a theologian works, nor because he is engaged in the always necessary task of prophetic critique. Farley is drawn to god-terms because of the particular problem posed for them in our advanced industrial society. Following Rieff, Marcuse, and others, Farley uncovers ways in which this society empties our conceptual and spiritual worlds of concepts like obligation, beauty, the sacred, personhood, dignity. Such words are meaningless to science and dangerous to the profit motive.

> The whole of recent western history is constituted by a shift, a transition to what we now call an advanced industrial society. This event or shift has discredited or rendered useless, passé, and powerless virtually all god-terms. If this is the case, rethinking the god-terms is up against something far more complex and devastating than the perennial dialectic of corruption and retrieval ever taking place in society and in religious communities. And this is

our theme, the atrophy of god-terms in modern and postmodern industrial society.[11]

God-terms are now suffering a double death. They are rightly and properly subject to rigorous and radical criticisms as vehicles of domination. At the same time, they are trivialized out of existence or reduced to impotent caricatures in a society that finds such words dangerous. They remain active in our culture primarily in the obfuscating rhetoric of the political right or as meaningless slogans pasted on the rear end of automobiles. This creates a peculiar and painful problem for feminist theologians and ethicists. Evoking the damage done by injustice requires a rich and profound sensitivity to the regions of reality for which the language of dignity, compassion, and beauty are ciphers. But to the extent this language has been appropriated for oppressive and patriarchal practices, they require criticism — the more radical the better. And yet it is only too easy for much-needed prophetic criticism to find itself having contributed to a situation in which words of power are most potent in the hands of those who use them to further erode the dignity of all persons.[12] The work of feminist ethics and theology is conditioned by two opposite corruptions present in our society: patriarchy and the reification of all reality by advanced industrial capitalism. Feminist theory may be vulnerable to a "double effect" that allows strategies for criticizing one corruption to serve the other.

In order to be most effective, ethical resistance might be mindful of its historical location at the end of modernity, in a post-industrial, capitalist moral wasteland. Reflection on this historical context should not be limited to the more characteristically postmodern one, but should include also a more overtly ethical one that examines the ways in which the very categories of ethical and religious existence are debased by our society.

Feminist Ethics in Post-Industrial Society

Patriarchy is not a static essence, uniformly stamped on societies throughout history. Resistance must be sensitive to the distinctive structures of oppression at work in different periods of history, as well as how oppression varies among women of different classes, races, religions, sexual preference, type of work, mothering experiences, and so on. Nonetheless, all these forms of domination are affected by their historical connection to industrial society.[13] One task of feminist scholarship is to track ways in which society is patriarchal, how it specifically harms women. But patriarchy is embedded in larger social systems that weave together many forms of domination. To expose general features of a contemporary logic of domination helps uncover distinctive versions of patriarchy at work in industrial society. Such an analysis may also suggest common ground among otherwise disparate forms of domination and in this way facilitate an understanding of both the irreducibility and relationships among different forms of oppression.[14] More pertinent for this discussion, it will suggest how the suppression of the category of truth and reality contributes to practices that oppress and destroy life.

Distinctive forms of domination characteristic of the contemporary Western world arise with the advent of modernity. The rise of modernity is almost infinitely complex, inclusive not only of many strands of Western culture (knowledge, religion, economics, politics, technology, and so on) but of antithetical tendencies (pulls in the direction of democracy and universal human rights together with pulls toward colonialism, slavery, racism, and misogyny, for example). But with modernity, a distinctive understanding of the nature of reality begins to emerge that is rooted in part in the conjunction of scientific method and capitalism.[15] The successes of science and capitalism are possible on the basis of the interpretation of reality as quantifiable. The twin engines that fuel an advanced industrial society, science and capitalism, though for different reasons, share a belief that *Being* is reducible to quantity, that is, to thinghood.[16] For science, such a reduction is at least at first methodological.[17] For good reasons and with frequently positive results (reliable birth control, inoculations against deadly childhood diseases, labor saving devices such as washing machines), science and technology abstract from entities those features that cannot be interpreted by or which are irrelevant to laboratory experimentation.[18]

What is real for the scientist is what is quantifiable and repeatable. By whatever strange coincidences that guide history, this methodological abstraction parallels almost exactly the moral requirements of capitalist industrialization. Reality is denuded of aesthetic and ethical dimensions as these are banished to the private, subjective, and "feminine" spheres. Cleansed of those features that would resist commodification, reality (persons, creatures, cultural artifacts, ecosystems) becomes both materially and morally passive. This artificially created plasticity allows all beings to be transformed into whatever the industrial machine needs them to be. The flattening out of reality into numbers creates ideal conditions for its domination. The complexity of beings is rendered invisible so that they can be mastered by thought; the integrity and intrinsic value of beings is dismissed as mere sentiment, freeing us from the ethical resistance beings exert against their own domination.

For science, the translation of beings into numbers occurs as the mathematization of reality; for capitalism, it is the transformation of reality into money. As Walter Lowe writes: " 'Business,' 'commodity'; with these terms a neglected dimension of the problem comes into view. This is the specifically economic dimension. In Western religious circles it is not sufficiently remarked that the historical Enlightenment and the rise of bourgeois individualism are profoundly linked to the rise of capitalism; and that it is in the nature of capitalism to reduce everything without exception to a single monetary framework."[19] Features of beings — that is, living creatures, animals, plants, human beings, cultures, ecosystems — that are irreducible to quantity (now not mathematics but money), become unreal and irrelevant. Repeatability becomes the essence of an entity: the capacity of a worker to repeat the same motion a thousand times a day; the capacity of one faceless worker to replace another; the capacity of a machine or process to infinitely produce the identical hamburger or piece of china marks a thing's reality and value.

This reduction means that "nothing is valued for its own sake, nothing has significance in its own right. All values are reduced to exchange value and in this sense every object becomes, at least potentially, a commodity."[20] Although contemporary thought dismisses ontology and metaphysics as so much poetry, a quite definite interpretation of being and beings is present in modern industrialized society in the identification of reality with quantity.[21] The very dismissal of ontology and metaphysics reflects this ontology: obligation and beauty are not *things;* they cannot be reduced to quantity and therefore can have no real being. The quantification of reality becomes commonsensical, as obvious as gravity.

This reification of reality affects women and therefore feminist ethics and theology in many ways. Most simply, the reification of women is present in the identification of women with sexuality and beauty, both of which are central to advertising. Thus the commodification of women is the very life blood of capitalist image-making. But perhaps less overt and yet equally horrible is the transposition of ethical and fundamentally human issues into the logic of the marketplace. When this happens, not only are persons reduced to one-dimensional, degraded cartoons, but beauty, suffering, love, affection, life, birth and death, obligation vanish from the society's evaluative frameworks. This harms all living things, but it harms women in distinctive ways. One large corporation began experimenting with somewhat more generous maternity leaves and in-house day-care arrangements because a cost-benefit analysis revealed that having to retrain executives was more expensive than granting maternity leaves. While this might be hailed as an advance for working mothers (at least those at the executive level), should the possibility of caring for a newly born child be dictated by the benefits it produces for a large corporation? That cost-benefit provides the only conceivable grounds by which women can campaign for work patterns that make family life possible or humane exemplifies the ways in which ethical discourse has simply ceased to operate in our society. That we are not shocked and outraged by cost-benefit arguments for or against health care, maternity leaves, environmental protection, support for the arts, or nutrition programs for pregnant women and young children suggests how thoroughly the lie of quantification has invaded our capacities for ethical existence.

The success of the quantification of reality in producing a form of knowledge on the one hand and money on the other produces a social world intolerant of all "god-terms," that is, a social world in which ethical dimensions of reality, together with aesthetic dimensions and the sacred, become inarticulate. This intolerance is not corrected but obfuscated by the current anti-ontological or anti-metaphysical mood of contemporary thought.[22] Because reality is construed as a quiddity in our advanced industrial society, the struggle against oppression and dehumanization is therefore not only at the level of particular practices and policies but also at the level of metaphysics or ontology: it occurs as a struggle to acknowledge persons and beings as possessing a kind of reality that is harmed by commodification itself, harmed by having to live in a world emptied of the sacred, of beauty, of compassion.

Patriarchy in a post-industrial context threatens women not only in the familiar — if deadly — ways of violence, poverty, exclusion. It threatens women by emptying moral language of its power. How can we cry out the sacredness of human dignity when both the sacred and dignity are empty sounds? How can we speak of the fragility of nature when beauty means only prettiness? How can our weeping over humiliations, the suffering of our children, or the violence endured by our sisters be anything but water if personhood and the anguish attached to it are shadows of dreams? The surrender of the questions of being and reality forces critics of a logic of domination to cede in advance most of the universe to the very powers that are busily annihilating moral discourse.

In this context, to contest the identification of being with thinghood or with the effects of power can be an act of resistance and protest. A too-hasty and too-comprehensive embrace of the anti-metaphysical mood tends to forget that

> reflective ontology is itself a polemic, negation, and disruption of other cognitive styles, especially those that quantify knowledge and reality, which have arisen with advanced industrial societies.... If human reality is merely an object that occupies this or that causal system of its environment, there would seem to be no criteria by which subjugation and violation could ever be recognized, much less opposed. Thinking from the mysterious center of human reality, reflective ontology works to uncover what violates and corrupts human reality. Hence the critical disruption it perpetrates not only targets quantifying reductions of human reality but ex-

ploitative social systems that would profit from obliviousness to
the density and mystery of human beings.[23]

Whatever shred of hope there might be that feminism could help to
shift our society away from its deadly and violent practices will lie in
part in its ability to carry on the work of the "god-terms."[24] In doing so feminist theology and ethics refuses the trivialization of itself as
merely "politically correct" or as one of many competing "interests"
with which a tepidly pluralistic world must deal. In this effort, feminism
is no mere academic or social fad, but a prophetic calling of our society's "deepest corruptions to account." It is a witnessing to the deepest
convictions that life in its infinite diversity is beautiful, that the anguish
of injustice is essentially, violently wrong, that disrespect for any form
of being is a deep violation of the very fabric of reality, that a thirst
for compassion is more satisfying and humanizing than the satiation of
possession.

Part of the work of feminist theory will be not only criticisms of patriarchal theologies, philosophies, thoughts, practices, social institutions.
It will include also struggling to see and describe and relate to reality in ways that counter our society's all-pervasive reification of reality.
One witnesses this fecundity of feminist thought in the work of Sallie
McFague, Katie Cannon, Mercy Amba Oduyoye, Sharon Welch, and
countless others. In conjunction with these other efforts, I am propos-
ing a model for interpreting the role of truth in the struggle for justice.
As women and as feminists, women are well placed to know the infinite plurality of reality: we know the importance of the differentiation
of the human race by gender as well as by innumerable other modes of
concreteness: ethnicity, race, historical location, type of work, region of
the world, types of education, family relations, and so on. The patterns
of thought through which we seek to oppose the logic of domination
will therefore not themselves be univocal or require an allegiance to the
"same." They must express our passion for the truth presupposed by
any resistance to oppression and suffering, but in a way that permits
the complex and beautiful plurality of reality to shimmer forth. As an
illustration, I will propose eros as providing a cognitive and ethical disposition toward the world in which truth and plurality require rather
than exclude one another.

Eros of the Broken Wings

In the *Phaedrus* Lysias advises a young man to prefer the non-lover
to a lover because "what is wanted is that the business should involve no harm, but mutual advantage."[25] One should engage in sexual

congress in ways that do not drag one into embarrassing or burdensome relationships. Socrates attacks Lysias as a traitor to Love and all human lovers alike.[26] He personifies "broken-winged eros in love with its own passion" (Buber). For the seducer, the other person remains at best a shadowy reality. The exteriority of the other's body is necessary for his pleasure, but the seducer remains completely absorbed in himself. Lysias's seducer is a metaphor for a mode of existence in which nothing beyond egocentric experience has meaning. Others are merely instruments of my will and pleasure. Extrapolating this logic beyond individual egotism, the same pattern can be seen in other relationships of domination: patriarchy, capitalism, racism, totalitarianisms of right and left. In each case, others — including the whole world outside the system of value and power — can be encountered only in relation to the defining whole. This allegiance to what Levinas calls the "same" extinguishes the possibility of recognizing the meaning, value, or a point of view of other beings. What cannot be absorbed into the "same" is rejected as illusory, unreal, or evil. In its celebration of radical egocentrism and in its objectification of and alienation from others, Lysias's speech epitomizes this mode of relationship.

This reduction of others to a passive instrument of a totality is a diseased form of relationship in which the motion to the other has been inverted. In it, other beings have meaning only in relationship to some artificially absolutized one: the ego, the economic or political system, religion, method, and so on. This One functions as the source and center of reality, the sun that rules and illuminates the shadows beneath it. Correlative to this idolatry of the one is the denuding of all other beings of their reality and value. Nature, ideas, persons, nations, religions are flat and passive images waiting the rising sun to write their meaning on them. This kind of relationship, whether present in a philosophical system, a science, labor practices, or interpersonal relationships is simultaneously illusory and evil. It is illusory because the reality, the real being of the other remains concealed. It is evil because alienation from the kind of reality another person or being has is itself a kind of violence that generates and justifies violence. The full and distinctive humanity of women cannot be acknowledged within a system that has become structurally incapable of recognizing a human being in a woman's face.

This blindness is illustrated by the reception to Sojourner Truth's "Ain't I a Woman?" speech. She stood before a room of men, describing her work, her hunger, her anguish at the loss of her children — but stones and statues would be no less blind and deaf to her than the men to whom she spoke. This ignorance of the other culminates in two forms of violence. First, it makes possible all kinds of acts of destruction. If others are neither real nor valuable no sense of obligation arises in relation to them. The inability to recognize a black woman as a human being becomes enacted in a history of racism and sexism that shows no signs of relenting. But blindness does not only make possible violence against the other; it is itself a kind of violence. To stand in the presence of another person without evoking recognition of one's person is a profoundly humiliating and excruciating ordeal. To see oneself reflected back from the eyes of another — or in the institutions that shape one's life — as a thing, an obscenity, an absurdity inflicts a wound difficult to heal.

Eros for the Other

Audre Lorde knows another meaning of eros. Rather than using another "as we would use a kleenex," through eros we encounter another in the mystery and joy of her otherness.[27] Eros is a disposition toward others that no longer requires that other beings function as parts of an alien system. Lorde describes it as a "sharing of joy, whether physical, emotional, psychic, or intellectual [which] forms a bridge between the sharers which can be the basis for understanding much of what is not shared between them, and lessens the threat of their difference."[28] This connection with others, rooted in a deep consciousness of their independence and differences, gives to eros an orientation toward truth or reality. "The erotic is the nurturer or nursemaid of all our deepest knowledge."[29] Others, precisely in their unique and irreplaceable concreteness, different from all others, beautiful and exposed in ways distinctive to themselves, can emerge from the shadows and dreams in which hostility and exploitation cast them. Eros, for which otherness is the occasion of positive delight, allows us to recognize one of the most fundamental realities of our existence: as Hannah Arendt phrases it, that "plurality is the condition of human action because we are all the same, that is human, in such a way that nobody is ever the same as anyone else who ever lived, lives, or will live."[30]

The effects of eros are felt not only in relations with others but in relation to oneself.

> For as we begin to recognize our deepest feelings, we begin to give up, of necessity, being satisfied with suffering and self-negation, and with the numbness which so often seems like their only alternative in our society. Our acts against oppression become integral with self, motivated and empowered from within. In touch with the erotic, I become less willing to accept powerlessness, or those other supplied states of being which are not native to me, such as resignation, despair, self-effacement, depression, self-denial.[31]

Lorde emphasizes that eros is a form of joy that overcomes our hostility toward others, toward difference itself. Resistance to oppression arises out of this shared joy and respect that empowers one to resist what thwarts personhood — one's own or anyone else's.

Farley offers a much more comprehensive account of the "elemental passions," although like Lorde, he sees eros directed toward the self, toward others, and toward the world.[32] Part of the significance of his analysis of the passions is to retrieve from instrumental reasoning dimensions of human existence and its world that are lost and distorted by reductionism and cynicism.[33] One of the reasons these are elemental passions, rather than passing desires, is that they are "never terminated. Their drive is ever beyond their present realizations. Thus, their imagined objects or references are always penultimate."[34] Desire and its objects break up the notion of a perfect adequation between subject and object. Such an adequation requires objects whose reality can become transparent and fixed to a knower or experiencer, that is, quiddities. The kind of being that desires past every particular fulfillment is not driven only by biological compulsions or market-created cravings. Desire as infinite, as elemental, is the orientation not of things but of *persons* to their world.

Desire that moves past and through particular fulfillments is, correlatively, in relation to its world not as a series of items that serve certain pragmatic functions. It relates to the world as mysterious, beautiful, perplexing. "Meant reality always has a surplus, a more. And this surplus draws the biologically rooted orientation to reality past the sheer presentation into explorations that have no set limits."[35] The correlation between subject and object presupposed (in different ways) by various strands of modern thought is challenged by this account of desire.[36] Nothing is purely "present": a fixed, static, identity that is passively delivered of its entire reality to the system of knowledge or society that grasps it. The world and its inhabitants are always more than what can be experienced or known about them. They transcend the knower by defying any concept or system that would pretend adequately or perfectly to contain them. But this transcendence of pure presence evoked by desire does not mean a pure absence, as if the world were nothing but illusions, fictions, or socially constituted chimeras. "There are satisfactions intrinsic to these experiences. Meanings enable us to experience reality not just as useful but as beautiful. . . . Through meaning the passion for what is so, born amidst the pragmatic needs of life, lures us toward the mystery and beauty of the world."[37] An analysis of eros dissolves false epistemological alternatives between complete or absolute knowledge and resigned or cynical agnosticism. Both, in different ways, imply that what is known is static, thing-like: either perfectly transparent to knowledge or utterly absent. Eros reveals that other beings are not thing-like and that relationship to the world and its inhabitants is therefore not marked by perfect possession or nihilistic absence. Others are both real and mysterious, beautiful and perplexing.

By appropriating these different analyses of eros, a feminist theology can suggest how eros's turn toward the reality of others simultaneously generates understanding and ethics. Knowledge of other beings is not only of their mystery and beauty; it is awareness of others as vulnerable to harm and to suffering. Objectifying knowledge of others is knowledge of beings as things; almost by definition things do not suffer. Objectification of the other is a lie about the *kind* of being others have that prevents attention to their suffering from occurring and therefore precludes the question of obligation toward the other from ever arising.

In contrast to this form of awareness of others, erotic knowledge lures us toward the world through its intrinsic interest and value. In becoming alive to the reality and loveliness of others we are awakened both to truth and to obligation.[38] Eros is born as delight in others that cleaves the hegemony of any artificial totality or whole. The self-transcendence accomplished by eros permits others to appear for themselves, *kath auto,* as Levinas says. They are not simply images fabricated by the hopes and fears of a self-absorbed ego or faceless integers in a philosophical or political system. Erotic relation to others permits a proximity in which a deeper understanding of them and their situation is possible.[39] Out of this understanding of their situation as it is *for them,* and not determined by one's own, a less paternalistic form of responsibility emerges.[40] This approach to others that allows their perspective to shape one's own generates the possibility for a practical wisdom. In this way one might discern what is required in this particular situation, with respect to these particular people.

Through eros, understanding and obligation are deeply linked. In permitting something of the mysterious reality of others to appear, the concreteness and plurality of others becomes more evident and, together with these, their distinctive beauties and vulnerabilities. If eros is to maintain its turn toward reality in light of suffering, it must call upon all of its courage. But if eros survives this deepening awareness of the anguish of the sufferings and fragilities of others, it produces on offspring of its own: from the delight and pain of eros, compassion is born.[41]

Desire is a feature of world-relatedness that perhaps most fundamentally orients human beings to *reality:* to the beauty, mystery, and, ultimately, suffering, of all of those beings who remain irreducible to my consciousness or to society's regimes of power. It is for desire that the otherness or transcendence of the world emerges. The implications of this alterity return us to those problems we face at the end of modernity. When beings are understood to have existence, reality, and beauty in themselves, the increasingly radical erasure of beauty, obligation, and truth by modern and postmodern modes of thought and society is challenged. Beings *in themselves are* beautiful, complex, plural. The integrity and rightness of their existence are not contingent upon participation in any particular economic or social system, nor accessible through the privileges of any single method or point of view. In paying attention to the concreteness of beings, the vitality of reality, its lovely richness, its crushing fragility come into view. With this overwhelming sense of the density of reality — of all creatures, cultures, ecosystems, cultural artifacts, particular persons — comes an increasing sense of the illusions of post-industrial society. This appalling gap between the conventions of our society and the reality of the beings it exploits tends to be further obscured by philosophical rejections of the category of truth. If truth and reality are nothing other than social conventions, then within corporate capitalism, ecosystems are really nothing other than raw materials for profitable enterprises; within patriarchy, women are really nothing other than instruments of male desire; within racism, Jewish or African or Asian peoples are really nothing other than the refuse of subhumanity, fit only for service or death. Against these fictions that have been writ large in the history of Western culture and on the bodies of its victims, the reality of beings protests. An analysis of eros provides a way to articulate the reality of beings against systems that defraud them of meaning and, in more extreme cases, existence itself. Eros does not *possess* the objects of knowledge or experience but makes possible an orientation that, precisely in its recognition of the non-possessability of reality, its non-identity with any method or mode of relation is "on the way" to truth in a way that fictions of total knowledge or power are not.

Conclusion: Feminism as Metaphysical Ethics

Eros is a passion for reality that allows others to emerge from the shadows and dreams of egocentrism and socially constructed illusions. Eros's journey toward others is a pilgrimage toward a truth that is always exterior to the ego and to the regimes of power that shape it. The practices of eros permit the reality of others to emerge in at least two senses. The *kind* of being the other has can be recognized. The other is not a thing, an object of use, or an anonymous, threatening power. The other is beautiful, mysterious, and vulnerable. Eros provides knowledge of the *kind* of beings that inhabit the world. But eros is always directed toward concrete others and is therefore also knowledge of and obligation toward these particular creatures, threatened in particular ways, with unique capacities for suffering, resistance, and joy. In this sense, eros also provides a practical wisdom, discerning possibilities of action and relationship in concrete situations.[42] Analysis of eros assists feminist theory in overcoming a series of bifurcations that cripple modern thought: oppositions between knowledge and ethics, between ontology or metaphysics and praxis, between the universal and the concrete, and between truth and justice. Such an analysis does not simply paste together two halves of a whole, but reinterprets the nature of these phenomena as richly multidimensional, infinitely pluralistic, and enacted in the concreteness of history, culture, and environments.

In raising questions about the kinds of beings that inhabit the world, feminism engages not only in the critical task of revealing the limitations and corruptions of philosophy, religion, and society. It contests a lie about the nature of reality with an alternative vision. Ideologies and social structures that enact a belief that women are less capable of works of reason, or courage, or compassion are not simply different points of view in the great cacophony of competing interests. They are lies. The more comprehensive defrauding of all reality of beauty and mystery by an advanced industrial corporate capitalism is, again, not an interesting play of difference. It is an enactment of a mendacious, immoral ontology.

In addition to its other work, it is fitting for feminist thought to compete against these lies with claims about the nature of reality that is rooted in a passion for truth. In this way feminism takes on the work of "god-terms" that have been discredited by contemporary society. It engages in the perennial task of calling society to account for its corruptions, its preference for lies, its injustice, its self-imposed ignorance, and its alienation from the beauty of things. By reclaiming words of power — truth, desire, compassion, beauty, reality, personhood, dignity, responsibility — we are refusing to collaborate with a society that empties these words of meaning even as it empties us of our humanity.

NOTES

1. See, for example, *Good and Evil: Interpreting a Human Condition* (Minneapolis: Fortress Press, 1990), chapter 1.

2. In this he is very much in the lineage of continental philosophy, which combines criticisms of absolutizing reason with retrieval of the category of truth. See, for example, Karl Jaspers as illustrative of this same effort to overcome the stifling oppositions between absolute truth and total relativism. "The metaphysical or gnostic 'total' knowledge of an event of Being is no more than an evil or beautiful dream" (Karl Jasper, *Reason and Anti-Reason in Our Time*, Stanley Godman [London: SCM Press, 1952; German ed. Munich: R. Piper Verlag, 1950], 36. And yet the absence of total knowledge does not reduce all to irrationality. See his descriptions of reason as ethical, fragile, historical, always restless and moving on, methodologically aware, and so on, e.g., in this text pp. 39–65. These themes are present as well in concise form in

Karl Jaspers, *Reason and Existenz: Five Lectures*, trans. with introduction by William Earle (Noonday Press, 1955, from 3d ed., Bremen: Johs. Storm Verlag, 1949, originally published Groningen: J. B. Wolters, 1935).

3. *Good and Evil,* chapter 5.

4. See *Ecclesial Reflection* (Minneapolis: Fortress Press, 1982) for a criticism of authoritarianism and an analysis of a more appropriate sense in which the Bible and tradition serve as authoritative in the Christian community. See *Good and Evil,* especially chapter 14, for his analysis of social oppression, chapters 15 and 16 for the redemption of community.

5. See, for example, "Introduction: On Cognitive Style," *Good and Evil,* especially 8–11.

6. For another version of this objectivity of personhood and, correlatively, of obligation, see Simone Weil. This theme is characteristic of much of her writings; see especially "Human Personality," "Factory Work," and "*Iliad,* A Poem of Might" (*Simone Weil Reader,* ed. George A. Panichas [New York: Moyer Bell Limited, 1977]). The philosophy of Emmanuel Levinas is perhaps the most comprehensive and radical effort to articulate the objectivity of both other persons and the obligations they evoke. See in particular *Totality and Infinity: An Essay on Exteriority,* trans. Alphonso Lingis (Pittsburgh: Duquesne University Press, 1969), and *Otherwise Than Being or Beyond Essence,* trans. Alphonso Lingis (The Hague: Martinus Nijhoff Publishers, 1981). From a quite different direction, the work of John Cobb can be understood as a defense of ethical realism; see, for example, "In Defense of Realism," in *Theology at the End of Modernity,* ed. Sheila Greeve Davaney (Philadelphia: Trinity Press International, 1991).

7. Levinas argues that gratitude reflects a "return to the same" and is therefore a violation of ethical existence (Emmanuel Levinas, "The Trace of the Other," *Deconstruction in Context: Literature and Philosophy,* ed. Mark C. Taylor [Chicago: University of Chicago Press, 1986]). The general point may be to distinguish disinterested ethical actions from those that impose a debt. But in making the point so categorically, Levinas leaves no avenue for one to express the quite proper experience of gratitude. Perhaps in continuing the work another helped to make possible, one enacts a gratitude that cannot be spoken.

8. This quote is from "God-terms in Atrophy," 1; it is taken from a series of lectures Farley gave at Trinity College at the University of Toronto in 1992 entitled "Re-thinking the God-terms." They are now being revised and, together with a second series on the same topic, will constitute a forthcoming book tentatively titled *Words of Power.*

9. "God-terms in Atrophy," 1.

10. For Farley's analysis of the several reasons for and senses of this corruption, see the opening pages of "God-terms in Atrophy," 1–3.

11. "God-terms in Atrophy," 3.

12. Kathleen Sands points out the way in which the current campaign against efforts to be more inclusive of human persons employs the language dearest to Americans: "One such prolonged offensive is the current campaign against 'political correctness,' which invokes ideals of freedom and equality to oppose precisely those policies that could actually promote practical increments in free-

dom and equality for marginalized peoples" (*Escape from Paradise: Evil and Tragedy in Feminist Theology* [Minneapolis: Fortress Press, 1994], x).

13. For the way industrialization intertwined with patriarchy to produce distinctive forms of domination in modern society, see, for example, Zillah R. Eisenstein, ed., *Capitalist Patriarchy and the Case for Socialist Feminism* (New York and London: Monthly Review Press, 1979); Paula Giddings, *When and Where I Enter* (New York: William Morrow and Co., 1984); Beverly Wildung Harrison, "The Effect of Industrialization on the Role of Women in Society," *Making the Connection: Essays in Feminist Social Ethics* (Boston: Beacon Press, 1985).

14. My point here is that oppression occurs simultaneously at different levels of generality and concreteness. Oppressions in any large society will be characterized both by distinct mechanisms and by common features. Racism is irreducible to sexism, patriarchy irreducible to class conflict, imperialism distinct from racism. At the same time, domination will be structured in similar ways in any society or historical period. The racism and sexism of late twentieth-century America will have features in common that neither share with the racism and sexism of feudal Japan. Resistance can benefit from understanding all levels of oppression and their interaction, even if particular persons and groups will, naturally and properly, emphasize one dimension over others.

15. Countless analyses trace the connections between science and capitalism in the rise of modernity. See, for example, Max Horkheimer and Theodore W. Adorno, *The Dialectic of Enlightenment,* trans. John Cumming (New York: Herder and Herder, 1972, from *Dialektik der Aufklarung,* 1944, German reissue, 1969). For the distinctive conflation of philosophy, science, and technology in producing a logic of domination over the natural world, see William Leiss, *The Domination of Nature* (Boston: Beacon Press, 1972). For the role of capitalism in producing both a logic as well as institutions and practices of domination see Hannah Arendt, *The Origins of Totalitarianism,* part 2: *Imperialism* (New York: Harcourt, Brace, Jovanovich, 1948).

16. This reduction of being to thinghood has been, if anything, more severe in the Soviet Union and China. The point is not that capitalism alone produces a logic of domination. Rather, we are seeking distinctive ways in which capitalism, the central power of our own culture, produces structures of domination and oppression.

17. See, for example, Gabriel Marcel, *Man against Mass Society,* trans. G. S. Fraser (Chicago: Henry Regnery Company, 1962; first published in Great Britain, 1952) for a distinction between methodological abstraction and abstractionism. Also, note Edmund Husserl's analysis of the tacit movement in modern thinking from an appraisal of science as a method to a grid that itself defined being and the real. See Parts One and Two, *The Crisis of European Sciences and Transcendental Phenomenology,* trans. and introduction by David Carr (Evanston, Ill.: Northwestern University Press, 1970).

18. Notwithstanding the criticisms I am making, it cannot be overlooked that at least some women have been the benefactors of the scientific method as much as anyone has, as my examples suggest. See the section on "The Societal

Tragic," in Farley's "God-terms in Atrophy," for the interdependence of goods and corruptions in our society.

19. Walter Lowe, *Theology and Difference: Wound of Reason* (Bloomington: Indiana University Press, 1993), 6.

20. Ibid., 6.

21. Horkheimer and Adorno in *Dialectic of Enlightenment* note the way in which industrialized, capitalist society makes criticism difficult by erasing those dimensions of thought that are irreducible to calculation. Metaphysics, aesthetics, morality itself become "meaningless prattle" (*Dialectic*, 25) when thought is understood exclusively instrumentally and, likewise, thought's referents are objectified, reduced to static, one-dimensional quiddities. Note the parallel point made throughout Herbert Marcuse's *One-Dimensional Man: Studies in the Ideology of Advanced Industrial Society* (Boston: Beacon Press, 1964), especially chapters 6 and 7.

22. The words "ontology" and "metaphysics" have multiple meanings, of course, slightly different in the hands of every philosopher who employs them. For Heidegger or Derrida, for example, metaphysics carries something of the same condemnatory implications as Levinas's "ontology," while for Levinas, the term "metaphysics" refers to the (ethical) transcendence of persons from the historical or philosophical totalities that deface them. Resistance to the language of ontology or metaphysics is quite widespread, including many otherwise competing schools of thought: postmodernism, pragmatism, positivism, Barthianism, neo-Kantianism, narrative theology. My use of the terms here is intended to be general, referring to modes of analysis that permit the irreducibility of beings to be recognized.

23. *Good and Evil,* 11.

24. Farley uses the metaphor of recalling a tune to describe this work of recovering dimensions of reality evoked by "god-terms." "Common is the experience of being unable to recall a tune we know. The tune is there. We would recognize it if someone else whistled it. But for the moment, the tune is only there in our memory bouncing among other tunes. I did not invent this metaphor. Recall the pathos of one of Israel's exiled poets. I paraphrase the poet's cry. In this strange land, a land that is not given to us, a land without any fixed place of the Lord's presence, the temple, a land whose stories are not our stories, a land of strange armies, rulers, customs, and languages, how can we sing the Lord's song? Can we only put away our musical instruments and not even try to recall the tune? In very different historical circumstances the Christian movement in the industrialized west is experiencing something like that. Its god-terms are tunes it cannot quite recall" ("God-terms in Atrophy," 15).

25. *Phaedrus* 234c, trans. R. Hackforth (Cambridge: Cambridge University Press, 1952).

26. "Yes, dear Phaedrus: you understand how irreverent the two speeches were.... Suppose we were being listened to by a man of generous and humane character, who loved or had once loved another such as himself: suppose he heard us saying that for some trifling cause lovers conceive bitter hatred and a spirit of malice and injury towards their loved ones.... Wouldn't he utterly refuse to accept our vilification of Love?... Then out of respect for him, and

in awe of Love himself, I should like to wash the bitter taste out of my mouth with a draught of wholesome discourse" (*Phaedrus* 243 cd).

27. Audre Lorde, "Uses of the Erotic," *Sister/Outsider: Essays and Speeches* (Freedom, Calif.: Crossing Press, 1984), 56.

28. Ibid., 56.

29. Ibid.

30. Hannah Arendt, *The Human Condition* (Chicago: University of Chicago Press, 1958), 8.

31. Lorde, *Sister/Outsider*, 58. Lorde's description of eros, like that of most feminists, emphasizes its humanizing affects on the self as well as the other, that is, the integration or necessary simultaneity between self-respect and respect for others. This is at least rhetorically in marked contrast to the phenomenologies of Levinas, who emphasizes so strongly the asymmetry between self and other as fundamental to ethical existence.

32. Farley describes three elemental passions: the passion of subjectivity, of the interhuman, and for reality. These are not exhaustive, but he does understand them to be characteristic of human beings, however dramatically these passions may vary in concrete experience and across cultures. He is not describing them as constituents of human nature but perhaps closer to what Hannah Arendt describes as the human condition. See Arendt, *The Human Condition,* especially 8–10.

33. See *Good and Evil,* 98–99.

34. Ibid., 100.

35. Ibid., 107.

36. Note Emmanuel Levinas's similar analysis of metaphysical desire that is directed toward an infinite other (*Totality and Infinity,* 33–35). For Levinas, too, the analysis of desire is part of a challenge to models of knowledge that presuppose a correlation between subject and object, knower and known, an adequation that Levinas believes obscures the infinity of the other (and with it, the infinity of obligation to the other).

37. *Good and Evil,* 108.

38. Note Whitehead's parallel account of the value-ladenness internal to all reality. His essay "Importance" offers a succinct expression of this point (*Modes of Thought* [New York: Free Press, A Division of Macmillan Publishing Co., 1938]).

39. Note Max Scheler's analysis of sympathy as that form of relation in which the other's grief or humiliation (or happiness) is understood *as* belonging to them, in their own terms. "Can one ... commiserate more deeply than for his having to suffer as he does, *being the sort of man he is?*" (*The Nature of Sympathy,* trans. Peter Heath [Hamden, Conn.: Shoe String Press, Archon Books, 1954], emphasis added).

40. Beverly Wildung Harrison emphasizes the need for an interactive sense of responsibility to displace paternalism and tacit domination. She describes ethics as conveying "the implication that 'good' action is a mode of 'doing for' others rather than 'acting with' them. In contrast, victims of oppression need an ethic grounded in images and concepts that affirm reciprocity in action. If our moral language is ever to interpret self/other duality in terms that affirm and embrace

mutuality and support the whole spectrum of human fulfillment, autonomy, and as yet unrealized possibility, all of us must learn to envision all action as genuine *inter*action" ("Sexism and the Language of Christian Ethics," *Making the Connection: Essays in Feminist Social Ethics,* 39).

41. Farley has developed a very rich phenomenology of obligation in his work on words of power. In it, he argues that though obligation is a "tug" toward the other, it is not in itself a desire for the other. In linking desire and obligation more closely, I am not disputing that the actual content of obligation is distinguishable from that of desire. But I do want to emphasize the origin of ethical existence in the intrinsic value of other beings and therefore as intimately related to the delight in being characteristic of desire. This intimacy between desire and obligation points to ethical existence as requiring not self-abnegation but a fully functioning and self-respecting self. This point is one central to Farley's phenomenology. The differences between our accounts are largely of emphasis rather than content.

42. Putting it this way implies an opposition between two poles: a universal or ontological pole and a concrete one. This would falsify the situation, I believe. It is more helpful to think of dimensions or levels of concreteness than of two opposite poles. Existence always occurs in utterly concrete and irreducible beings. But each being is constituted by the interaction of several other levels or dimensions of generality: "woman" is less concrete than a particular person, but more concrete than human being. Human being is less concrete than womanhood and more concrete than living being. Womanhood itself interacts with one's religion, race, parenthood, work, historical period, geographical location, and so on in the constitution of any particular person. There are lots of good reasons for abstracting some level of concreteness to examine features of this form of existence, especially to understand distinctive ways it evokes oppression. Existentialism focused on the individual in order to protest the totalizing effects of philosophy and society; feminism focuses on issues of gender to protest the distinctive oppressions experienced by women; reflective ontology focuses on features of human being in order to resist the quantification of reality in advanced industrial society. But it does not seem legitimate to me to identify any level of existence with reality itself in a way that would preclude the significance of any of the other levels.

⇛ 3 ⇚

The Face and the Spirit

PETER C. HODGSON

The Face and the Spirit

Two remarkable stories are found in the book of Exodus about Moses' encounter with God. When commanded to leave Sinai and lead Israel into the land of Canaan, Moses asked to be shown the divine glory, a request that was denied with these words: "You cannot see my face; for no one shall see me and live." But God promised to place Moses in a cleft of the rock and cover him with a divine hand "while my glory passes by.... Then I will take away my hand, and you shall see my back; but my face shall not be seen" (Exod. 33:20–23). God shields the divine face by the divine body, that is, by God's worldly embodiment. The world is God's body, God's back. We cannot see God's face directly but only as reflected in a multitude of worldly shapes and faces. Yet, something apparently *can* be seen of the divine glory. God also appeared to Moses on Mount Horeb in the form of a flaming fire that burns without consuming. Moses turned to gaze on this sight, but after seeing it "hid his face, for he was afraid to look at God." Then he received the divine name and the divine commission to gather the people and lead them out of bondage (Exod. 3). This fire became for both Jews and Christians a symbol of the love and Spirit of God. It is the worldly manifestation of the divine face, possible to see but awesome. The love that burns without consuming is the agapeic communion in which intense reciprocity occurs without otherness being reduced to the same. Edward Farley calls it the community of the face. I shall call it the community of the Spirit, for the Spirit is the divine power and presence that engenders agapeic and liberating communion.

These stories serve as an apt introduction to a discussion of aspects of Farley's theological anthropology as set forth in *Good and Evil: Interpreting a Human Condition.*[1] I regard this work as the most important and creative theological anthropology of our time. I have learned a great deal from it and am in substantial accord with its detailed descriptions

40

of good and evil. Yet my own approach to theological anthropology differs from Farley's in important respects, and it may be worth the effort
to expose some of the issues involved in this difference.[2] The fundamental question is how, where, and even whether *God* appears in relation
to human life. Is Farley's anthropology a truly *theological* anthropology? This question is pursued in the next section by asking two further
questions.

Anthropology and Theology

1. *Is Relatedness to God a Structural Sphere of Human Being or a
Contingent Feature of Religious Faiths?* In the first part of *Good and
Evil,* where Farley develops a reflective ontology of human being, three
spheres of the human are identified: the interhuman, the social, and the
personal. Lacking is a sphere of transcendality, openness, or relatedness
to God such as might be indicated by understanding human being as the
imago Dei. Farley does refer to an "eternal horizon," which is an im-
plicate of the elemental passions that pervade the personal sphere, but
the "eternal horizon" is not a term for God; it only permits the question of God. The eternal horizon appears as an actual, sacred presence,
that is, as God or perhaps better a *trace* of God, only in relation to the
experience of redemption as mediated by determinate communities of
faith (28–29, 111–13, 144–46). The trace of this presence, as we shall
see, is the "transregional" or universal face that appears in "communities of the face." The only references to God in this work occur in
connection with the elemental passions (111–13) and the experience of
"being-founded" (150–53, 272), the latter being Farley's way of talking
about the occurrence of redemption in the Hebraic-Christian paradigm.

Thus God-relatedness is an ontic, not an ontological feature of
human being. It is not entirely clear why Farley takes such a position,
especially in light of his defense of reflective ontology in the introductory
chapter. Perhaps he concedes too much to the postmodern critics of this
ontology and is wary of introducing explicitly theological claims into an
ontological scheme. Perhaps this is his way of avoiding "ontotheology."
But if one wishes to do theology, *can* it be avoided? If theology is not in
some sense ontotheology, it is likely to evolve into anthropotheology or
ethicotheology in the Kantian sense.[3] This is the danger I perceive in Farley's approach, yet I believe it is one that he himself wants to avoid. Of
course, to advance ontotheological claims today would require a fairly
radical revisioning of *ontos* — that is, of what we understand "being"
to be and of God's relationship to it. If God were to become the central theme of theology, and spheres or patterns or elements of the divine
life (rather than of human life) its organizing principles, then human be-

ings along with all other finite beings would be understood to exist in
a constitutive relatedness to God — a relatedness that is capable of being distorted or broken as well as redeemed or healed. The condition of
possibility for both evil and good in the world would be this pervasive
God-relatedness. I believe this is implicit in Farley's treatment of good
and evil, but he does not provide the necessary theological foundation
for it.

The difference between the two approaches to theology that I have
described thus far might be viewed as another version of the difference
between Schleiermacher and Hegel — the difference, that is, between
an anthropological and a trinitarian philosophical theology. Farley is
probably the most creative contemporary representative of a Schleiermacherian approach to the theological task. But in one important
respect he differs from Schleiermacher. The experience of being-founded,
which I shall discuss more fully below, seems to correspond to Schleiermacher's feeling of utter dependence. But for Schleiermacher the latter
occurs as a universal ontological or generic structure of human being, whereas Farley's being-founded is set forth at the ontic level and
seems to be confined to a specific religious paradigm. This raises a number of questions in light of the multiplicity of religious faiths and the
universality of religious experience.[4]

2. *Is Redemption a Divine Action and Presence in History or an
Interhuman Transaction?* A subsidiary form of this question is whether
christology and pneumatology are reducible to strictly anthropological
categories. Farley's answer seems to be clear. He intends to translate
the language and symbolism of salvation, associated by Jews and Christians with the coming of the Messiah and the presence of the Spirit, into
"a theology of the human condition as historical freedom" (117). From
his point of view, the "cosmic narrative of divine acts," focusing upon
Christ and the Spirit, does not add anything essential to the Christian
paradigm of good and evil as derived from a strictly anthropological
analysis (140). In this he is very close to Schleiermacher, for whom the
three dogmatics forms — self, world, and God — are ultimately reducible
to and derivable from the first, namely, states of self-consciousness.[5]

The essential meaning of salvation, according to Farley, has to do
with the experience of "being-founded," which is formulated by him
in terms of the interpersonal metaphors of compassion and forgiveness. Robert Williams summarizes the core of Farley's argument this
way: "Evil is a weakness, an inability to abide chaos and an open,
unsecured existence. Being-founded is the power to live in the condition of tragic vulnerability without insisting upon absolute idolatrous
self-securing. It is the condition of historical freedom and courage."[6]
Farley's exposition of courage as the condition flowing from the experience of being-founded is truly excellent. He offers it as an alternative

to the traditional piety of guilt and repentance, which presupposes the notion of sin as rebellion against a cosmic monarch and of salvation as forensic acquittal. Being-founded breaks the logic of divine sovereignty and the juridical metaphor, which have long played a destructive role in the Western theological tradition. It opens up new possibilities for understanding what redemption actually means with respect to human historicity, the elemental passions, bodily existence, interhuman relations, and social institutions (chapters 8–14).

But the wealth of analysis on these matters contrasts with the paucity of Farley's treatment of being-founded. It is not entirely clear, for example, whether courage entails a consent to chaos (as something that is simply endemic in our cosmos) or a refusal of chaos (a refusal that belongs to the elemental passion for the eternal). Is chaos the supreme reality? Or does sacred presencing provide the power to refuse chaos without appeal to false absolutes? Assuming the latter, what then *is* this power? Where is it generated and how is it mediated to us? Presumably it is not simply autonomous human power but some sort of divine empowerment. It has a sacred, transcendent, even spiritual quality, but Farley's theology remains largely silent about it. What is needed, in my judgment, is *an ontological clarification of the being that founds* (that is, a doctrine of God), together with a christology and a pneumatology that articulate the historical mediation of founding power, and do so in such a way that it is not simply derivable from anthropological categories. Perhaps this will be provided by Farley's future work.

The Face

A hint of the direction in which Farley is moving is provided by his analysis of the face. I believe that this hint, if pursued to its limits, would yield a theology of the Spirit.

The face appears in the interhuman sphere, which has three dimensions: alterity, intersubjectivity, and the interpersonal. Alterity points to an inescapably solipsistic separation of persons such that the other remains other and elusive, not reducible to a sphere of my own. But every individual is always already intersubjectively formed by postures, languages, roles, agendas, etc., so that the gulf to the other is already bridged, and no one needs a proof that the other actually exists. Finally the interpersonal refers to the actual encounter and dialogue among different but not isolated selves; this is the locus of the face.

The face presents an ethical summons and criterion. "It is the face that shows the other as one who can be murdered, violated, and manipulated, and as one to whom we are responsible. The face is the agent's own face discovered in the alterity of the other and the other's face

44 PETER C. HODGSON

experienced in the agent's own sphere" (288). In Part One Farley follows Emmanuel Levinas in his stress upon an asymmetry that grants unqualified priority to the face of the other, but in Part Two he modifies this asymmetry in the direction of reciprocity and compassion. Levinas was wary of reciprocity, but for Farley this is not a self-seeking but an other-seeking reciprocity founded in courage. What is discerned in the face is not only a stern summons but a beauty and loveliness that call forth affection and compassion. In any event, the face discloses what is most intimate, essential, unique, and inviolable about a human being. In seeing the face we see the character and heart of a person.

Likewise, the divine face discloses the very heart of divinity, its "glory," and thus it cannot be seen; it is too overwhelming, too consuming, too radiant and blinding. The human face can be seen only with difficulty; gazing upon it is an awesome but not annihilating experience. The question whether the face of the human other acquires an unqualified priority or enters into a relationship of reciprocity with other faces applies also to the divine face. Must we simply bow down before and avert our eyes from this face? Or does the divine face too enter into relationship with other faces and become visible among them? Is God an inaccessible monarch or an available friend?

Evil affects a disconnection from the face in various ways. In the personal sphere it is blotted out by egocentrism and idolatrous self-securing; in the social sphere it is obliterated by institutional anonymity and social stratification. Thus redemption requires a reconnection of the spheres with the face. Farley writes:

How can the face be released from its capture by the determinacies, loyalties, and commitments of specific social locations? The face transcends these regions only if it manifests something that pertains to the good of the total human life-form, and beyond that to the good of all life-forms. In the Christian paradigm of redemption, the transregional face is experienced in connection with the experience of the sacred.... It is the sacred manifested through the face that lures regional (familial, national, tribal) experiences of the face toward compassionate obligations to any and all life-forms. (289)

The communication of a "transregional" or "universal face" calls for a distinctive social and historical mediator, the "community of the face."

The Community of the Face

Face-to-face relations transpire in all actual social groups, but only a few of these are a community of the face. The latter, says Farley, is a community "whose raison d'être as a community is the mediation and attestation of the universal face" (290). The universal face is one that lures regional experiences of the face toward a compassionate obligation for all of life, human as well as non-human. The experience of the universal face, Farley argues, in accord with Levinas, is connected with the experience of the sacred, and the embodiment of this face occurs through the ritualization of the sacred. He does not elaborate on what this means. It is unclear, as Williams points out, whether the universal face is directly theological — that is, an actual presence of God in the form of community — or whether it is only a "trace" of the sacred (Levinas) or an "appresentation" of God (a concept Farley derives from Husserl).[7]

Assuming that it is in some sense directly theological, what concept of God is implied by it? Given Farley's critique of all forms of absolutism as idolatrous, we must assume that his God is also not absolute, at least in the traditional sense of an unrelated, non-reciprocal, utterly transcendent supreme being. How, then, does relationality enter into the constitution of God's being? Neither Schleiermacher nor Levinas is helpful at this point. Schleiermacher's God is an absolute causality unaffected by relations with the world, while Levinas's account of the asymmetry of the interhuman parallels the traditional non-reciprocal conception of the God-world relation. Farley will need to look elsewhere for a concept of God adequate to his own theological criteria — perhaps to Tillich, or Hartshorne, or Whitehead, or Hegel, or the Neoplatonists.

Tillich and Hartshorne were two of the theologians studied in Farley's first published work, *The Transcendence of God*.[8] The book analyzes the impasse between apologetic and kerygmatic theologies and their corresponding emphases on human experience and divine revelation. In the first, the Transcendent is conceived as Limit (beginning, end, depth, height); in the second, as God (creator, fulfiller, preserver, the holy). Farley agrees that divine revelation occurs, focused upon the Christ-event, but he insists that it comes into and is surrounded by "preceding structures." These structures are themselves manifestations of God's grace, as is everything in the created world, and Farley proposes an "analogy of grace" as a way of overcoming the tension between the two theological approaches. God's free grace has its norm in Christ, but "it exists as a forgiving and transforming redemption that transforms and utilizes *everything* human."[9]

It is clear that in his most recent work Farley favors the first of these approaches. The *face* is now conceived as the Limit in which the Transcendent is appresented. But is it also self-presented? Is it really present as efficacious redemptive power, as grace, so that we can speak of the Transcendent as God as well as Limit? To affirm this, something of the second theological type needs to be reappropriated. It is unlikely to take the form of the kerygmatic christocentrism that echoes in the early work. It would be more consistent with the basic impulse of Farley's thought to move in the direction of a theology of the Spirit, as I shall attempt to show. And as yet Farley has not worked out the relational ontology needed to understand what it means to say that God's essential nature is *gratia ipsa*, grace itself.

The primary example of a community of the face offered by Farley in *Good and Evil* is that of the Christian ecclesia. "Ecclesia" refers to an ideal type of community "whose primary aim is to embody and attest the face for any and all and to press all autonomous and local social powers to open themselves to the face" (291). In its actual historical embodiments, ecclesia appears in a mix of "natural centrist communities that serve racial, ethnic, and gender loyalties." Thus a tension exists between the historical churches and their ecclesial essence, a tension that might be described in terms of the traditional distinction between the church visible and invisible. This way of understanding the ideality of the church means that its primary purpose is oriented neither to individual spirituality nor to sociopolitical mission. Its primary reality is that of mediating "agents-in-relation under the face and before the sacred" (292). Spirituality and politics are important derivatives of this primary reality but must not be allowed to substitute for it.

The Community of the Spirit[10]

Farley's "community of the face" corresponds anthropologically to what can be named theologically the "community of the Spirit." Spirit is a community-creating power; spiritual presence engenders spiritual community. The intrinsic sociality and relatedness of Spirit is a central theme of modern philosophy from Hegel on. Hegel understood Spirit (*Geist*) to be the result or accomplishment of reciprocal recognition, and therefore to be essentially a holistic, social, intersubjective category. The individual subject is at most a phase in the development of Spirit, an abstraction from the larger concrete social whole. Individuals are not ontologically prior to the social but are always already embedded in and dependent on a social matrix. This matrix, which Hegel sometimes referred to as "objective Spirit," is not something mysterious and mystical, such as a group mind or consciousness, but is simply the "spiritual air ... in which we breathe," the sphere in which we are situated and nurtured by culture, customs, language, ideas, values.[11]

According to Hegel, there are two kinds of community, or two ways of conceiving community. One is an aggregate of atomic individuals who exist mostly in isolation, and from whom social unity must be coerced, so that community is essentially heteronomous, limiting autonomous freedom. The other is a communion of freedom, a community of free communicative praxis, in which individuality is not suppressed but elevated to a higher cause, that of freedom and truth, the consciousness of a free people.

Only the latter is a spiritual community. It is spiritual because it is grounded in acts of mutual forgiveness and releasement, allowing the other to be other while remaining in relation to the other. God as Absolute Spirit *is* the event of reciprocal forgiveness, releasement, and love that makes community possible. Love is at one with its object, neither dominating it nor being dominated by it. In love the separate remains, but in union. Hegel in his *Logic* describes the Absolute or the Universal as "the free power." "It is itself and overreaches its other, but not in a dominating or forceful way.... It could also be called free love and limitless blessedness, for it is a relating to its other only as itself. In its other it has returned to itself."[12] Robert Williams comments:

> Love transcends the standpoint of domination, and allows the other to be free. In such absolving love, there is no reduction of the other to the same or exclusion of difference from totality, but rather solidarity with the other. Self-recognition in other presupposes and requires that the other remain distinct, even as it is no longer purely other. Love transforms identity into a holistic conception that not only preserves, but requires otherness.[13]

The holism that constitutes Spirit entails a triadic rather than a monadic or dyadic social structure. It is not a matter of an absolute ego (I = I) positing the other as merely the self-othering of the ego, such that the other is reduced to the same. This is the received opinion about Hegel, but it is a false reading, a confusion of Hegel's position with that of a Kantian or Fichtean transcendental idealism. Nor is it a matter of an I and a You standing in infinite, irreducible otherness to each other (I vs. You). This is the position adopted by Levinas over against what he terms Hegelian "totality." Rather it is a matter of a triple mediation in which I and You remain other yet related in a third, a We (I-You-We). The Spirit is the third, the We, the community. The We is no undifferentiated fusion of persons but a reciprocity of recognition that produces a new kind of differentiated wholeness, a liberated communion of free persons. This is the authentically Hegelian philosophy of Spirit.[14]

What God does in the world as Spirit is to engender spiritual community. The term "spiritual community," while a central concept for Paul Tillich,[15] was earlier employed by the American philosopher of religion Josiah Royce, who in turn borrowed and refined it from Hegel. Royce has a very suggestive theory of community. Communities depend on acts of interpretation, and interpretation involves a triadic process, namely, the introduction of a third, comparative idea or deed into a

dyadic relationship, a third perspective that creates a unity of consciousness and action in the form of insight or vision. Creative insight comes
from those who first compare and then mediate, who first see two great
ideas at once, and then find a new third idea that mediates between and
illumines them.[16]

Now God, according to Royce, is "the Interpreter who interprets all
to all," the infinite Third that is present in every mediating idea.[17] The
divine Spirit is the third reality, the living power unifying the many into
a one, while the members as such remain individually distinct. A *divine* unifying power seems to be needed because of the individuality
and conflicts that pervade the human social world. A unity that does
not destroy but embraces finite entities, healing their mutual hostility,
bringing good out of evil, seems to be attributable only to a transcendent cause, not to immanent human resources. An Interpreter is needed
who breaks through the blockages and isolation of human existence
and interprets "all to all." "Interpreter" is Royce's ingenious equivalent
for the traditional name of the Holy Spirit, "Paraclete" — an advocate, intercessor, intermediary, interpreter. It needs only to be added
that such interpretation has not only a reconciling but also an emancipatory effect in the world since it is above all conditions of systematic
exploitation that block communication. Thus the spiritual community
is not only a beloved community (an expression borrowed from Royce
by Howard Thurman and Martin Luther King, Jr.) but also a liberated,
free community.[18]

God's face cannot be directly seen. But it appears in the flaming, non-
consuming fusion of love that is the presence and power of Spirit in the
world. Developing such an idea requires moving from anthropology to
theology proper — in my view, to a trinitarian theology that understands
Spirit to be the shape of God that emerges out of interaction between
God and the world, the gestalt that mediates God to the world and the
world to God. For Christians the world assumes its most pointed and
poignant expression in the one face of Christ, where the consequences of
evil and the power of good are definitively revealed. But the face of the
Spirit is a *multiplicity* of human faces, interacting in communal domains
of resonance[19] in which each face reflects and echoes the others and all
are drawn together to form a universal and interpersonal face, a We that
is the shape of God in human shape. To be sure, the Spirit is the Spirit of
Christ, but the Spirit also transcends Christ, bringing his one face into
play with the many faces.

Spirit also appears in the multiple faces of nature — in those of
animals and flowers, trees and mountains, wind and water, stars and
planets. We know these faces far less well than our own, but as we come
to see them more clearly and learn to read them we may recognize the
divine countenance in them as well.

Hopefully these brief reflections will serve as a fitting tribute to Farley and his thirty-five years of imaginative theological work. By the time they are published he may already have offered to the public a doctrine of God that addresses all of these and other questions. If not, perhaps these reflections can assist his own.

NOTES

1. Minneapolis: Fortress Press, 1990. Page references to this book are placed parenthetically in the text.

2. Some of the material contained in this essay comes from my book *Winds of the Spirit: A Constructive Christian Theology* (Louisville: Westminster John Knox Press, 1994), chapters 14, 17, 18. © 1994 Peter C. Hodgson. Used by permission of the publisher.

3. For a detailed analysis of Kant's anthropo- and ethicotheology, see Walter Jaeschke, *Reason in Religion: The Foundations of Hegel's Philosophy of Religion,* trans. J. M. Stewart and P. C. Hodgson (Berkeley and Los Angeles: University of California Press, 1990), 68–81.

4. Robert R. Williams points this out in his excellent review article, "Good, Evil and the Face: Edward Farley's *Good and Evil,*" *Philosophy Today* 36 (Fall 1992): 281–93; see 286–87.

5. See Friedrich Schleiermacher, *The Christian Faith,* ed. H. R. Macintosh and J. S. Stewart (Edinburgh: T. & T. Clark, 1928), §30.

6. Williams, "Good, Evil and the Face," 286.

7. Ibid., 292. Williams mentions that the connection of the universal face with the sacred can be traced back to Nicholas of Cusa and Jonathan Edwards. Farley himself does not explicate this connection.

8. Edward Farley, *The Transcendence of God: A Study in Contemporary Philosophical Theology* (Philadelphia: Westminster Press, 1960). The other subjects of this study were Reinhold Niebuhr, Karl Heim, and Henry Nelson Wieman. The work originated as a doctoral dissertation at Union Theological Seminary–Columbia University under the direction of Daniel Day Williams and Robert McAfee Brown.

9. Ibid., chapter 7, especially 218–19.

10. The following draws directly from material at the beginning of chapter 18 of my *Winds of the Spirit* (293–95).

11. See Robert R. Williams, *Recognition: Fichte and Hegel on the Other* (Albany: State University of New York Press, 1992), 191–93 (the quotation in the last sentence is from Nicolai Hartmann). Hegel first developed the social concept of *Geist* in chapter 6 of *The Phenomenology of Spirit* (1807), trans. A. V. Miller (Oxford: Oxford University Press, 1977).

12. G. W. F. Hegel, *The Science of Logic,* trans. A. V. Miller (London: Allen & Unwin, 1969), 603. The passage as quoted is translated by Williams.

13. Williams, *Recognition,* 198–99, 206–11 (quotation from p. 211).

14. Ibid., 254–56, 265–66, 270, 286, 297–301. Steven G. Smith attempts to mediate between what he regards as Hegelian totality (no radical otherness)

and Levinasian philosophy of absolute otherness. His own proposal is to define spirit as "the intentional togetherness of beings who are for themselves 'I' and for others 'You,' that is, other to each other." The "intentional togetherness" is the We that relates the I and the You without destroying their otherness. Smith thinks it is better to describe spirit as "togetherness-with-others" rather than as "unity in difference." But his proposal is not far from Williams's reading of Hegel. See *The Concept of the Spiritual: An Essay in First Philosophy* (Philadelphia: Temple University Press, 1992), 27–30, 35–43, 49–71, especially 63–65.

15. Paul Tillich, *Systematic Theology,* 3 vols. (Chicago: University of Chicago Press, 1951, 1957, 1963), 3:162ff.

16. Josiah Royce, *The Problem of Christianity* (1913) (Chicago: University of Chicago Press, 1968), 298–307.

17. Ibid., 318–19, 339–41.

18. Mark Lewis Taylor points out that the theme of emancipation is insufficiently developed in Farley's theory of the interhuman. See "Reflective Ontology in the Land of Postmodern Suspicion," *Journal of Religion* 72 (October 1992): 578–79.

19. This idea is developed by Michael Welker, "The Holy Spirit," *Theology Today* 46 (1989): 5–20.

⇛· 4 ·⇚

Issues of *Good and Evil*

WALTER LOWE

Well into the body of *Good and Evil* there is a footnote in which Edward Farley locates his theological project within a larger tradition. The tradition is that of Schleiermacher, whose thoughts on (religious) experience Farley distills into a striking aphorism: "that about ourselves which is utterly dependent is our freedom..." (113). *Good and Evil* may be read as an extended reflection on this dictum.

But it is reflection of a vigorous, constructive sort. A sort of compassionate rationality — sharp-edged conceptual discernment in the service of a deeply humanistic sensibility — makes this a work of major importance. There are, specifically, at least three respects in which Farley extends the Schleiermacherian aphorism. Methodologically, he draws from Maurice Blondel an appreciation of the centrality of human agency, and from Edmund Husserl a rigor in the delineation of the structures of experience. Fusing these two sources is an accomplishment in its own right, a persuasive demonstration that the often conflicting themes of agency and structure can in fact be complementary. Second, Farley surpasses Schleiermacher (and Husserl) in the richness of his palette, giving prominence to themes of *passion* and *tragedy*. (One of the secondary pleasures of this book is seeing the often austere method of phenomenology operating at full stretch.)

In sum, dependence is inseparable from vulnerability. Indeed the effect of *Good and Evil* is to reformulate the Schleiermacherian dictum to read: that about ourselves which is utterly *vulnerable* is our freedom. To this revision may be added one more that is perhaps less obvious, relating to Farley's deft use of a certain notion of *horizon*. The notion is important as the pivot by which Farley will introduce his theological claim; the usage is deft in not presuming that a description of the human horizon is itself necessarily theological. The treatment of horizon is guided by the thesis that it is the nature of our fundamental passions to "desire through and past" their particular objects; "their reference is

51

an infinite resource, an eternal horizon" (112). But the terms "infinite" and "eternal" notwithstanding, the horizon is not itself God.

The nature of the relation to that horizon is more desire and passion than dependence. In my judgment, dependence becomes an explicit theme when the eternal horizon *ceases* to be a mere horizon and is manifest as the sacred, that which in some way does ground and fulfill the passions. (113, emphasis added)

As I understand it, Farley is saying that the horizon per se, "mere horizon," is one thing, while an explicit, thematized awareness of absolute dependence (or of the sacred, or of God) is another. The notion of horizon thus opens a space in which one can affirm a longing for "something more" without being peremptorily informed, as in some overly hasty apologetics, that one has thereby acknowledged the existence of God.

That is not to deny that Farley's own aim is ultimately apologetic. But it is an apologetic that, to put the matter paradoxically, respects the integrity of human brokenness. Delineating brokenness without retreat to reductionism, whether positivistic or theological, demands patience and discernment. These virtues prove their worth as the book unfolds. It is a major contribution to theological anthropology — and, one might say, to theological honesty as well.

Of the twofold thematic of passion and tragedy, it is *tragedy* that predominates in Part One of Farley's two-part study. The contemporary theologian Dietrich Ritschl has remarked that "theology, especially in the protestant tradition, likes to avoid the concept of the tragic."[1] Tragedy is a hard topic in any case. Theology for its part has been particularly resistant to the notion that suffering might be ineradicable; for this has seemed tantamount to saying, unredeemable and unredeemed. Clearly Farley is at grips with a boundary issue here. It is well that he proceeds so judiciously. (A propos of tragedy in particular, there are stretches in which Farley's argument recalls that of Tillich: Tillich with less panache, perhaps, but greater precision.)

To begin with the "human condition," which figures in the subtitle: the term describes "not so much a collection of features of human nature, as what we are up against in our environment, the situation that evokes our typical efforts as living beings" (27). That is to say, our most essential condition is already, of itself, profoundly relational — and profoundly poignant. What structure it has lies neither within us nor outside us. Our human condition is "what we are up against"; perhaps better, it is *the particular shape and context of* of our being-up-against. To say this is already to suggest that, for all its harsh givenness, the situation is not irrational; it is not impervious to reflection. Bearing in mind that abstractions have their limits but also their uses, Farley is arguing that we may treat this condition-of-being-up-against as a single pervasive situation; and further, that we may see it as eliciting from us certain "typical efforts" (cf. Blondel), certain intelligible patterns of response. Here is a refreshing affirmation that there is, after all, a certain shape to what it means to be human.

Farley's exposition of this shape proceeds in two parts. These stand in roughly the same relationship as Paul Ricoeur's two volumes, *Fallible Man* and *The Symbolism of Evil*. That is to say, the first addresses the *preconditions* of evil; the second, evil's *actuality*. In phenomenological terms, the first abstracts from the reality of evil whereas the second removes the brackets, admitting what had been previously disregarded. Or, in the problematic but familiar mythological terms, the first stands "before the Fall," the second "after." As important as the formal parallel, however, is the tacit dispute between Ricoeur and Farley regarding the extent of the shift, fissure, or break between the first condition and the second. For Ricoeur the break is radical. There is a strangeness or otherness that has to be recognized and respected the moment one confronts the reality of evil. To put the matter methodologically, there is a chasm that concept and logic prove unable to traverse unassisted. Thus Ricoeur's hermeneutical turn at the beginning of *Symbolism of Evil* from the relative autonomy of (phenomenological) reason to the resistant but fructifying obscurity that is uniquely conveyed by symbol and myth.

Farley, in contrast, has greater confidence in the capacity of conceptual reflection to hold its ground without compromising alliances, even in the face of a subject as daunting as the irruption of evil. His reason for taking this position has already been shown; there is a coherent, univocal "human condition" that perdures though the worst occur. Because it perdures, it can serve — and indeed for Farley it *must* serve — as the determinative context within which the deliverances of symbol and myth are to be set and by which they are to be judged. One sees the criterion functioning as Farley shows himself considerably more inclined than Ricoeur to pick and choose among the elements of symbol and myth. The effect is a sort of demythologization. A further consequence of the phenomenological adhesion to the guiding thread of the human (albeit always the human in relationship) is the crucial fact that in *Good and Evil* the concept of evil is pretty much coterminous with moral evil or, in theological terms, sin. (What is often called "natural evil" Farley includes under the heading of "the tragic," which, I take it, he is precisely concerned *not* to call evil, lest the human condition itself be thought evil.) This is another divergence from Ricoeur, for whom any purely anthropological understanding of evil must inevitably run up against a surplus, a surd, which resists so monothematic an account.

•

This is perhaps an appropriate point to register my impression that there is both gain and loss in Farley's approach. Pure gain is the fact that Farley compels classical Christian theology to confront its deeply rooted penchant toward a certain escapism, the impulse, which Ritschl remarked, to deny the harsh reality attested by the tragic vision. Challenged by Farley's argument for relative continuity, much of the tradition shows the marks of discontinuity run amok: Eden is free of suffering, all suffering is the result of the Fall, and with personal conversion, on some accounts, all real suffering is removed. On this telling, as Farley observes,

> suffering succeeds evil as its punishment. Accordingly, the tragic cannot be sin's context because it is its consequence. Sin thus is contextless, and its only motivation is simply its own formal possibility. (129)

Theology proceeding by way of phenomenology is sometimes charged with anthropocentrism. But in Farley's hands phenomenology serves to show that it is the common reading of the tradition that is anthropocentric; for its story turns on a contextless will, voluntarism pure and simple, whereas phenomenology traces the complex web of human relationality. Will acting without context, transcending limitation, and, by the same gesture, delivering itself from pain — this is the gnosticism that constitutes, if Harold Bloom is right, "the American religion." Such homegrown escapism is very difficult to defend in light of Farley's critique.

So much is gain. At the same time, it may be that Farley's very strength, his unblinking lucidity, entails a limitation. Ricoeur's well-known formula is that "the symbol gives rise to thought," with the implication that it does this again and again: thought constantly returns to the symbol in order to be renewed. But increasingly as one witnesses the steady progression of Farley's thought, one is moved to say that here the symbol does not so much give rise as give *way* to thought. To be fair, Farley does affirm that the symbols of Hebraic culture did make a contribution to human understanding that is distinctive and crucial. The symbols made a firm "differentiation between imperiled finitude and evil" (126). But the force of this affirmation seems to be that the symbols and stories were, historically, the original vehicles for this "insight." But it would seem on Farley's account that once the insight has been gained and the distinction firmly made, then it becomes possible for reason to proceed apace without requiring further reference to the genre from which the insight originally sprang. In the language of Kierkegaard's *Fragments,* symbol is here understood to function in the manner of a Socratic teacher; in time it becomes dispensable.

Thus there is little suggestion in *Good and Evil* that evil might be in any strong sense of the term a mystery; or that symbols might convey such mystery through a surplus that resists translation. (Pressing this point need not amount to special pleading for the Hebraic or Christian perspective; classical tragedy, in its own fashion, resounds with a sense of the imponderable.) In allowing the actual incursion of evil to remain a surd located "between" two books, Ricoeur acknowledged a space in which reflection must fall silent. Such recognition is not prominent in Farley's account.

Having registered this reservation, let me conclude this assessment by saying that I had not originally envisioned an extended comparison with Ricoeur. But in reflecting on *Good and Evil,* one naturally turns to Ricoeur — simply in order to find anyone else who has worked on such an extraordinary scale and yet has done so with such incisiveness.

Returning now to the argument: there is "a human condition" that perdures though the worst occur. After all, we continue to speak of "human being" before, during, and after the bracketing of evil. What Farley proposes is simply a judicious exposition of the continuity of sense that is implied by this univocal usage.

And what is this golden thread? In *Good and Evil* the good news that there is a sense-making continuity running throughout human affairs is inseparable from the hard news that the name for this continuity is "the tragic." Both points are in evidence when Farley states that "aside from the paradigm of evil and good, the tragic is the most general and *unifying* feature of our condition..." (28, emphasis added). Tragedy is not adventitious, an affliction from without. The book is relentless in pressing the full logical force of tragic *necessity.* "Human condition is not tragic simply because suffering is an aspect of it but because sufferings of various sorts are necessary conditions of creativity, affection, the experience of beauty, etc." (29). We find egress neither backward by retreat to Eden nor forward by divine deliverance. In words anticipating his own description of salvation as graced existence (and recalling Tillich's "courage to be"), Farley writes that "historical freedom is not a release from vulnerability and the tragic but *a way of existing as* vulnerable and...tragic" (118, emphasis added).

Thus while it is true that in Farley the chasm of "before" and "after" is reduced and a certain continuity affirmed, it is also true that the note of conflict is retained, even heightened, and the field of conflict expands. There is less offense to reason, but now tragedy is all-pervasive — precisely because it is inherent and reasonable. All this Farley readily affirms; for the same gesture that so extends the realm of the tragic serves, ipso facto, to restrict the realm of *evil.* The logic, as I understand it, is this: Apart from the tragic, which is its precondition, evil remains incomprehensible. Uncomprehended, evil exceeds all bounds, seeming ontological. The human seems evil by nature. But once the full sway of tragedy is avowed, acknowledged as "a human condition," then (moral) evil makes sense as a human, all too human *response to* the inherent given. It itself ceases to be inherent.

One might perhaps say that the irrational gap has been tamed to a rational distinction, namely, that distilled from the Hebraic "differentiation between imperiled finitude and evil." "Human evil as an individual response is constituted by a distinctive dynamics, and as such is to be differentiated from tragic existence and its vulnerabilities..." (117). But it is a distinction that makes all the difference — opening space for freedom and hope. "Human reality is redeemable, transformable toward the good, because the dynamics of evil at work in each sphere have no necessary status in that sphere" (118).

That affirmation — "the dynamics of evil...have no necessary status" — is the good news of *Good and Evil.* To live by that word is to exist in freedom. But the living requires grace; and an understanding of grace requires a further engagement with Farley's text.

•

Part One of *Good and Evil* treats "Three Spheres of Human Reality." We may provisionally regard these as the realms of the one, the two, and the many. They are the personal sphere (the realm of individual agency), the interhuman sphere (or the interpersonal), and the social sphere. In the process of fleshing out these abstractions, Farley marshals an extraordinary range of human experience. There are reflections on compassion, obligation, temporality, determinacy, transcendence, and much else. An entire chapter is devoted to the biological aspects of personal being. Uniting it all, however, is the theme of the human's structural vulnerability. Indeed that phrase distills the movement that each chapter manages, *mutatis mutandis,* to trace: from eidetic *structure* to the consequent concrete *vulnerability.* Thus, for example, the movement from "elements of social reality" (power, society) to the social world and systems; and thence to a consideration of the incompatibilities inherent to the social world and social systems — which eventuate in specific forms of human suffering.

Thus tragedy is the *telos* of each of Part One's chapters. But it is not quite the *telos* of Part One itself. For, while tragedy has had the foreground, the part's logic has been throughout one of tragedy and *desire.* For one state of affairs is hardly tragic unless another is desired. Now, at the end of Part One, this generative tension is foregrounded and intensified under the heading of "tragedy and *passion.*" The final chapter introduces three "elemental passions of personal being": the passion of subjectivity (cf. the realm of personal being), the passion of the interhuman (cf. the second sphere, pressing into the third), and the passion for reality. At first these seem to function as simply a further

turn of the descriptive screw, for they do have the effect of intensify-
ing, painfully, the human's awareness of exposure and loss. The passions
"are our deepest motivating inclinations. Yet they cannot be fulfilled"
(111). But in and through their unfulfillment, the passions introduce
something new, as reflected by the fact that after the penultimate section on "the tragic structure of the elemental passions" there appears
a further section entitled "Eternal Horizon." By virtue of passion the
tragic is intensified, no doubt; but also by virtue of passion, tragedy is
situated, and even relativized, against a larger backdrop. It is here that
Farley's notion of horizon comes into its own. It is sheer "beyond," de-
void of material content or moral assurance. It is not God; but if there
is a God, it opens in that direction.

Thus it is ultimately by a process of triangulation — tragedy, desire/
passion, eternal horizon — that Part One anticipates Part Two of Farley's diptych, "A Paradigm of Good and Evil." Pivotal in this respect is
the lead chapter of the second part, "Idolatry." Surveying the various
forms of human suffering, Farley notes that they do not necessarily issue
in unrelieved misery or despair. What *can* be taken as a necessary result, and thus as a firm point of reference for theological reflection, is a
certain "timbre of discontent." The point is delicate; theology has often
leaned heavily on dilemma and guilt to tilt reflection toward a celestial
remedy. Farley's sensitivity is exemplary. "Tragic vulnerability effects a
tone of discontent and anxiety" (131), which becomes acute when it is
set where life sets it, amid the elemental passions. "Subjectivity yearns
for its confirmation and securing"; but "whatever clues there might be
to our place in the scheme of things, they are not built in" to the various
dimensions of our experience. "This is not to say that there *is* no meaning in the totality of things," but it is to say that such meaning as there is
"is not itself contained in the act of existing." The result is that "hiding
at the heart of things *appears* to be chaos" (131, emphases added.)

These anxious reflections bring us to the very precipice of moral evil.
In describing the next step, Farley is concerned, as he is throughout
Good and Evil, to show how understandable, how pitiable, is the moral
lapse. The book, for all its intellectual rigor — or rather, in and through
its rigor — stands as a work of compassion. Having called theological
escapism to account in Part One, he is equally unsparing of a certain
theological vindictiveness in Part Two. This is the tendency, in the name
of divine goodness and sovereignty, to so dissociate God from the circumstances of moral evil that the human individual is subjected to an
incomprehensible and near-irredeemable guilt.

This long overdue correction is, one may say, the raison d'être of the
book. It is a major contribution to the discussion of moral evil, to be
received with gratitude. At the same time, however, if we read Farley's
text somewhat against the grain, we find it attesting to another real-

ity as well — namely, the reality of guilt and its resistance to rational understanding.

Resuming our exposition, there "appears to be chaos." It is not necessarily anything more than an *appearance*. But it is the appearance of *chaos:* the apparent futility-of-all confronts us constantly, implacably, with no label saying "mere appearance." It is proof of Farley's continuity that the entire approach to evil, including the encounter with apparent nonsense, makes sense. Only now, at the ultimate moment, does the text register a tremor of the inexplicable. The situation described is, Farley writes, "the one situation we human beings seem incapable of accepting." He does not explain why we are incapable. The word "seem" suggests a hesitation, reintroducing the possibility that we are not really incapable. And hesitation is in fact in order; for if we are truly *incapable* of withstanding this situation, then we cannot logically be blamed for giving in.

What has happened, I think, is that Farley has carried logical explanation to something like its limit, an extraordinary achievement. But at the decisive moment, through a matter as slight as the word "seem," evil's absurdity reappears. And with that absurdity, it seems fair to say, the classical debates of Augustine and Pelagius, Luther and Erasmus, become pertinent again.

In another summary statement, Farley writes that "human passionate existence...cannot accept its own ultimate nonsignificance" (132). Again one senses a textual/logical unease. Recent theology has frequently endorsed, often for good feminist reasons, the importance of a certain self-affirmation; and indeed Part One makes a similar argument. Thus it seems inconsistent for Farley now to imply that humankind is blameworthy because it "cannot accept its own ultimate nonsignificance." Surely resistance to utter non-significance is a legitimate act, an affirmation of self-worth. (There is also the ambiguity of "cannot," echoing the earlier "incapable.") Soon there will be passages in which Farley will be prophetic in condemning the consequences of moral evil. But precisely in the measure that moral evil is so condemned, it becomes important that the present argument not reinforce theology's penchant for imputing false guilt. Yet that, it seems to me, is what happens when "human passionate existence" is condemned because it "cannot accept its own ultimate nonsignificance." Truer to Farley's intent, perhaps, is to focus the critique upon the human failure to stand firm in the face of the ambiguous *possibility* that our existence might ultimately be futile. Truer still, perhaps, would be to say that the (famously elusive) authorial intention is in tension, tugged by conflicting requirements that are the evidence of a surd. "Cannot accept...*nonsignificance*" makes the transition from precondition to actuality of evil, from "before" to "after," smoother, more logical; but it renders moral responsibility problematic. On the other hand, not accepting the *possibility* of non-significance is something an agent can be more readily blamed for; but it leaves unresolved, obscured by the ambiguous "cannot," the question of why humankind responds not with reasonable acceptance, but irrational flight.

There follows Farley's most explicit fingering of the culprit — "through this weakness, this incapacity to tolerate a clue-less world enters the initial act of the dynamics of evil..." (132). The break, chasm, or fissure has been crossed; we find ourselves east of Eden, bearing, if not the full knowledge of good and evil, at least a working criterion by which the terms can be understood. Evil is, or springs from, a refusal to accept vulnerability, a fierce determination that vulnerability be expunged. "Driven by this insistence, we thus move through our times and places alert to anything that might fill our existentially hungry maws" (133). Grasping at anything, asking of the objects of experience an assurance they cannot give, we "relate to the mundane good as if it itself were the eternal horizon"; "we collapse the horizon into these goods" (134). Or rather we try to do so. Horizon remains horizon, particular good remains partial — yet our choice of stance toward these abiding facts, these continuities, does have its effect. For if it is true that that about us which is utterly vulnerable is our freedom, then freedom is diminished when vulnerability is denied. Trying to bend the finely poised concept of horizon into something more or less than it is, trying to make it a thing or a god, we deny ourselves the precious opening, the sort of edenic latitude, that it can properly provide.

Whence the morphology of distortions that constitutes much of Farley's Part Two. "Distortions" is preferred to "vices" as a term that, even in naming the wrong, invokes the rightful structure in light of which, only, the malignancy makes sense. (Farley is explicit here about his debt to the virtue tradition [156]). The three elemental passions, each confined to a subsection in Part One, now get a chapter each: it is almost as if the passions were not really interesting until they got distorted. But this is unfair, for each distortion is paired with a positive counterpart, a turn to the good. And what makes this turning possible? Farley speaks of the experience or occurrence of "being-founded."

> The eternal horizon as such does not found since it is simply the term for the undesignated referent of the elemental passions. The eternal horizon founds (locates the human being in the midst of chaos) only in the form of an actual presence, or in other words, the sacred. (144)

We noted at the outset that the notion of horizon provided an opening in which inchoate longing could reside without being overinterpreted, without having to speak of God. Recently we have seen that in actuality

humankind does not sustain such openness, does not endure the longing, but chooses rather to shrink horizon to the shape of some imagined
god. Now in the notion of "being-founded" the terms of horizon and
divine, which were first distinguished and then collapsed, find at last, in
encounter with the sacred, their appropriate convergence — horizon is
concretized.

   This event or succession of events shapes the chapters that treat the
various passions. We witness the movement from the passion of subjectivity to its corruption, and thence to the freedom of vitality; from
passion of the interhuman, through distortion to the release of agapic
freedom; and from passion for reality through distortion to the freedom
of wonder. The book then concludes by exploring the specifically social
form of the tragic as well as social redemption.

                                    •

In the remainder of this essay I propose to treat a notion that orients
much of Farley's thinking, giving his book its strong humanistic appeal.
This is the notion of the interpersonal, or more concretely, following
Emmanuel Levinas, the encounter with "the face." As regards method,
I propose to press further the practice of occasionally reading "against
the grain." Doing so is an indirect gesture of respect, as it is only with
a finely executed text that such an approach proves interesting. Where
thought has been vigilant, any residual incoherence suggests less of an
authorial lapse than of a resistance in the subject itself. In eliciting such
points of resistance, deconstruction may be said to strive for a certain
objectivity. A part of my purpose is thus to suggest that elements drawn
from deconstruction can coexist and interact with a traditional reading
of the text.

   The importance Farley attributes to the interpersonal is measured by
its role in resisting "a prevailing dualism" that he sees as debilitating
much of contemporary thought. This is "the dualism of the individual
and the social. Like most dualisms, it distorts a legitimate distinction —
one that in fact structures a good deal of Part One. To forestall the
distortion, Part One treats not two "spheres of human reality," the
individual and the social, but three. The first to be discussed, "the
interhuman," is precisely that which exceeds and undercuts any binary
opposition of the other two.

   To elucidate the interhuman in all its irreducibility requires phenomenological effort, because the distinctiveness of this sphere is not
immediately obvious. It is marginalized by the commonsense alternatives
of the one and the many, which readily turn to an all-encompassing opposition in the current culture of alienation. In face of such distortion,
phenomenology assumes a social-critical role, cracking the resistant shell
of "the natural attitude" in order to elicit awareness of that which is

truly original and generative. In the face of the other person one encounters a "primordial summons" to "compassionate obligation." The summons is not derivative from culture; it is rather "the basis of the values in the normative culture" (41).

One can only applaud Farley's reclaiming of the interpersonal in deliberate resistance to "the oppressive de-humanization of advanced industrial society" (25–26). But precisely because the Levinasian testimony is so crucial, to Farley and to us, we need to attend to it closely, hearing it in its strangeness. Nothing is accomplished by receiving the testimony patronizingly, secure in the assurance that we in our good humanistic hearts already know what it is about.

As antidote to such assurance, a passage from Jean-François Lyotard is, I think, suggestive. Lyotard asks:

> what if human beings, in humanism's sense, were in the process of, constrained into, becoming inhuman (that's the first part)? And (the second part), what if what is "proper" to humankind were to be inhabited by the inhuman?
>
> Which would make two sorts of inhuman. It is indispensable to keep them dissociated. The inhumanity of the system which is currently being consolidated under the name of development (among others) must not be confused with the infinitely secret one of which the soul is hostage.[2]

While it is perhaps wiser to use the term "nonhuman" for the second case, Lyotard's distinction may indeed be important, even "indispensable," to our time. There may indeed be an "inhumanity of the system which is currently being consolidated..." — which is what both Farley and Lyotard oppose. But there may also possibly be an other-than-human that proves as ingredient to our humanity as "the human" itself. Raising this possibility, Lyotard ventures beyond what Farley has said.

If there should be such non-human reality, Farley would yet be vindicated in one sense at least: for even in that hypothetical realm there would persist the themes of ambiguity and vulnerability. The inhabiting of the human by the anomalously non-human might be a susceptibility to the destructively inhuman. And yet that same strangeness might also be a resistance against an all too knowing humanism that can, unfortunately, become another form of reductive inhumanity. With such possibilities in mind, let us return to the text.

Farley stresses that the interpersonal is not to be approached lightly; awareness of this reality "requires a reflective break." Just how radical a break Farley makes evident as he quotes approvingly Gabriel Marcel's assertion that such awareness requires "a kind of redemption" (38). This is strong rhetoric, aimed at making an ethical point. But if one takes it seriously, as it asks to be taken, one has to find it daunting. For how then is one to proceed? Specifically, does the break required by the interpersonal entail a break in method? Farley writes,

> the interpersonal is something disclosed in concrete human acts and relations. Thus, for Buber, it happens as a turning to the other and a becoming aware which breaks the order of mere observing and onlooking. (137–38, emphasis added)

It is impossible not to endorse the sentiment here, impossible not to wish to honor the interpersonal in its uniqueness. But *how* does one do this? According to the Buber paraphrase, one does it by breaking with "the order of mere observing and onlooking." But as I understand phenomenology, it *is* precisely a discipline of "mere" — cf. strict — "observing and onlooking." Certainly as regards its *subject matter,* phenomenology can treat anything, no holds barred. There can be a phenomenology of passion or a phenomenology of apathy; a phenomenology of observing and onlooking, a phenomenology of utter engagement, a phenomenology of the break that leads to the interpersonal. It is the glory of phenomenology that all of these things are possible — as regards the subject treated. But as regards *method,* phenomenology lives and breathes, or one might say it gets its breathing space, by virtue of a certain bracketing. Any phenomenon may present itself; but as long as the brackets are maintained, all that presents itself is regarded as phenomenon, i.e., as occasion for pure description. Thus the phenomenologist who does that describing remains — as phenomenologist — in a posture of "observing and onlooking." In this sense one might speak of a certain "coldness" of phenomenology. For all the humanness of its purpose, its method necessarily retains an element of the "nonhuman."

Thus a dilemma. *Either* phenomenology sets firm limits to the "reflective break," keeping it within the brackets and not allowing it to affect the method as such, in which case it opens itself to the accusation of denying in its very method the reality it professes to respect; *or* phenomenology allows the break to exceed the brackets, to affect the method itself, in which case the mode of investigation becomes something different from what is commonly meant by phenomenology. Farley's preference, I think, is for the first option, and that is fair enough. Being open to an accusation is not the same as being guilty of it. But then it must be said that Farley's references to break and conversion have the effect of obscuring a critical distance or "coldness" that is perhaps endemic to reason, and specifically to phenomenology.

Now Farley himself has recognized and affirmed a certain otherness within his account of the interhuman. An early signal that Farley is up to something distinctive in Part One is the subsection entitled "Alterity." At the same time, however, this is one subsection among three, reflecting "the triadic structure of the interhuman"; and it would seem that of the three it is not the most fundamental; for it, along with the always already thereness of the social, represents a somewhat formal element that does not achieve full significance until anchored in the concreteness of interpersonal encounter. Farley's text makes it clear that the alterity of which he speaks is the alterity of the (other) person; and that the place where that otherness finds its natural setting — better, the place where it occurs — is the interpersonal encounter.

This is well and good. But can alterity, once introduced, be confined to the task that Farley stipulates? In *Good and Evil*, alterity applies specifically to the other person, the individual; it is, if you will, a humanistic alterity. But the other, counterbalancing notion with which it is linked — namely, the always already thereness of language and sociality — is that not itself a form of "difference"? Is it not a web of deferral that, exceeding my grasp, constitutes another sort of alterity? If so, then Farley's delimitation of alterity may actually mask something more fundamental.

Talk of coldness and the non-human is inevitably off-putting. Let us conclude by turning to Levinas, a figure compelling in his undoubted humanity. In the decisive paragraph in which Farley gives his most concentrated account of the reality of the interpersonal, he approaches the topic from two angles. The first cites Levinas in particular; it speaks of "the 'face' (*visage*)" as "the 'infinitely strange' and mysterious presence...an unforeseeable depth..." (39). The second invokes Buber in particular, speaking of mutual relation. The clear implication is that the two thinkers converge, perhaps even coalesce. Here one must ask: can the ethical *asymmetry* of Levinas in fact be contained within the dialogic *symmetry* of Buber? I sense in Levinas's invocation of the face something absolute, "infinite," and absolutely demanding: something that calls upon me to expend myself absolutely, without reserve. The stringent asymmetry falls from view when themes of mutual relation are invoked, as in Farley's grouping together of Buber and Levinas as "philosophers of dialogue" (39).

The difference between Buber and Levinas may be pertinent to "the inhuman," Lyotard's first, negative term. Between the publication of *I and Thou* and the appearance of *Totality and Infinity* there lies the reality of Nazism and the Holocaust. It may be that Levinas was inclined to speak in terms of mutuality and reciprocity, in terms of symmetry, but that he found himself driven to adopt terms more difficult for our ever-equilibrating minds. Farley's acknowledgment of alterity (34–36) notwithstanding, there is in his adoption of Buber an implication that interpersonal encounter is in some sense a knowledge of "like to like." In Levinas one encounters the radically "unlike" — I am finite, the other is "infinite" — something that is perhaps more akin, for all the difference in mode of presentation, to Kant's relentless imperative. Could it be that it is only by such non-human strangeness that the human, or interhuman, is truly affirmed?

NOTES

1. Dietrich Ritschl, *The Logic of Theology: A Brief Account of the Relationship between Basic Concepts in Theology* (Philadelphia: Fortress Press, 1987), 192.
2. Jean-François Lyotard, *The Inhuman: Reflections on Time* (Stanford, Calif.: Stanford University Press, 1991), 2.

5

Beyond Good and Evil

A Conversation about Reality

CHARLES E. SCOTT

One of the privileges, Ed, of writing for a volume such as this one is that a contributor may address directly the volume's subject. You are, in my address to you here, primarily a philosopher. We are in broad agreement that philosophy properly arises from and addresses the ideas, meanings, and attitudes in which we live. The "we" in that sentence, of course, means that thought is always contextual and that it arises from our everyday lives. One aspect of the context of my own thought in this discussion of your work is our common background in continental philosophy. Another is my admiration for your clarity of mind and care of scholarship, your remarkable range of knowledge in the history of Western thought, and your requirement of exactness in agreement as well as in argument. More than any other theologian whom I know, you have read classical phenomenology with a depth of understanding that allows you to think with it and through it without superficiality as you have formulated your own reflective agenda. I shall attempt to think with you in the context of your originality by addressing the question of "reality" as you conceive it. I shall carry out this address by attention largely to your *Good and Evil: Interpreting a Human Condition* (whose page numbers I will occasionally note in the text in parentheses).

I do not wish to deny your claims for reflective ontology, particularly at a time when ideology and interest in power often thoughtlessly override the discipline of thought while attempting to change practices and stratifications in our culture: a dangerous way to proceed — thoughtlessly — when at least a small revolution is afoot both in theology and in Western society generally. Such revaluation is composed of a bundle of changes in which you and I are willing participants. But without careful thought? With a fervor and certainty that compare in their intensity to that of the Children's Crusades and the witch hunts of not *so* many years ago? Confidence, the rightness of the victims, overriding

65

interest in power — without careful, disciplined, patient, very well educated thought? We have good reason to be worried that in such passions one kind of racism will replace another, domination will replace domination, tribal identities will be preserved *über alles*, and self-deception will rule many values. I am a part of such dangers, but I also agree with you that careful thinking, while itself constituting a danger, provides possibilities for understanding and action that are missing from the passions of overwhelmed and committed individuals.

I wish to show, with considerable reliance on reflective ontology, that your reflective ontology requires more of itself than it seems prepared to be. By using the word "be" in this moment, I intend to suggest the importance of attention to the performative aspect of thought. Thinking is a praxis that creates sight, value, and knowledge. Although I will not elaborate this claim, I should say for the sake of orienting my remarks, that I believe that fundamental "symbols" in a culture often arise from still more fundamental thoughts, that just as thinking can carry out the subtle and often indiscernible direction and power of symbols, so some symbols also carry out the overdetermination of thoughts in the power of those thoughts to generate meanings and identities. The thought of continuing presence, for example, seems to me to have produced the very idea of *symballon*. In this essay, however, my parameter is narrow, and I shall ask only about the manner in which your thought performs its closeness and its distance to certain aspects of what it knows to be "real." In this process I hope to call into question the manner in which you thematize good and evil.

Skeletal thinking. Thinking that looks at the structures of things, that attempts to see the bones bare of the skin and tone, of the voluptuousness, the attraction and repulsions, the sensualness, and above all the self-interested desires that hold "us" hostage to the flesh. I believe that Nietzsche is correct in finding such thought to be a major progeny and carrier of the ascetic ideal, a child of the resentment in Western moralities and religions that create meanings and invest them with images of deathless being. The ascetic ideal is the moving force that attempts to separate reality in some essential way from the meaningless beginnings, sensations, sufferings, and deaths of bodies. I also believe that such thought provides an avenue through itself and beyond itself. I will say more about that later. For now I want to emphasize how important such thinking is. I have seen you many times quietly eye a complex situation, gently pull at your mustache, smile slightly, and see beyond the covering, x-ray-like, to the bones. I have also seen you look for the skeletal structure when it was not clearly manifest, or look for the stress fractures, the strange mutations, and the missing joints. I have seen people withdraw and flee as though physically threatened by your quiet desire to see the structures that hold a thing together.

Skeletal thinking, I believe, both expresses a passion and restrains many passions. It expresses and constitutes a desire to see things as they "really" are, to see things *in* their definitive being, to avoid deception and the seductions of rhetoric, special pleading, and well-dressed muddled-headedness. But such thought also restrains us and interrupts the significations of common practice and ideological affirmation. It is so irritating to be interrupted in the act of passionate self-expression, particularly when it is for an obviously good and right cause! In your practice, skeletal thinking can liberate us from what offers itself unthinkingly as liberation, can let us see the hidden and required attachments. Before such discomforting thought as yours can be, some people want to know what happened to faith as the origin of reflection. What happened to worship as the figuration of proper theology? And what happened to the Bible? etc., etc. You, however, give us a new version of Christian humanism by means of discerning what I believe I can fairly call historical universals in human experience in connection with primary symbols in Christian faith. You show Christian intention and meaning in its presentation of human reality.

Although *I* think it is obvious, let me say what I have just done: by this aside I want to emphasize the performative aspect of thinking, its practice and, in your terms, its "reality." I affirmed the importance of reflective ontology in the form of skeletal thinking with an ambiguity that I believe is part of *its* skeleton. I attempted to write in this ambiguity as I linked it to the ascetic ideal, by emphasizing its questionable connection to meaninglessness, sensuality, and death, and by also connecting it to "genuine" insight that in its enactment can free us from all manner of half-baked conceptions, practices, and bondings. I took a light tone to offset a predisposition to weighty seriousness that I believe is part of our usual attitudes toward death, meaninglessness, and what is really "real," an attitude that perpetuates an anxious emphasis on the importance of essences. I invoked Nietzsche in order to suggest in an initial move that the anatomy of skeletal thought has a genealogy that provides both its value and its danger. Throughout the paragraph I maintained a posture that I believe can be spelled out and justified only by the use of something like skeletal thinking. And finally, I noted in this context the import of the words "presentation of human reality" for your project.

In *Good and Evil*, when you consider deconstructive thought, you caution against throwing the baby out with the bath water. We should address with severe criticism — relative criticism, you call it — whatever distorts "reality." But we should not condemn the carrier of those distortions, a carrier such as reflective ontology (17–18). I am on the way to supporting the genealogical claim that our ability to reflect as we do — our reflective capacity — itself has a history of development that

reflective ontology can to some degree uncover. By such analysis reflective ontology can put itself in question, and when it does, as it occurs in
question, it approaches something like an origin in its own occurrence
that is, in your terms, paradigmatic and expendable. In this endeavor,
I do not want to support those kinds of criticism of your work that,
like regional ontologies at play in power games, use limited descriptive claims to enhance this or that special interest. But I do want to
show that the "origin" and "reality" of rational ontology are not found
in essences but in paradigmatic presentations that give most value to
human subjectivity in the shading of a Greek-oriented rationality.

As you know and say in effect in *Good and Evil*, you and I are in
discourses that are different enough to be immune to any "refutations"
that one might make of the other. Even the names we choose for the
other's stance will lack resonance enough to carry the power of *proper*
names: we would not recognize ourselves clearly in the other's nomi-
nation. In part that is because I do not find your preferred traditions
persuasive in their theories about "reality" and reason and symboliza-
tion; hence, in the realism, idealism, and theologies that form in part
my ability to think I want to find the conflicts, interests, and countermovements that give force to their transformations and mutations, find
their "questionability" without belief or trust in grounding "reality" of
any kind. There are strategies and economies of thought and practice —
very powerful ones — that constitute us, some of which have weakened
enough to become optional. In the balances and disequilibriums of those
strategies and economies that constitute us, a person is more or less inclined to desire and trust "a reality" or the possibility of the grounding
and unifying "reality" that occurs outside of the clear figurations of
our perceptions (occurs, you have said, appresently). Such desire and
trust are not lively enough or productive enough of things that I want
to value to merit a much longer life. But — and this is a hermeneutical "but" — this difference, as I see it, makes continuing talk possible.
Not so much argumentation as conversation. I doubt that ontology as
a means of perception will bridge this gap since, to be convincing, it
requires a view and use of reason that are part of the question. But
we can continue to compare notes, suggest modifications, and present
what you call paradigms in their productive differences. In our continuing conversation I read you with an emphasis on what makes optional
the definitive and hence necessary experiences, concepts, and agency in
your rationality and faith. I look for the powers internal to them that
will overturn them. I find that you read texts on my side of the divide
in a way that dulls the sharpest edges of their difference and that places
them — holds them — in the very kind of thinking and observing from
which they take their departure. But distortion, as you say, is part of the
thinking process, and I believe that neither one of our distortions much

surprises the other. Yet in spite of the genial spirit of our encounter, the stakes are high. I believe that we are addressing the basic human experiences of life and that the manner of our encounter with them can come to be a stabilizing or destabilizing part of those experiences. Our basic human experiences are always available for transformation. None is stabilized by simple or non-historical essences (you can see that before this discussion is finished I will question your idea and image of the faith), and our encounter can be a moment in which those experiences, for the moment, alter decisively or hold their course in traditional self-repetition.

"Paradoxically we must distort reality in order to know it" (10). This paradox, which is important in your assessment of the limits of rational ontology, means that our successes in interpreting and thinking are at best provisional and partial. You are clear that neither your thought nor anyone else's escapes situational limitations even in its most fundamental axioms. Thinking always includes distorting. Hence you appreciate the importance of the consequences of thought. If your reflective ontology or the very thought of reflective ontology were to lead to unacceptable ethical or religious practices, you would want to change your thought. I understand this conviction to function like a principle of self-correction that defines rational ontology on your terms.

Your thought — that is, your distortion — is pervaded, you say, by a "guilty conscience" (1). In your "guilt" you place a strong emphasis on the agent as well as on "reality" as such, i.e., on things and people in their own presence. I believe that I can say appropriately for your thought that agency and reality as presence are two of the primary axes for your rational ontology (God or the Sacred — presence necessary to itself and to other presence — I believe is another and closely related, if less mentioned axis, but I will have little to say about that.) So guilt and your experience of agency and presence presumably make an important combination in the formation of the "skeleton" of your reflection. And that places you squarely, and I assume happily, in the center of Judaeo-Christian reflection: agency is experienced and thought in its difference from and in its guilt before an unreducible other, however alterity is otherwise conceived. This acceptance of guilt in the agency of your thought I take to be an indirect acceptance of something approximate to original sin in the sense that your agency is in its distortion always already indebted to the other-to-*be*-thought or known.

There are, of course, other ways to experience difference and identity than the way tinctured by guilt — an enjoyment, for example, of creation and distortion *without* a sense of violated nature, as one might find in Homer (and hence, Odysseus), or perhaps in Picasso, or in Nietzsche's ideal of the artist and philosopher. Or one might attempt to overturn the experience of guilt from within its own occurrence, as Heidegger does in

Being and Time. But your reflection reveals its guilt on its own terms by falling short of the "reality" of whatever it "grasps."[1]

The dyad of "reality" and grasping is both definitive of your thought and optional for a thinker. Viewed in the economy of agency, one's "reality" is active and to an extent oppositional to whatever one takes or grasps in regard of the other. The agent's self-enactment is at once a loss of the other's reality in the agent's recognition or appropriation of the other. A certain prefiguring of evil and need for redemption that are found in agency as distortion in the enactment of the agent's "reality" spells out loss and immediate denial of the other's *own* being. A nascent cruelty lies there, curled up as Sartre says, like a worm in the apple's core. Somehow the agent's "reality" needs a revision of its own nature to avoid its natural and depleting distortion, a revision that it, of course, fails to accomplish in any further (distorting) self-enactment. Maybe the face will help us here — we will see.

Hence, as I understand your "cognitive style" (2, for example) you appropriate the abstractness of cognition along with its specific situatedness: your thought, on its own terms, is an actual moment that expresses a highly complex history in the disclosive and distorting power of an abstracting agency. In such activity one comes to see the structure of focused things, and this seeing shows and hides what is there in a thoroughly incomplete presentation in both the reflective agency and the reflected subject.

This revealing-concealing activity — this distorting presentation of "realities" — can take place within the "paradigm" of good and evil as it has developed within the Hebraic-Christian tradition. I understand "Hebraic-Christian" to mean the Christian tradition with special note given to its Hebraic lineage, although the word "paradigm" suggests a certain privilege for the Greek component in Christian experience and thought. Levinas, for example, would surely find himself lost to his faith in a paradigm that included him. But that is part of the distortion. You do not claim to escape at least a prefiguration of evil in your account of good and evil. To the contrary, your presentation is one that owns its distortion of "reality" — owns the evil that takes place within it — and that indirectly, at least, opens itself to something that it cannot accomplish, to a coming of redemption before the face of the other. The focusing, abstracting, and selecting that compose your reflective ontology manifests the prefiguration of evil, if not the evil of ontology, as surely as your ontology shows the good that comes to human being. As your thought "grasps" and "exhibits" human "reality" within the Christian paradigm, the tragic drama of evil takes place within the shadow of redemption. "Reality" drains from its reflective presentation; that drama has, as one of its actors, the distortion of evil's "reality" along with the loss of "what" will not be a part of focusing and abstracting and selecting. Reflective ontology *presents* its need for redemption before the distorted other that reflective ontology knows itself to have wronged badly in its effort of faithful presentation. Hence your suspicion of those confident articulations of values that, in their sense of right, seem to have no attunement to the cruelty that indwells their bright truths. In your thought, "paradigm" happens in guilt and distortion before the loss of life-giving creation: *in* your thought's creative work, careful, even loving presentation of what is presented loses something of its life, is maimed in its being. And the hope that indwells your paradigmatic thought happens here in its failure, for reflective ontology knows about its evil, and that knowledge is like a clearing for a less contaminated option. It does not expect to be fully true — or it expects to find its truth in its terrible limitation — but it also finds in its presentation of "realities" the hint, at least, of presentation, viz., creation, that gives life rather than takes it away.

While thought and knowledge are always distorting and contingent, "reality" is of another order in comparison to them. I have marked "reality" with quotation marks throughout this essay because it is so important for your thinking and because I doubt that the word appropriately names anything. Or at least the word distorts badly what it names. In this context I want to address your understanding of agency. I give emphasis to the issue of agency because in your thought the various "spheres" of human being and the problematic of good and evil are determined by the thought of agency. As I see it, the formalism and structural emphasis in your thought are not at all its most questionable characteristics. *The* question addresses the "reality" of agency-in-the-world.

I note in passing that considerable work has been done and is being carried out in efforts to let the priority of subjectivity — i.e., agency — overturn in our thought and values. In saying that, I do not mean that your thought of agency or the way you think it are passé. To the contrary. Most of the continental philosophers whom I know are persuaded that our political and ethical hope lies in our shared "human reality," which is thought in terms of agency and subjectivity. They share with you the belief that without a full and careful account of human subjectivity one cannot properly understand either our human condition or the basis for our best hope and strategies for well-being. Nonetheless, in both the Heideggerian and in genealogical and deconstructive thought a de-structuring of the idea and experience of the priority of agency has been necessary for the development of ways of knowing and thinking that are at least partially outside of the polarities, representational reflection, and hierarchies that are required in that priority. I note this work, which is often classified and dismissed as "postmodern" in order to indicate where lies the major contributions of options to thought that is carried out in the priority of subjectivity. By such exploratory shifts in the experiences of language, tradition, and value one finds a shifting of the problematic of good-evil, and I wish to speak to you out of that turning — a turning through the experience of the priority of subjectivity in thought and knowledge, a turning to thought outside the polarity of good and evil.[2] As I see it, a "condition" for our thought and for the structure of world-presentation is found in the passing away of experiences of transcendental "realities" and "truths." But that is another story.

You make a strong case for "reality": oppression is "real," differences are "real," suffering is "real," just as are agency and personal being. As we think and experience we are before something, in touch with something. As philosophers we wish to think appropriately in relation to what is the case, to what is happening and to what is there. If rational ontology is to be rejected, it will be rejected because it is not able to take account of certain "realities" that can be perceived and addressed in other, more appropriate ways. So you set about to show in a systematic way the "reality" of various spheres of human life. If someone thinks that redemption, for example, is not real, let that person show what is the case, show that redemption "really" does not happen and that something else does happen. Even deception has its "reality," we saw, and, strangely, if we fail to perceive that "reality" we fail to grasp the limits of our reflective endeavors.

I understand one aspect of your concept of "reality" to be grounded in (i.e., to have its rational basis in) presentation. I do not think that you claim, for example, that a redemptive community pre-exists in a fully constituted, essential state. It arises out of what you call the paradigm or vision that developed vis-à-vis commonsense experiences with "real" things in a tradition that we call Hebraic-Christian. In living in and through this paradigm, people find the world appearing in terms of a special kind of affirmation and in terms of certain values that define for them how to live and define, as well, what is most important and what is most characteristic for human lives. "Reality" occurs both before and *in* this living paradigm. It would not be too much to say that this paradigm gives "reality" in the paradigmatic presentation of "real" things and that "real" things come to be the things that they are in their presentation. A "real" thing, for example, is different in *its* "reality" if it happens as God's creation as compared to a thing that happens only for the sake of the efficiency. The thing that is already "real" is also given "reality" in its presentation. The presenting paradigm or intention gives the thing to be as it is, and the "real" thing performs its own presentation.

You are not saying, as I understand you, that single individuals *make* such presentations. Presentations come from structures that are social and historical and that transcend the acts of individuals by defining the very "reality" of those acts. "Reality" viewed in this aspect *is* presentational and hence is not individually perspectival. So by *reality* we do not exclusively mean something already constituted and pre-presentational, something in itself and outside of time. Rather, "reality" is, in your terms, socially constituted in the sense that *what* occurs happens as structures of presentation that in their organic complexity have a history of formation and that vastly transcends the individual agents who live in and through such structures.

But this historically formed complex of structures of presentation does not absolutely define or exhaust what appears through it. "Reality" outside of time *could* appear in time — "outside of time" in the sense that it is manifest as pre-existing its presentative occurrence. Such occurrences would be like hints or indications of something more than the "reality" of the presenting occurrence. Yet I hesitate to say that you should say in your terms that whatever transcends presentation is thoroughly "real." I suspect that you do not share my hesitation. I suspect that you want to think of whatever transcends the presentation as "real." If I am right, this double sense of "reality" — "reality" as presentative and "reality" as transcendent of presentation — points to an ambiguity in your sense of "reality" that I want to say more about.

I assume that a paradigm gives us to be more or less alert to transcendence of paradigmatic presentation, that a paradigm is not innocent of implication in the experiences of transcendence. A paradigm, for example, might give us to know of sin and redemption, of human worth, and so forth. The paradigm, as we have said, gives some "reality" to whatever appears within its jurisdiction and seems to give "reality" to what it presents as though it were "real" before it was manifest. We could say, for example, that a certain community of redemption gives "reality" to a loving and forgiving God, but would you, as a philosopher, want to say that such a God is appresently "real" outside of the paradigm that gives such presentation? Is God not a presentation that performs a lineage of experience and meaning? Is God's "reality" paradigmatic? When we speak of God's "reality" are we not speaking paradigmatically? And is that speaking not within a very Greek lineage?

As I understand you, the world of common sense gives us our sense of reality that functions largely unnoticed in our everyday lives. In that sense we know that things *are* and are in certain ways: trucks and puppies and crevasses and doors, etc. Our sense of reality begins in our lives with things, and our theories and knowledges arise from this world. In their thereness and just-so-ness things for you are not only presentations. There is a pre-presentative aspect of "reality." You appear to say that our commonsense lives are in contact with things — and here I am unsure of whether to say that things in themselves (a phrase that I believe you prefer to avoid) or things as they are presented in commonsense life. (If I said that, I would say that things in their just-so-ness are presentations.) The side of your thought that is close to empirical realism finds hardness and distance and oppression to be "real" as they *are* and, in this regard, being (the *are*) seems different from your phenomenological sense of "reality." Things *are* before they are presented. And yet I do not think that you want to say that the commonsense world is without paradigms; rather, the commonsense world presents things that *are* before they *are* thematically presented: the hardness of the church door, for example, or the genetic structure of an individual.

Thus, we can have a passion for reality that is not only a matter of wanting to understand a paradigm but is rather a matter of wanting to behold the thing in its own process of being. For you, is that process of being not a process of presentation? Are things in their pre-thematic presentation, as you see them, not presented in their meaning and value, in their space and time? Does their presentation not constitute them in *their* "reality" before you thematize them? We are able to transcend our use and abuse of things and stand before *them* in wonder that they are, to participate in their reality. "Reality" before any kind of presentation? This paradigmatic metaphysical feeling (one formed in a complex Greek lineage) is called good by you because, could I say, it allows things to *present* themselves? To be present in their pre-thematic presentation?

My primary question regarding your account of the "reality" of things is this: what paradigms and lineages have produced *this* knowledge of "reality"? It seems to me to be saturated by such paradigmatic factors as the conviction that "reality" is positive and in some sense good, the Greek values of harmony and ascetic participation with things, the separation of experience and the thing experienced, a Greek-based sense of transcendence and the modern experience of subjectivity. That does not mean that you are wrong (or right). It means that what you call the sense of reality is a historically formed sense and that "reality" is its object, that the self-presentation of things was incubated in ascetic Greek experience, that even here at the rock bottom of commonsense life "reality" is a presentation and that in principle it ("reality") is subject to fundamental change: a strong "paradigmatic" shift would change "reality" considerably or eliminate what *we* know "reality" to be. If I am right in saying that "reality" is historically formed, it too is more like a watery, undulating play of shades, a performance of paradigms, than it is like something foundational and self-identical. The sense of reality is no less a historical formation than are the paradigms that arise through it and from it in regard of it. That sense performs a highly complex (and conflicted) lineage, a lineage that is also enacted in your knowledge and in the "reality" that you behold.

Yours is a subtle concept of reality, and I do not do it justice in writing of it in so abbreviated a way. I want, however, to interrupt my expository narrative to ask, not so much about deception in the formation of "reality," but about creativity in paradigm formation. For the moment I shall accept the coherence of "reality" and presentation and ask further about "reality" as a highly complex, historical creation — I would rather say "production" — that has within its formation all manner of values and experiences that countermand the paradigmatic "reality's" dominant meanings. I ask about the contamination of paradigms and hence about the contamination of "reality" in its occurrences. If the paradigms and "reality" are as contaminated as I think they are, reflection approximate to them will need to be filled with countermovement, lack of harmony, and reversals. Otherwise one's thinking would carry out a distortion of its own presentational basis.

It seems to me, for example, that Greek and Hebrew elements within the paradigm you emphasize are in considerable conflict and that Levinas (as I indicated earlier) would find himself at considerable odds with your descriptive claims. Even your confession of guilt in your rational ontology in its Hebraic lineage does not replace, on Levinasian terms, the radical interruption of grammar, subjectivity, and meaning that Levinas carries out in his de-structuring of Western ontology. Such de-structuring, especially in *Otherwise Than Being,* occurs for him in the Hebraic experience of God's call to a people who, in His call, can never confront or otherwise directly find Him.[3]

I am well aware that Levinas is not *the* spokesman for Judaism, but his radical attack on ontology and reflection in our Greek lineage nonetheless arises from our Hebraic-Christian tradition as surely as your and my thought do. And as does Nietzsche's thought, which finds our lineage in its own movement of self-overcoming and in a consequent transvaluation of our paradigmatic values into a transitional time marked by God's corpse and "man's" possible transformation out of what we call humanity. Contamination. Most of our (radically) different positions and their sometimes embarrassing similarities arise from and through the Hebraic-Christian tradition and contaminate each other. They constitute a flow that is multiply crossed by opposing paradigms and anti-paradigms, by oppositions and alignments more complicated than Greece's tenth-century pantheon. Our lineage *is* a performance of contamination and disjointure.

I am suggesting that there is no singular Western paradigm for "reality" and that the Hebrew-Christian one that you favor is not only one among many others that indwell *its own composition* but also that it carries some of its opponents in hostile servitude, and that they, like Levinas, have their own bases of power such that your (and my) leading organization of values and meanings, i.e., our paradigms, suffer definitive reorganization in foreign recognitions that arise from *within* the conflicts and countermovements that compose both our paradigms and our sense of "reality." Your paradigm is thoroughly contaminated by opposites and does not enjoy the harmony that you seem to require of it. That means, I believe, that clarity of division and meaning constitutes in your rational ontology an important part of its distortion, and that *distortion* itself might appropriately name the presentation of the movement of our lineage in its multiple plays of opposites and in its chaotic lack of harmony: *if* your clarity celebrated its own distortion, it might well reflect, in its celebration, its ontology more appropriately than it does in its gift of dominance to harmony and meaning.

I am also saying that such thoroughgoing strife is in the presentation of the world, is a definitive part of historically developed world-disclosure, hence is intrinsic to our everyday world, is outside of the good-evil paring, and, thus, that "reality" is a misleading term if it suggests a certain priority of identity and essential (or definitive) meaning. As I see it, the crossing, exorbiting, and mutating flow of paradigms, structures, ethea, practices, deaths, and all else that come in the disclosure of things — such de-organizing flow presents/de-presents in no dominant meaning or paradigm. Thus *para-digma* is not an appropriate word for the "structures" of presentation, and hence that "reality" names an abstract cut taken out of the disclosure of things, a cut that might suggest, in its abstraction, agency, but one that requires for this suggestion a paradigmatic control over most differences and over the absence of meaning that composes the presentations of things.

The "reality" of agency thus finds its distortion when the presentation of the world is thought primarily by reference to the self-enactment of a subject or of subjectivity. More and more your paradigm looks like a historically formed perspective on presentation and presence that requires for its validation the suppression of meaningless difference, meaningless power, and meaningless coming to be and passing away by the elevation of self-consciousness — meaningful human self-enactment — over its absence in the disclosure of the world.

Is *what* I say that you leave out of your paradigmatic perspective "real"? Am I not saying that there are things that are different from agency, "really" different in the presentation of the world, and that you are not taking adequate account of them? Not quite. I am saying that the name "reality" has functioned in our heritage and functions in your knowledge to favor substantive identities and fundamental harmony, to minimize not-reality in the occurrence of things; that transformation, mutations, dying, loss, and absence "are" not really "real" because they are not subject to identity or the logic of identity; and that reality-based thought is now legitimately and productively in question. Were I to carry this direction further, I would turn to poetic thinking, the performative dimension of genealogical thought, and explorations by thinking *in* the loss of some of our previously dominant experiences and values.

But that is enough for now. I will do no more than suggest such directions by a concluding observation concerning your discussion of the face.

"The face is a *criterion* for individual agents because one of the agent's elemental passions is for communion with the other" (288). You have defined the face as " 'the infinitely strange' and mysterious *presence* of something which contests my projecting . . . " (39). I have emphasized "presence" in order to emphasize how far removed your understanding of face is from that of Levinas's. In the first quotation I emphasized "criterion" for the same reason. Your account of the face is, I believe, a creative version of Christian humanism, instead of a contribution to the overthrow of humanism in the manner that one finds in Levinas's thought and, in quite different manners, in the thought of Heidegger, Foucault, and Derrida (as well as Nietzsche). The face, you say, is a "humanizing criterion." In Levinas's thought, however, particularly in *Otherwise Than Being* (as you know), one-before-the-other loses the control of criteria as surely as the Hebrew lost reason's control in God's call-in-absence-before-them. "Presence" is for Levinas a term of subjectivity, and the other withdraws presence from the experiencing subject (a thought that Levinas, embarrassingly enough, seems to have learned in part from Heidegger). You, to the contrary, understand the face to manifest "the presence of the sacred" (289). And by invoking presence, the sacred, individual agents, and humanism in the context of reflective ontology you indicate your overwhelming preference for the lineage of Greek metaphysics and its affiliation with the philosophy of subjectivity. Indeed, the face *can be* a criterion for people *because* of the subject's ("the agent's") elemental passion, i.e., the individual subject is the condition for the possibility of the face's criteriological power. You are saying, I believe, that human subjectivity is the presentative occasion for the self-disclosure of the infinitely strange and the sacred. That is very different, of course, from saying that the presentative occasion is *dasein*, as Heidegger has it, or the-one-for-the-other according to Levinas, or the loss of presence in language as Derrida has accounted it, or the ascetic ideal's lineage in Nietzsche's thought. In your thought alterity in its mystery comes through the agency of the subject's elemental passion.

How, then, are we to assess the "reality" of the other? As far as I can tell, the agent's elemental passion is, for you, about as fixed a state as we are going to find: it may be historical, but we should not expect change any time soon. This historical, universal condition is the presentative agency for the self-presentation of the other, and the other is the presenter of the sacred. Although I am fully aware that you see the other and the sacred as elemental "realities," they appear to me, in your thought, to be thoroughly presented in their "reality," not even as much "to themselves" as the hardness of the church door is, but paradigmatically saturated in and through the agent's passion and the Greek lineage.

It might be the case that elemental passion, the other, and the sacred are given before all paradigms and that the Hebrew-Christian paradigm in your thought shades their "reality" in a particular way. That seems to be so far from accurate as to make it doubtful that you would claim such a thing. All three terms — elemental passion, the other, and the sacred — are themselves paradigmatic perceptions within a lineage, as I see them. The "reality" of the other in its redemptive possibility is presented in the Hebraic-Christian paradigm that organizes your thought, and it is not presented (in its redemptive possibility) outside of that paradigm. Presumably an individual agent's passion would have to be turned to and into this paradigm in order for the other's redemptive possibility to be presented in the agent's world. That seems to mean that this redemptive power becomes "real" only in the agent's presentation. Does that not mean that redemption is paradigmatic in its "reality"? That good and evil are paradigmatic constructions *in* their "reality"? That when the operative paradigm for agent changes, the "reality" changes? That your elemental realism takes a back seat to the subject's presentative power? And that the Hebraic aspect of your paradigm is considerably subjected to its Greek counterpart?

We usually end with questions when we talk and are sober. I do like the more Dionysian moments when the structures waver, and laughter, rather than reason, fills the gaps. But even sober, I find it at times remarkable when we have spoken in Nashville or on Falls Branch Road of presence and withdrawal of presence in the coming to pass of human life. You are quite sure that it is "real" — human life. I am not. I am at times astonished by the figure of Apollo with a cross who seems to lead if not to rule your thought and who defines human "reality" too cleanly, too morally, and too exactly for me to recognize it. But I also find in your work and thought a relentless effort at honesty whose passion exceeds the limits of honesty toward creativity, and that, combined with your passion for writing as well as for music, makes your work rather more than "real" as far as I am concerned: it shows a passion for good and evil that is beyond good and evil.

NOTES

1. I wonder about falling short of the "reality" of falling short in this sense: our knowledge of falling short of realities presumably distorts that falling short because falling short too is agency-turned-object. And since the falling short occurs *in* this very turning, our reflection, which distorts reality, distorts itself

in its knowledge of itself. We lose to some extent our own reflective "reality" in reflecting it. So presumably the "reality" of distortion is distorted. Distorting the otherness-of-distortion — in relation to distortion — is an interpretation of something like original sin, is it not?

2. The absence of a sustained encounter with Nietzsche in your thought is remarkable. I suspect that his significance is seriously underestimated in most theological circles; people often read him only in their adolescence and do not get beyond the feeling of a creative rebelliousness in his work and do not reach the kind of affirmation in his work that Foucault, for example, articulates in his "Nietzsche's Genealogy" (Michel Foucault, *Language, Counter Memory, Practice* [Ithaca, N.Y.: Cornell University Press]). I believe that his is for the twentieth century the initiating encounter with transvaluating movements within Western values and beliefs, movements that redistribute our various transcendental orientations in a loss of the value of transcendence and that reveal the mischief generated by our best values and highest "realities." His descriptions of emerging transformations of mythologically based culture, his accounts of the structures of guilt and of the good/evil dyad, his style of language and thought, his formulations of questions regarding tribal heritages of belief and practices, and his rigor in allowing processes of self-overcoming in his own thinking — his thinking *is* a process of self-overcoming — all have considerable import for your thinking and require a full encounter in their lineage if you are to address the strongest differences between your own position and one of the cutting edges in twentieth-century thought.

3. It is true that Levinas also has a sense of the irreducible other, but his reasons for not interpreting the other in the language of "reality" are germane to the criticism that I am advancing: for him the lineage of "reality" shares responsibility with the lineage that gives priority to subjectivity in losing an ethical sense of alterity and of good and evil. Although I do not suggest that you adopt his thought of alterity, I believe that he has a good descriptive basis for rejecting "reality" as a proper name for "what" is there. Heidegger too has effective, if different descriptions that lead him to hold "reality" in suspicion because of its affiliation with truth as correctness and with being conceived as presence. Your account of "reality" seems to accept uncritically the experiences of being as presence and of alterity as "real" presence.

❧ 6 ❧

Tragedy, Totality, and the Face

ROBERT R. WILLIAMS

Edward Farley's *Good and Evil* is an important book. It is a theological anthropology that develops the program set forth in his prolegomena, *Ecclesial Man* (1975) and *Ecclesial Reflection* (1982). It is more than an anthropology because it offers a theological analysis of redemption. In *Good and Evil* Farley moves beyond prolegomena to the construction of a position that, while serious theology, does not resemble any traditional theological literature and may appear bewildering to those accustomed to references to Scripture, to christology, and to other theologies. This book is not easy, but, in an era of deconstructive erring and aesthetic play of differences, it stands out as one of the most substantive constructive theological proposals since Reinhold Niebuhr's *Nature and Destiny of Man* and Paul Tillich's *Courage to Be,* and it combines important elements of both. It also stands in the lineage of Schleiermacher and Troeltsch, who seek to distinguish theology from ontotheology and metaphysics and to translate it into the idiom of historical being-in-the-world.

The aim is to interpret the human condition by drawing upon a paradigm of good and evil retrieved from the Hebraic and Christian heritage. The book is divided into two parts. The first is an existential-phenomenological anthropology that sets forth three spheres, personal agency, the interhuman, and the social. Here Farley undertakes a reflective ontology of human existence. The cognitive style of the book is informed by continental philosophy, with an expository style modeled after Gabriel Marcel.

Farley identifies the sphere of the interhuman or interpersonal as primary to the spheres of personal agency and the social. His discussion of the interhuman draws upon the discussions in continental philosophy from Husserl through Levinas. Nevertheless, the concern is not simply another traversal of problems of intersubjectivity, but to develop an ontology of tragic finitude as the background for the retrieved Hebraic-Christian paradigm of good and evil.

80

Part Two of *Good and Evil* is the specifically theological part of the argument, a theology of the human condition as historical freedom, susceptible to evil and yet capable of redemption. The move is from a general ontology of human being in the world to determinate analyses of freedom as idolatrous, corrupted on the one hand, and as liberated to theonomous freedom on the other. The generic universals of the inter-human, personal agency, and the social now appear modified, under the Hebraic-Christian paradigm, by the concrete determinacies of evil, or idolatry, and good, or being-founded.

Farley presents an analysis of reconciliation and redemption without any overt reference to christology, traditional or revisionist. In short, he presents a systematic theology without christology, or even a developed doctrine of God. I for one find this a refreshing and illuminating reconstruction of Christian faith. What follows is an inquiry into Farley's transposition of theology into historicist modes of thought, which distances his theology from traditional ontotheology, and his acknowledgment of a tragic dimension of existence while continuing to maintain the central Hebraic-Christian distinction between sin and finitude. Farley proposes a theology that incorporates a tragic view of things, while continuing to maintain a conception of redemption and theonomous freedom. Further, Farley appropriates and transforms Emmanuel Levinas's concept of the face. The face functions as both a philosophical criterion (Part One) and a theological criterion (Part Two). This complex normative status of the face — as at once philosophical and theological — ties the two parts of the work together and is an application of Farley's methodological principles of positivity and determinate universality.

Reflective Ontology, Postmodernism, and Deconstruction

It is a telling commentary on the contemporary state of theology that a book on philosophical theology must begin with an apology and defense, not merely of its own enterprise, but of the enterprise as such. The discrediting of philosophical theology, not only in the general intellectual community, but especially among theologians themselves, makes it appear as if philosophical theology has become an oxymoron. In view of the contemporary consensus against philosophical theology, a work such as *Good and Evil*, which stands in the lineage of Schleiermacher, Troeltsch and Tillich, appears to be museum piece or just quaint naivete. The "flip side" of such discrediting is that much contemporary theology has abandoned the truth question and a corresponding corporate-public role. But when theology embraces aestheticism, play, and difference, it ceases to inform or challenge and appears to be toothless in the face of evil.

Recent disenchantment with ontology seems to have overlooked that reflective ontology is itself a polemic against cognitive styles that quantify knowledge and reality. This polemic has a moral aspect, for if human reality is simply an object that occupies a place within some causal system or environment, there would seem to be no criteria by which its violation or subjugation could be recognized, much less opposed. Thus if theology makes assertions about evil, corruption, and liberation, then it presupposes that there is something in human being that makes it vulnerable to evil and corruption and capable of redemption. And this means that theology requires a reflective philosophical ontology of human reality in order to uncover and discern whatever violates, corrupts, or subjugates human reality. Granting that reflective ontology is indispensable to theology, is it still a viable enterprise?

Farley's defense of reflective ontology deals in part with the contemporary consensus against ontology's stock in trade, the universal or essence. The objections are many: the universal freezes reality, and it can do so only as an abstraction from the temporal flow of events. If the universal so abstracted is granted independent ontological status, then it is ahistorical. It seems to exist apart from world participation and is not subject to it. It floats above time and history. Further, the abstracted universal stands in contrast to particulars that are caught up in flux; thus a distinction is drawn between universal and particular. In short, a binary is perpetuated. This establishes a preference, a ranking that favors one side over the other. Thus, say the critics, ontology is inherently oppressive and dominating. The abstract universal is characterized by simplicity, purity, and self-identity. Its pure self-identity, as simple, excludes difference and reduces the other to the same.

The foregoing account depicts the abstract universal. The abstract universal, when reified, violates the axioms of determinacy, concreteness, change, and relativity. But the universal may be reformulated in such a way that these axioms are not only not violated, but become constitutive of the universal itself. The concrete universal does not exclude particulars or contingencies; rather it is the enduring element in and is mediated by the temporal flow. It is not something already existent apart from particulars, but rather the pattern, the continuity or perduring, of concrete diverse phenomena. The universal that Farley defends is a historical conception, a life-world universal. The ontological reflection he undertakes is an inquiry into enduring features of human beings that are already part of commonsense discourse, including the commonsense discourse of deconstructionist critics of ontology. Farley's life-world ontological claim is that there are such things as agents, face-to-face relations, social organizations, events, processes; agential features such as temporality, emotions, and postures; and social features such as power and subjugation. He notes that the writings of those who repudiate ontology, metaphysics, truth, and representation, retain, make use of, and require these concepts. This is a structural incoherence that gnaws at deconstruction and obscures whether it is a repudiation or correction of reflective ontology. Farley believes it should be interpreted as the latter rather than the former.

This observation presupposes that our commonsense world of everyday life and discourses about such are, because unavoidable, in some sense foundational and normative. This does not mean that everyday opinions (*doxa*) are beyond correction or criticism. Rather it means that the life-world is presupposed by the most technical theoretical scientific and philosophical undertakings, including deconstruction. If life-world commonsense convictions were absolutely false, such that there is no meaning and no presence, or if it were the case that there are no agents, persons, postures, subjugations, etc., then no cognition whatsoever would survive. An absolute cognitive skepticism loses the possibility of being self-reflexively self-conscious and even of making a case for its own preferability.[1] Farley deploys on behalf of reflective ontology self-reflexive transcendental arguments to show that those who repudiate reflective ontology nevertheless make use of what they repudiate in order to make their case. For Farley, the criticisms brought against reflective ontology are not absolute repudiations, but are, from the standpoint of reflective ontology, relative criticisms that call for corrections of the ontological enterprise.

Being-Founded: Some Preliminary Issues

Farley's aim is to interpret the human condition by drawing upon a paradigm of good and evil retrieved from the Hebraic and Christian heritage. The argument of *Good and Evil* follows a two-step pattern similar to Schleiermacher's *Glaubenslehre:* Part One sets forth a reflective ontology of the human condition, followed in Part Two by an analysis of the human condition as qualified and determined by the Christian paradigm of sin and redemption. However, Farley differs significantly from Schleiermacher in that he does not seek to establish as a general ontological principle that human being is fundamentally religious, utterly dependent or ultimately concerned, or derive doctrines of creation and preservation from a general ontology of the God-world relation expressed in the consciousness of utter dependence. Instead Farley's reflective ontology in Part One is confined to an anthropological level and standpoint.

To be sure, Farley does have a conception like Schleiermacher's feeling of utter dependence, which he calls "being-founded." But where Schleiermacher's utter dependence and Tillich's ultimate concern are expounded as borrowings from the philosophy of religion and defended as explicitly universal ontological or generic structures and elements of life, Farley's being-founded is set forth at the ontic level, i.e., within the body of his constructive theology. That is, being-founded is set forth not as part of a universal ontology of God, human being, and world (as in Part One of Schleiermacher's *Glaubenslehre*) but rather (in Part Two of *Good and Evil*) in reference to the Hebraic-Christian paradigm. This seems to confine it to determinacy and an ontic, anthropological level. It is as if Schleiermacher had discussed the feeling of utter dependence only in the body of his theology as qualified by the contrast between sin and grace.

Eschewing an ontological philosophy of religion in favor of an ontic theological account of the determinate Hebraic-Christian paradigm, Farley's account of sacred presencing that founds freedom and courage is thin and minimal. Yet Farley is no less concerned than Tillich or Schleiermacher to criticize ethnocentrism and provincialism, and no less universalistic in his claims about the sacred as that which lures us beyond regionalism and parochialism toward compassion for all of life. However, for Farley *theological universality* resides in the determinacy of the Hebraic-Christian paradigm, and not simply in a universal ontological scheme and vehicle. This is the lesson of Ernst Troeltsch's inquiry into the essence of Christianity. Nevertheless, his methodological commitment to determinate theological universality places Farley in the position of having on the one hand to contend for reflective ontology against contemporary anti-metaphysical bias, deconstruction, and the like, and on the other hand to defend his ontological commitments from within the apparent confines of a particular religious-theological paradigm. This prompts some questions.

Does Farley mean that being-founded belongs exclusively to the Hebraic-Christian paradigm? If so, then is it the case that only Christians are courageous? Not only would this seem too parochial, it would make being-founded virtually synonymous with reconciliation, which is only one of its elements. Moreover, to place such constraints on being-founded by confining it to the ontic level would appear to stand in tension with the general thrust of Farley's defense of reflective ontology. On the other hand, if being-founded is more inclusive than the ontic, more inclusive than reconciliation, then this theology, like Schleiermacher's and Tillich's, would appear to share some generic structures with the philosophy of religion. This would imply the possibility that being-founded and courage, or something analogous to these, might be present in and shared by other faiths and paradigms.

A second question concerns the scope of the claims Farley makes on behalf of his reflective ontology. On the one hand he defends reflective ontology against contemporary anti-foundationalism and de-construction. He does not do so only as a philosopher, but also as a theologian. Thus he is closer to Schleiermacher and Tillich than to Karl Barth in seeing an affirmative relation between theology and philosophy; as a philosopher he would reject both foundationalism and anti-foundationalism. On the other hand, his exposition of re-flective ontology is from within a particular paradigm of a historical faith-community. As noted above, Farley propounds something like Schleiermacher's feeling of utter dependence, namely, being-founded, but treats it only at the level of ontic historical determinacy, i.e., as a historical conception and reality.

Thus Farley seems anti-foundationalist in a way that Schleiermacher is not, and yet also foundational in some sense. In the traditional conception of metaphysical theology, ontotheology is inherent in the conception of creation, the claim that being has a theological ground. Such a foundational conception underlies and extends into the monar-chical metaphor, the judicial metaphor, and theodicy — all of which are targets of Farley's *theological* critique. His alternative concept of being-founded "is a founding that is not founded" (182). The founding that is not founded suggests an implicit criticism of classical theology and metaphysics, an apparent alternative to ontotheology. The precise meaning of this dialectical conception can be determined only from his determinate analyses of good and evil, including his concept of courage. Nevertheless we can ask, If theology is not ontotheology, what is it? Does Farley accept, reject, or reconstruct ontotheology? Can there be a non-foundational theology? If so, what would it look like? But before we take up these questions, we must first note the levels of the problem of evil to which the concept of being-founded is addressed.

Tragic Finitude Differentiated from Sin and Evil

In one of the richest, most astute theological anthropologies since Tillich's *Courage to Be* or Niebuhr's *Nature and Destiny of Man*, Farley depicts three fundamental dimensions of human being: the personal, the interhuman, and the social, each of which has a corresponding elemental passion and vulnerability. The elemental passions have a fundamentally tragic structure in that they are marked by vulnerabilities, incompati-bilities, and an irreducible gap between desire and its fulfillment. For example, the passion of the interhuman seeks an unqualified reciprocity, a relation of mutual acknowledgment that preserves genuine otherness and yet exhibits total empathetic understanding and affection. But what we actually experience are relations darkened by misunderstanding, ego-oriented intentions, and incompatible agendas with their attendant antipathies (110). Farley characterizes this gap as tragic because we cannot have the fulfillments without the passion, and the existence of the passions requires some fulfillments (111). His point seems to be that human existence, while not without its joys and satisfactions, is characterized by a fundamental discontent. The tragic dimension of existence means that the very conditions of well-being are also conditions of limitation, conflict, discontent, and suffering.[2] However, this discontent and vulnerability are *not* sin or evil, but preconditions of such.

Farley's acknowledgment of a tragic aspect of human finitude constitutes a revision of the theological tradition. Let us recall that the classical account of evil includes seven features: (1) the distinction between sin and finitude, (2) sin as a distortion of human reality, (3) sin as theological, arising from a skewed passion for the eternal, (4) a comprehensive cosmological narrative framework, (5) a quasi-biological transmission of sin that served as the explanation for its empirical universality, (6) a monarchical metaphor for the relation between God and world, (7) the exclusion of the tragic from the origin of sin; insofar as the tragic dimension of finitude is acknowledged, it is viewed as the consequence of sin that distorts not only human reality, but the world as well.[3] Where the tradition sought to derive evils, including the tragic, from sin, Farley identifies a constitutive tragic vulnerability in human existence that, while distinct from sin, is its background and condition. Sin and evil are thus no longer interpreted as sheer willful acts of pride and rebellion against God the cosmic monarch; rather they are responses to and an inability to accept and abide by finitude and its discontents. Although sin is not to be identified with finitude, the tragic dimension of finitude influences and conditions sin. How does this happen?

In response to this question, Farley introduces another, somewhat more obscure, tragic motif, namely, chaos. This motif seems to be cosmological and not merely a disproportion in the elemental passions. The tragic aspect of existence means that there is chaos lurking at the heart of things, "and this the one situation we human beings seem incapable of accepting. Because of the intensity of the passions and their discontents, we find this situation to be intolerable" (131–32). The concept of chaos is elusive. On the one hand, if there really is chaos lurking at the heart of things, such that at the beginning and end of things there stands meaninglessness and ultimate insignificance, this seems close to nihilism. There are passages in *Good and Evil* that reflect this conception (131–32). This is the "continental thought" strand in Farley's argument (Nietzsche, Tillich, Ricoeur). In this strand, chaos is "ontological" and structural and tends to undermine meaning. This strand tends toward nihilism, if not Manicheanism. On the other hand, Farley does not embrace a tragic vision of things (being as tragically flawed, a tragic theology, etc.), but defends instead the proposition of the essential goodness of being, which means that

> the total complex of reality with its self-initiating entities offers to its participants environments that constitute conditions of survival and well-being....If this is what the goodness of being means, it should be clear that this principle does not exclude chaos, suffering, and tragic incompatibilities....In fact, without chaos and randomness and therefore incompatibilities and suffering, there can be no self-initiating beings, nothing available for use, and nothing that can give pleasure and meaning. (149)

This passage reflects the Edwardsian-Whiteheadian-pragmatic strand in Farley's argument. This conception of chaos is more dynamic, historical; chaos is almost synonymous with creativity. Better, it can be both creative and destructive. Meaning is both constantly destroyed and recreated. Here the tragic aspect of chaos in the first sense is all but set aside.

How to explain and relate these two conceptions? Are they inconsistent? I am not sure. It would seem that while Farley asserts a tragic *aspect* of existence, he does not embrace a "purely tragic" view such as described by Paul Ricoeur.[4] Nevertheless, Farley is committed to some extent to a tragic view because he holds that the conditions of well-being are also conditions of limitation, conflict, and suffering. Perhaps the difference between his two accounts can be sorted out by noting that the first account of chaos as meaninglessness occurs in the context of Farley's discussion of idolatry. Evil is due in part to an inability to tolerate a tragic finitude, i.e., a refusal to exist in the gap between elemental passions and their fulfillment. Therefore, viewed from the perspective of the idolatrous self that demands absolute unambiguous meaning, chaos is viewed as larger and more serious than it really is, i.e., tragic. But would not tragic chaos undermine all meaning, relative as well as putatively absolute meanings? Conversely, the Whiteheadian notion of chaos is presented from the perspective of being-founded and courage. Courage relativizes the self and its metaphysical urges and thus makes possible consent to and acceptance of chaos as a condition of freedom and creativity, a condition of creation and destruction. Thus the difference of the context and perspective of Farley's diverse assertions concerning chaos may mitigate the appearance of inconsistency. But I am not sure that it removes the inconsistency. In the one scenario, meaning is undermined (Nietzschean nihilism); in the other it is both destroyed and created. The creation of meaning suggests that tragic chaos in the Nietzschean sense can be set aside.

Whatever chaos ultimately signifies, it is something that human beings refuse and resist. We refuse this radical disorder, refuse ultimate non-significance. But this refusal is not yet sin. The Hebrew-Christian paradigm requires a differentiation of sin from tragic finitude and suffering. Sin enters the picture with a specific refusal of tragic vulnerability, namely, one that demands absolute security and an absolute that secures. The human being searches for something that will remove the chaos and suppress the tragic vulnerability of the human condition. We want something that will transform tragic vulnerability from something constitutive, necessary, and inescapable, into something contingent, manageable, escapable (132–33). In short, we want to be founded: we want the gap between desire and fulfillment closed; we want to be elevated above the vulnerability of finitude. Evil is thus a kind of weakness, an incapacity to abide chaos and unsecured existence (144). This weakness alters the relation of the self to itself, to others, to the world, and to the eternal horizon. The desire for an absolute foundation forces something mundane into a founding role.

This insistence that chaos be removed, the self absolutely secured, and the gap between desire and fulfillment be closed is at the same time a demand that eternal horizon merge with a mundane good at hand; the result is an "absolute" that temporarily satisfies the infinite passion for the eternal. Thus idolatry arises. The idol must defeat chaos and so cannot itself be subject to chaos; it must be beyond chaos, corruptibility, and criticism. There is a pathos of idolatry: the idol, which is supposed to defeat chaos, is itself subject to chaos. Farley's account of idolatry is important because it shows that idolatry is not just a quaint cultic issue about "false gods," but rather retrieves classical prophetic insights into the connection between moral and political corruption and the act that substitutes a mundane good for the eternal.[5]

Being-Founded as Alternative to Idolatrous Self-Founding

Idolatry is a desperate search for an absolute foundation that presses a mundane good into a foundational role to close the gap between passion and fulfillment. It is "necessary" to close this gap in order to nullify or exclude the tragic dimension of finitude. This "necessity" shows that evil is a weakness, an inability to abide chaos and an open, unsecured existence. Idolatry seeks an absolute, ahistorical foundation and thus appears to be a flight from history on the part of a desperate absolute self-securing. In Sartre's language, the self seeks to be god, to be its own foundation, and fails. In contrast, being-founded in Farley's normative sense is the power to live in the condition of tragic vulnerability without insisting upon absolute idolatrous self-securing. It is the condition of historical freedom and courage. It is important to note that being-founded in this historicist sense is an alternative to idolatry.

In traditional theological terminology, being-founded might be regarded as justification by faith. But the problem with the traditional conception is its use of a juridical metaphor and what Ricoeur has called the myth of punishment.[6] Traditional Christian thought seems to have been unable to think of grace and salvation apart from a moral-legal vision of the world. Accepting Nietzsche's and Ricoeur's critique of the moral view of the world, Farley prefers to formulate being-founded apart from the juridical-forensic metaphors and by employing an interpersonal metaphor wherein God is portrayed as loving spouse (143). Being-founded, and not partaking in acquittal, is the primordial event of agential freedom. As such, being-founded is linked with relationship and with courage.

In the Christian tradition the sacred is known and interpreted in connection with the experience of the hold of evil, its tie with idolatry, and the breaking of these powers. Accordingly, being-founded arises with the breaking of the dynamics of evil. Being-founded means a power or ability to live in the condition of tragic finitude and vulnerability without insisting on being absolutely secured by goods at hand. Being-founded has negative and positive aspects. Negatively it breaks the hold of the dynamics of idolatry. Positively it is a way of existing as fragile and vulnerable amid the sufferings and tragic incompatibilities of the world. Farley observes that "this way of existing appears paradoxical because it is both a resistance to and realistic acceptance of chaos and vulnerability" (146). Courage relativizes finite goods on the one hand, and on the other consents and accepts the tragic character of being, the element of chaos that resists the creative power of the sacred (148).

Note that here chaos is not simply identified with creativity and randomness, but is something that resists the sacred. For this reason, chaos must be resisted. However, the various resistances to chaos have not yet been distinguished or sorted out. For example, natural subjectivity resists meaninglessness as something that thwarts the possibility of fulfillment. Idolatry also resists chaos and meaninglessness, but in a different way. Instead of being a relative struggle against erosions and competitions of world process, idolatrous existence assumes the shape of an intense and desperate defense of an idol threatened on all sides with contingencies (174).

There is yet a third type of resistance to chaos on the part of courage. In general courage is a response to tragic existence. It negates the absolute self-securing of flight and idolatry and restores to goods at hand their historical character, contextuality, and fragility. Courage implies and leads to a consent to being, which includes an existential acceptance of its tragic character. Courage's resistance to chaos seems to be a rel-

ative resistance, which is grounded in an appreciation that chaos can
also be creative and productive of novelty. However this concept of resistance is problematic, because being-founded, which participates in the
sacred presence, apparently consents to chaos, not merely in a somewhat
neutral sense of randomness and creativity, but in the sense of being that
which *resists* the ordering power of the sacred (148). Would not chaos in
this sense be something that threatens the very notion of being-founded
insofar as this is grounded in the forgiving sacred presence? If chaos is
lurking at the heart of things such that it is contingency "all the way
down," what is left of being-founded? Would not consent to chaos turn
into a resignation to fate? Farley rejects this interpretation: fate is a category that describes the already defeated self. Part of the interpretive
difficulty is that Farley discusses courage as an existential and not as a
cognitive conviction or view of the world. Yet as an existential, a way
of being in the world, courage is not without ontological import and
implication.

The Bipolar Structure of the Elemental Passions and Its Transformation

Farley fills in his initial account of being-founded by an ambitious exploration of the new powers and possibilities of freedom made possible
by the breaking of the dynamics of evil. He interprets the traditional
concept of virtue (*habitus*) as something like an existential power or,
better, a determinate modification of an existential. Vices — which Farley prefers to call corruptions — are ways human historicity, biological
tendencies, and elemental passions undergo distortion. Virtues — which
he terms freedoms — are powers to effect the proper operations of
these anthropological dimensions, i.e., they are modalities of historical
freedom.

   In chapters 8–12 of *Good and Evil*, each corruption (vice) originates
in the dynamics of evil (idolatrous self-securing); unable to tolerate their
tragic vulnerability, agents insist on and find a way of securing themselves by goods at hand. This insistence on security forces the goods
at hand — people, tasks, experiences — into becoming instrumentalities
of the agent's self-securing. The goal of self-securing is to close the gap
between desire and fulfillment. If that gap were actually closed, the result would be to abolish the tragic structure and dimension of existence.
Viewing matters from the perspective of idolatry, the gap is apparently
closed. However the idolatrous insistence upon fulfillment does not in
fact close the gap between desire and its references or eliminate the
fragility of the goods at hand. But the desperate insistence that the gap is

closed constitutes the false consciousness of idolatry. False consciousness in turn generates false optimism.

Failure is built into false optimism. In spite of the optimistic expectation that the absolutized securing good has the power to hold all contingencies at bay, its existence remains precarious. The absolute resistance to chaos is a failing resistance, and its outcome can only be disappointment and disillusionment, or despair. Despair is not so much the experience of an actual defeat so much as a sense of being betrayed by what seemed to be most true and trustworthy. This dialectical duality of false optimism and despair is the basic bipolar structure of the corruption of the elemental passions, each of which has its own version of this falsely optimistic and despairing posture (175). The corruption of the elemental passion of subjectivity, for example, takes the form of a bipolar duality of false hope and ennui.[7] Similarly the corruption of the passion of the interhuman takes the form of a dialectical oscillation between false dependence and cynicism. I shall consider these in turn.

Unfounded, the passion of subjectivity exhibits a kind of benign natural egocentrism or solipsism. As egocentrism, the passion of subjectivity effects a division between the self and what is not-self. In this division, the self is caught in a bind between selfishness and altruism, a situation brought about by the egocentric structure of the passion of subjectivity. But in being-founded, Farley claims, the natural egocentrism and the bind between self and not-self are transcended in a new and higher vitality and freedom. Vitality is not a mere restoration of freedom to its "natural condition" minus sin, but a surpassing of both that introduces new possibilities of good (118).

Freedom (virtue) is a power to exist in the face of tragic vulnerability vis-à-vis a specific dimension of human reality. Such freedom is not a mere restoration of the original capacity of freedom as described in Part One. Something occurs in the breaking of the dynamics of evil that introduces a new set of possibilities and good in individuals and communities. Being-founded in its most explicit sense refers to these new powers and possibilities that are apprehended in faithful courage and that courage exploits. This is Farley's version of theonomy (157). Theonomous historical freedom (virtue) is not a release from vulnerability and the tragic, but a new way of existing as vulnerable and as tragic. This new way of existing is characterized in terms of vitality, courage, relativizing, and consent.

When courage enters the passion of subjectivity, the self undergoes a transformation. The passion of subjectivity is lifted beyond the either/or between the self and other. The other is no longer a mere means or instrument of the self's own securing. "The passion for life, is not just a co-option of the other for the sake of one's life, and the passion for meaning is not just a search for a framework of one's own meaning. It is a passion for life itself and meaning itself....It is neither a passion for the life of others at the expense of the self, nor a passion to live at the expense of what is other. It is a passion for the meaning and significance of things as such" (181). The passion for life, in other words, is a passion for the whole formed by and including self and other.

Farley claims that being-founded is a founding that is not founded, a founding that enables the acceptance of an eternal that does not serve our ends and fulfill our passions (182). Let us examine this paradoxical assertion more closely. Being-founded is a founding. This assertion is meant to rule out despair over the tragic dimension of life. The tragic dimension and vulnerability are there, but sin is distinct from tragic finitude. Idolatry cannot abide the gap between the eternal horizon and mundane goods and seeks to close it in a desperate act of self-securing. Being-founded is directed primarily to the sin of idolatry and not to the gap per se. Being-founded enables one to live in the gap in postures of courage and vitality. But being-founded is not itself founded, i.e., it is not a return to foundationalist metaphysics. That is, although it is a passion for the whole, being-founded does not remove the tragic or close the gap between passion and fulfillment. Rather it enables the subject to exist without possessing the eternal and without receiving from the eternal unambiguous life and meaning (182).

Farley provides a similar analysis of the passion for the interhuman. First, he identifies a natural solipsism and egocentrism that gives a certain priority to the self over the other. This egocentrism is not yet sin; however it can be inflamed by idolatrous self-securing into a bipolar opposition between false dependence on the other (the other is the utterly trustworthy one who secures the self absolutely) and cynicism about all relationship (the other is utterly untrustworthy) (188). This dialectic unfolds the corruption of the passion for the other, the passion for reciprocity. When corrupted, the passion for reciprocity becomes degraded into postures of control and domination. Conversely, being-founded and courage break this dynamic of evil, and, by relativizing it, open up new possibilities of relationship. Courage means living in a tragically structured world in postures of relativizing consent; this means that we relativize our own metaphysical need and problem of being secured and self-founding. Courage "takes egocentrism to a new plane where our desire is not merely on its own behalf, but merges with the desire of what is other" (190). Courage becomes agapic passion, for the other. This agapic passion is interpreted holistically as inclusive relationship: the relationship of the face, or the *face that evokes the face* (191). Agapic passion seeks an inclusive relationship exhibiting reciprocal affection and compassionate obligation.

Natural solipsism and egocentrism tend to give a certain priority of the self over others. In idolatry the self asserts an absolute priority, and benign domination becomes evil, as the other is reduced to an instrument of self-securing. The self and other are locked into an exclusive dialectic of either/or, either egocentrism (domination of other by self) or altruism (domination of self by other). The special power of freedom as vitality, coupled with the agapic passion lift the relation of self to other to a new level. This new level involves mutual mediation of self and other, which in turn includes de-absolutizing of the self, or, in Farley's terminology, relativizing. Here mutual exclusion is replaced by inclusive relationship. This inclusive relationship is founded on a passion for totality, a passion for the whole. In the case of the passion of subjectivity the whole is the meaning and significance of things as such. In the case of the passion for the interhuman, the whole is the evocation of the face by the face in reciprocal compassionate obligation and affection.

This analysis leads to the following issue. According to Farley being-founded overcomes the temptation of idolatry to close "the gap between desire and fulfillment. Being-founded and courage give the power to exist in that gap in relativizing consent. We are content to exist without possessing the eternal, *without receiving from the eternal unambiguous life and meaning*" (182; my italics). In short, being-founded is a *historical freedom* that is not a release from vulnerability and the tragic, but a way of existing as vulnerable and as tragic. On the other hand, as we have just seen, Farley conceives the founded *telos* of the passion of subjectivity as a passion for meaning and significance of things as such, which I believe is a holistic notion. Similarly, the *telos* of the passion of the interhuman is the face evoking face in compassionate obligation and reciprocity. This is likewise a holistic conception, although the holism does not become fully explicit until Farley's discussion of ecclesial community, which is the totality structured and shaped by reconciliation and agape (243).

Now for the question: Is there not a tension between historicity, which implies a denial of absolutes and/or totalities, such that the tragic dimension of existence, the gap between desire and fulfillment, cannot be overcome or filled, and the important claims about reconciliation, mediation, and totality? What sort of conception of totality is involved here, and how "total" is it? What sort of presence does such totality have? Further, if the only meaning received from the eternal is ambiguous, does this not affect, if not preclude, the meaning and possibility of reconciliation and totality? Does not tragic ambiguity preclude totality and vice versa? On the other hand, if being-founded really introduces a new set of possibilities and is not merely a restoration of the status quo ante idolatry, does this mean that the tragic itself is relativized, if not set aside?[8] If being-founded and reconciliation occur, doesn't this imply a meaning that is not ambiguous, and thus beyond tragedy? Is it "beyond history" as well? Or do historicity, ambiguity, and the vulnerability of tragic finitude affect, if not partially qualify or displace, the "founding" in being-founded? If existence really has a tragic dimension, why wouldn't this have a negative impact on the scope and possibility of historical being-founded and freedom?

The Face

Farley repeatedly emphasizes that historical freedom (vitality) set forth in Part Two is not merely a correction of the distortions introduced by evil (vice) that restores the generic existentials of human reality to its pristine condition. For if that were the case, then the content of historical freedom would be exhausted by the generic description of human reality set forth in Part One, minus evil. Instead, something new occurs in connection with the breaking of the powers of evil that introduces a new set of possibilities of good. What is the basis of this claim? In part it is the determinate historical Hebraic-Christian paradigm, but also important here is the face, which is the concrete event of interpersonal encounter through which the paradigm is communicated and comes to life. It is central in Farley's account of reconciliation and redemptive communities. The face is not an ontological structure, but an interpersonal event that cannot be cognitively or emotionally mastered, through which we are summoned to freedom and responsibility. The event of face, over which we have no control, is not only the phenomenological genesis of the novelty redemption introduces; it also provides a trace of the sacred.

The concept of the face is Levinas's contribution to Farley's account of the interhuman. Farley both appropriates Levinas's thought and transforms it; this transformation raises some issues. In Part One, Farley follows Levinas's account of the face, which exhibits a fundamental asymmetry that grants unqualified priority to the face of the other.[9] This asymmetry is the basis of the unconditional ethical summons of the face: you shall not kill. It signifies the priority of the ethical relation over its terms and renders reciprocity problematic. The other is an obligation prior to and independent of my freedom and breaks natural egocentrism and its presumption of neutrality. Farley follows Levinas when he characterizes the face as a primordial call to responsibility. "This primordial summons is the basis of values in the normative culture: the normative culture is not the basis of the summons" (41).

It is precisely on this point that Levinas has been criticized for having a formal conception of the face that is unable to ground any particular normative content. This is due to the fact that the face is pre-worldly, and its pre-worldliness reflects the height from which the other commands and obligates. This height implies asymmetry and non-reciprocity. Further, the asymmetry of the interpersonal implies an egocentrism that must be overcome and that is overcome by the event of the face, or the summons. But height and summons do not yet have a determinate content. If Levinas finds normative content in the face, e.g., the injunction against murder, it is because he tacitly appeals to or falls back upon his religious tradition. The normative content of the face then seems grounded in revelation, i.e., ethics is grounded in religion. Such a move sets infinity in opposition to totality, or faith and ethics in opposition to philosophy. Further, Levinas has been criticized for retaining the patriarchalism of his religious tradition.[10] I would add that he seems to retain a corresponding concept of the religious relation as asymmetrical that paradoxically reflects the traditional metaphysics he opposes.

Although Farley is also working within the Hebraic-Christian paradigm, he defends reflective ontology for theology, criticizes the monarchical metaphor and attendant patriarchalism, and transforms Levinas's austere account of the face *at the philosophical level*. Specifically, Farley's claim is that the face not only summons to responsibility, it also evokes compassion. The sphere of the face is a sphere of empathy, emotional participation, and compassion. Levinas's view of the strict asymmetry of the interpersonal undergoes modification. The modification Farley proposes is reciprocity: alterity is not just the cognitive elusiveness of the other or the height from which the other commands and disposes of my freedom, but a *reciprocity* of autonomies that discloses fragility (42, 103). Reciprocity and compassion are propounded as a philosophical-theological thesis that corrects and revises Levinas's formalism and assertion of an absolute priority of the other over the self. Levinas's view of the asymmetrical summons to responsibility is only a starting point for reciprocal mediation and a relationship that requires reciprocity.

Levinas rejects reciprocity in favor of a fundamental asymmetry of the interpersonal, because he fears reciprocity is the opening wedge for the hegemony of natural egocentrism. The face precedes and commands such egocentrism from a position of height and mastery. Hence the interpersonal, as primal ethical, must be asymmetrical, and asymmetry rules out reciprocity. But for Farley there are at least two sorts of reciprocity. The one is superficial, utilitarian, "tit for tat" reciprocity. This reciprocity is utilitarian, a form of self-seeking (not to be confused with idolatry or evil). It never gets beyond the egoism-altruism bind. Such utilitarian reciprocity must be distinguished from the reciprocity that is founded in courage. Courage means being freed from natural egocentrism, wherein the liberated passion for reciprocity becomes an agapic passion for the face. What dominates now is not the natural egocentrism of the subject, but what is discerned in the face, namely, a certain beauty and loveliness that calls forth affection and compassion (191). Face not only summons; it also evokes and calls forth face. This is the central core of Farley's theological treatment of the face, which makes the sphere of face and relation the primary sphere in his theological anthropology.[11]

The introduction of the possibility of reciprocity and the theme of compassion Farley introduces in Part One prepare the way for further theological transformation and development of the face in Part Two. At the risk of grotesque oversimplification, Farley shows that the face presents many faces. In addition to the vulnerable and destitute face described by Levinas, Farley speaks of a beautiful face and an accusing face. The beautiful face is Farley's interesting transformation of Levinas's stern moralism by appeal to the great American theologian Jonathan Edwards, who had much to say about the beauty and loveliness of interpersonal love and affection.

However Farley's transformation of the face raises questions about reciprocity and totality. Levinas's critique of Martin Buber's concept of relation is relevant, since Farley tends to side with Buber's view that relation implies reciprocity. Levinas criticizes Buber.[12] When Buber asserts that in the beginning is the relation, his concern is to criticize the view that individuals are absolute unrelated atoms, complete in and of themselves. On the contrary, they are what they are in relation. But Levinas would be cautious about assigning priority to relation, because this might suggest not only that the relation is prior to the *relata;* it might lead to the dissolution of the *relata* themselves. In other words, assigning priority to the relation might be another version of the priority of the whole over its parts. Thus totality, or holism, would undermine the priority of the ethical. Levinas believes this is what happens in Hegel, Heidegger, and the entire Western tradition.

For this reason, Levinas believes that if the asymmetry of the interhuman is transcended in reciprocity, the resulting reciprocity implies a co-equality that in turn implies that self and other are leveled and totalized. When totalized, the other is denied or reduced to the same. The other is neutralized by ontological universality and totality. To prevent such totalization, Levinas sought to distinguish the face of the other, as *infinity,* from totality. The face resists totalization. This issue is important at the philosophical level, where Farley tends to agree with Buber and with Hegel that relation, if genuine, must be reciprocal.[13] Although relation may begin in asymmetry, asymmetry must be transcended and transformed into reciprocity. If relation is reciprocal, then the *relata* do not persist unchanged or unqualified in spite of relationship. They undergo a mutual transformation. The *telos* of relation is a reciprocity of a certain sort, such that through reciprocal mediation the I becomes a We, a community. Relation leads to reciprocity, and reciprocity prepares the way for totality. But what sort of totality? Does Farley annul the important distinction between totality and infinity? To treat this issue, we must examine briefly Farley's account of the accusing face in his account of alienation and reconciliation.

Farley formulates sin and redemption in interpersonal terms and apart from the penal and forensic metaphors dominant in the tradition. The face is central to this interpersonal account of alienation and redemption. The face evokes both violence and compassion. Thus the face is what is violated, deprived of its powers of being. Violation means that the summons of the face is ignored and set aside. Violation is internalized by the violator as guilt and by the violated as resentment. Violation in turn creates a *second* summons, namely, to rectify the harm done, to heal the wound in the relationship. But rectification is never equivalent to the original wound. Hence violation effects an irreparable wound in the relationship that persists because of the inability of the violator to answer the second summons. The accusing face is the face of this second summons. It is not merely the face of the violated; it is the violator's own, self-accusing face. Forgiveness is a determinate interpersonal relation in which the hold of the violated and accusing face can be broken. Forgiveness means for the *violated* a transcending of the accusing face and the breaking of resentment; for the *violator* forgiveness means the acceptance of the impossibility of reparation and a transcending of its self-accusing face (248). The agapic relation manifest in forgiveness is the presence of the sacred in the interpersonal sphere.

The face, as it comes to expression in mutual forgiveness, becomes a principle of mutuality and totality rather than asymmetry and non-reciprocity. However, the community or totality that comes into existence through forgiveness is a community that acknowledges the dynamics of evil and idolatry and has experienced the breaking of the dynamics of evil, which includes the breaking of the hegemonic totality of idolatry. For this reason Farley's transformation of the face does not seem to lead back to the hegemonic totality that Levinas criticizes. Forgiveness is the "principle," as it were, of this "broken totality" or communion. That is, parochial particularism is transcended in principle through forgiveness. But how can the face be released from its capture by determinacies, parochial loyalties, and commitments of specific social locations? How can the face be transregional? Farley's thesis, similar to Levinas's, is that the transregional face is experienced in connection with the sacred. It is the sacred manifested through the face that lures regional (familial, tribal, national) experiences of the face toward compassionate obligations to all life. Thus Farley speaks of a universal face that is attested through and mediated by communities of the face. This interesting suggestion remains undeveloped.

However, the question concerning totality arises again at the level of the relation of the Christian paradigm to other paradigms. What sort of totality is meant by ecclesial community? If ecclesial community is a

universal community, is it nevertheless parochial in a certain sense, in
that as the expression of a single paradigm, it has an other? an outsider?
Can the outsider be given any affirmative theological basis and support
that is non-hegemonic, non-colonizing, and does not reduce that other
to the same? These questions are important in view of the fact that forgiveness and reconciliation are not unknown to other faiths, including
Judaism. It is difficult to determine whether Farley's transformation and
reconstruction of Levinas's concept of the face should be taken to imply
a separation of the Christian from the Hebraic paradigm on the issue of
reconciliation, or whether Farley's reconstruction posits a fundamental
continuity within a common paradigm. However problematic the claim
of a common Hebraic-Christian paradigm may be on the issue of reconciliation, the absence of any christological discussion by Farley in his
analyses of being-founded, courage, agapic passion, reconciliation, etc.,
is surely worth pondering.

Theology and the Tragic

I want to gather some of the questions previously noted concerning ontology, theology, and tragedy. Recall the questions: If theology is not
ontotheology, what is it? Can there be a non-foundational theology?
If so, what would it look like? Farley asserts that being-founded is a
founding that is not founded. Ontotheology seems to fall under Farley's
critique of the monarchical metaphor and the corresponding exclusion
of the tragic dimension of existence. A theology that, like Farley's, affirms a tragic dimension and insists that being-founded does not close
the gap but allows us to live in that gap in relativizing postures would
not be a foundationalist ontotheology in the traditional sense. If theology does acknowledge a tragic chaos as the condition, not the cause,
of sin, then the foundational character of theology undergoes a transformation: the sacred presence founds without itself being-founded. But
what does this mean? Is the sacred presence self-founding? That is the
anti-foundationalist move made by Schelling and Hegel, which Barth
appropriates.

Can theology embrace a tragic chaos at the heart of things without
ending in a tragic vision? Would not a theology that ended in a purely
tragic vision simply undermine good and redemption? Would it not violate the insistence of the Hebraic-Christian paradigm that tragic finitude,
while important, is nevertheless not the most important problem, but
that sin is, and that sin is distinct from finitude? Granting the Hebraic
and Christian distinction of sin and evil from tragic finitude, the question is whether this requires a distinction, if not complete separation, of
the problematics of salvation from tragic finitude as well. On the other

hand, if being-founded introduces a new set of possibilities into existence and is not merely a restoration of the status quo ante idolatry,
does this mean that the tragic itself is relativized, if not set aside? To set
the tragic aside would return to a triumphalism virtually indistinguish-
able from the traditional exclusion of the tragic that Farley opposes.
However, this seems to be a possibility, if not tendency, in the Whiteheadian strand of Farley's concept of chaos previously noted. If chaos is
part of the essential goodness of being, this would seem to neutralize the
ethically monstrous aspects of the tragic.

   But what would it mean to relativize the tragic dimension? Farley's
claim is that being-founded makes possible a way of existing as vulnerable and as tragic. This implies that redemption is not from the tragic,
but an alteration within tragic existence. If the tragic is not set aside
or suppressed, what is this alteration? Do goodness, salvation, etc., as
ontic, have any mitigating implications vis-à-vis the ontological tragic
dimension of finitude? If being-founded really introduces a new set of
possibilities, and is not merely a restoration of the status quo ante idolatry, does this mean that the tragic itself is relativized and set within
a larger ontological context? If being-founded and reconciliation occur
and break the dynamics of evil, doesn't this imply a recontextualization
or reinterpretation of tragedy at the ontological level? Or does tragic
finitude provide the ultimate framework and context for the new ontic
possibilities introduced by being-founded?

   For Ricoeur, such theological issues lie beyond the resources of a
philosophical anthropology. Nevertheless, these issues are raised by a
theological anthropology that sets forth both sin and redemptive existence and seems to be philosophically supported by Farley's endorsement
of reflective ontology, his acknowledgment of a tragic dimension of existence, and his important theological analysis of courage. These are
questions that clearly go beyond a theological anthropology to the level
of the doctrine of God. A new antinomy arises, this time in the concept
of God: chaos may be both an element in opposition to sacred presence
and yet an element in the sacred presence itself. It is worth recalling Ricoeur's observation that in pursuit of this question Job rediscovers the
tragic God.[14]

   If theology must incorporate a tragic element that deconstructs the
forensic juridical metaphors and penal vision of the world and must
make use of interpersonal conjugal metaphors to set forth the breaking
of the dynamics of evil and the authentic courage that consents to chaos
and tragic vulnerability, what theological conception brings the tragic
and the conjugal metaphors together? Can we discern a unified theological conception here at all? Or are we left with an insuperable antinomy?
Ricoeur formulates the antinomy and points a way to its possible resolution: "The tragic is invincible at the level of man and unthinkable at

the level of God. A learned theogony, then, is the only means of making tragedy invincible and intelligible at the same time; it consists, in the last resort, in assigning the tragic to the origin of things and making it coincide with a logic of being, by means of negativity."[15] This implies that there are negativity and suffering in God, a suffering that for Hegel is bound up with christology and the death of God. These distinctions in turn point to a developmental and relational concept of God, with attendant distinctions between God as Alpha and Omega (Schelling), God as substance and subject (Hegel), God as absolute yet related and indebted to all (Hartshorne). But do such developmental conceptions imply that tragedy is ultimately set aside, or *Aufgehoben?* Or is it rather a permanent but subordinate element in and condition of theogony? I believe that German Idealism, particularly Schelling and Hegel, points in the latter direction and provides one of the few conceptualities capable of acknowledging a tragic background and condition of evil while yet affirming the possibility of goodness and reconciliation.

NOTES

1. This defense is closely related to Husserl's claims for the priority of the life-world over abstractive theoretical reflections. Cf. Husserl, *The Crisis of Modern European Science and Transcendental Phenomenology,* trans. D. Carr (Evanston, Ill.: Northwestern University Press, 1970).

2. We shall return to these issues in subsequent sections.

3. According to Farley, 4 and 5 reflect discredited pre-critical modes of thought; 6 and 7 are theologically problematic. Thus only features 1–3 are retrievable.

4. Paul Ricoeur, *The Symbolism of Evil,* trans. E. Buchanan (Boston: Beacon Press, 1969).

5. At the same time Farley transforms this insight into a critique of classical religion and metaphysics — not unlike Barth's critique of religion — as a longing for absolute certainty and security.

6. *Good and Evil,* 143. Farley cites Ricoeur's essay "The Myth of Punishment" in *Conflict of Interpretations: Essays in Hermeneutics* (Evanston, Ill.: Northwestern University Press, 1974).

7. Tragedy and resignation to fate are thus interpreted as categories of the already defeated self.

8. Cf. Schleiermacher's claim that redemption is the completion of creation. Troeltsch criticized this notion as a peculiarly Christian attempt to overcome history through history. In *Ecclesial Reflection,* Farley carries out a similar critique of the traditional concept of salvation history.

9. Emmanuel Levinas, *Totality and Infinity,* trans. A. Lingis (Pittsburgh: Duquesne University Press, 1961), 215. Levinas speaks of the asymmetry of the interpersonal.

10. See Luce Irigaray, "Questions to Emmanuel Levinas: On the Divinity of Love," *Re-Reading Levinas,* ed. R. Bernasconi and S. Critchley (Bloomington: Indiana University Press, 1991), 109–18.

11. Redemption means the reconnection of the individual and social spheres to the face, so that they are humanized and become instrumental to historical freedom, rather than alienation, domination, and subjugation.

12. Levinas has written two essays that reach contradictory assessments of Buber. The first is "Martin Buber and the Theory of Knowledge," in *The Levinas Reader,* ed. Sean Hand (Oxford: England: B. H. Blackwell, 1989). This highly critical essay, which claims that Buber, by his tacit acceptance of the traditional philosophy of the subject, undermined the I-Thou as an ethical relationship, was written in 1958. Levinas offers a strikingly different, more positive assessment of Buber in a later essay, "Martin Buber, Gabriel Marcel and Philosophy," which appears in *Martin Buber: A Centenary Volume,* ed. H. Gordon and J. Bloch (New York: KTAV Publishing House, 1984). For a discussion of Levinas's complex and often changing relation to Buber, see Robert Bernasconi, "Failure of Communication as a Surplus," in R. Bernasconi and D. Wood, eds., *Provocation of Levinas* (New York: Routledge, 1988), 100–136.

13. See my *Recognition: Fichte and Hegel on the Other* (Albany: State University of New York Press, 1992).

14. Ricoeur, *Symbolism of Evil,* 319.

15. Ibid., 327.

PART TWO

Essays on
Historical Theology

⇒ 7 ⇐

Farley's Prolegomena to Any Future Historical Theology

Reflections on the Historicality of Theology's History

JAMES O. DUKE

Anyone who undertakes to judge, or still more to construct, a historical theology must satisfy the demands here made either by adopting Farley's solution or by refuting it and substituting another. To evade it is impossible. The double-play on Kant's words in this title and thesis statement[1] is patently un-Farleyesque sport. Farley eschews hype. He is well aware that the word-plays of theology's language-game(s) conceal as well as reveal and often take their cues from Gollum rather than Hermes or Jesus. By no means theologically risk-adverse, he is also aware that plays of this sort are likely to backfire. The last time rumors floated of a Reformed theologian who is to theology as Kant is to philosophy, theologians and philosophers alike took prompt evasive action. The full thrust of Friedrich Schleiermacher's thought was parried outside the Germanies by tagging it "too Teuton" and within them by intoning a mantra of *différence*: too philosophical for church theology *and/or* too church-theological for philosophy. Time alone will tell whether the more things change the more they remain the same once again.

It is then clearly not a natural but a moral impossibility of evading Farley's prolegomena to historical theology being spoken of here. In tune with the temper of our times, the only regulative principle to which appeal is in order is one honored as often by its breach as its observance — do not deceive. By that is meant in the context of the topic at hand to disavow any and every witting effort either to underestimate or overestimate the fragility of knowledge.

Farley signaled his commitment to this regulative principle often, as early as the telling book title *Requiem for a Lost Piety*.[2] The lead-in to the first chapter of *Ecclesial Man*, "Theology and the Problem of

Reality," was an apothegm from none other than Friedrich Nietzsche:
"Whatever a theologian feels to be true *must* be false; this is almost a
criterion of truth. His most basic instinct of self-preservation forbids him
to respect reality at any point or even to let it get a word in."[3] Although
respecting reality is by no means the leitmotif of today's Nietzsche
renaissance, it is noteworthy that Farley lets the past grand master of
the hermeneutics of suspicion get this word in. For their part, his various "genealogical" and "archeological" excavations of church as well
as his hard-hitting investigative reports on faith and its apprehended
and appresented "objects," theological criteriology, theological education, good and evil, metaphysics, truth, and topics in-between betoken
his resolve to grant the habit(us) of deception no quarter.

The resolve is manifest in Farley's many and varied efforts to descry
the process, structures, and elements constitutive of a historically determinate type of corporate human existence which in everyday language
is called the faith of the Christian church. My claim that these efforts
include prolegomena for any future historical theology arises from the
conviction that Farley's work directs the theological enterprise in toto to
own up to the historicality (*Geschichtlichkeit*) of its subject matter, and
so its inquiries and their results as well. This conviction is here reduced
to a shamelessly *fachgemäss* (if not *fachidiotisch*) frame in which theology's history is thematized as a subject matter to be explored by a fabled
inquiry with the name historical theology.

The term "historical theology" is a latecomer to the study of theology,
first making its appearance at *theologia*'s early modern fragmentation.
(Before then theology's history was thematized in other ways and by
other names.) It has persisted despite failing to gain a secure disciplinary home by migrating within a limited habitat: to date, no more
apt name presents itself for hybrid inquiries that aim at searching out the
theological import of theology's history by rigorous historical thinking.

Such inquiries, neither fish nor fowl, have always been rather rare. To
historians qua historians, theology's history is a super-specialized topic
and in any case of concern because of its historical, not its theological
import. Theology, however, lives in a perpetually unsettled relationship
to its own history. Its history is its own, and so inescapable, and at once
a vital resource for and a drag upon its every undertaking. Theology
copes, by now owning some aspects of its past, disowning others, and
forgetting most. The realization that it is unable to do other than cope
is an "event" in theology's history with effects not yet accounted for
fully. Only when the tally is complete can theology even begin truly to
own up to its historicality. The several reflections on this task offered
here are hasty and rough ad-interim estimates. They are grouped under
four headings: (1) theology's problem with its own history; (2) reckoning
with that problem by historical theology; (3) historical theology as theo-

logical portraiture; and (4) remarks on the complexification of historical theology.

Theology and the Problem of Its Own History

Ambiguities attend the term "history" and its kin "historic," "historical," "historicity" (*Historizität*), "historicism," "historiography," and "historicality." Each of them presents Christian theology (the only sort of theology dealt with here) with certain opportunities and certain problems. One example must suffice, cited merely in passing: orthodoxy's claim of solidarity with "that which has been believed everywhere, always, and by all." This formula is a resourceful attempt on the part of at least some Christians to overcome history by history. As such, it has become historic. Yet failing the demonstration of the historicity of anything Christian believed everywhere, always, and by all, one may begin to wonder if the claim is a historical claim at all. Is it perhaps, instead, by virtue of the odd logic or miracle of theological discourse only quasi-historical, viz., an article of faith, a doxology, or a rule of theological grammar cloaked in historical garb?

Theology's history is riddled with such apiorias, or ploys. Distinguishing what is and what is not historical about theology is an undertaking more like that of Sisyphus than Hercules or Judith. Questions of historicity per se have proved to be among the least of the challenges. In the main they (along with many other questions of various sorts) surface at the "instant" of theology's history, the immediacy of some moment, and as such are handled — swept up or swept aside — as the history of theology runs its course. The immediacy of a moment, however, is a deceptive abstraction: the "this, here, and now" of every instant is a mediated immediacy, always already historically constituted. Awareness of the historically constituted mediated immediacy of every instant is itself a historical event. This event has been swept up into history books, where it is usually told of as stories about "the rise of historical consciousness." However lengthy the overture, the story-line itself gets underway in the aftermath of the Enlightenment and moves on — extending, deepening, complicating, and radicalizing itself — thereafter. (In many accounts, the erstwhile protagonist "consciousness" is flung out of the story during a radical turn along the way.)

The term "historicality" is a neologism, a linguistic innovation generated by historical consciousness raised to the "x" power in order to identify a thematic "object" for which no other name available will quite do. Historicality itself is nothing new, having been always already there unnoticed or in some partial (dis)guise. Its thematization, however, is ongoing twentieth-century news. One way to put the matter is to say that historicality is a world-structure: the condition of being-there in-the-world with-others amid-care-laden-time. Yet another way, more brief and slightly closer to ordinary language and hence inviting, is to speak of the condition of belonging to history.

Something of what is meant by this phrase is indicated by now commonplace references to the "historical" finitude, flux, contextuality, and relativity of human being and all that is human. Much more is to be gathered from phenomenological and post-phenomenological explorations into the temporality and linguisticality and enigmatic presence/ absence of the Being of beings. Without ignoring such concerns, attention will focus here on a penultimate matter: the historicality of structures of the social world. These reflections return to Farley's point of departure — the "concept" of a determinate social world in chapter 4 of *Ecclesial Man* — and only occasionally and all too casually press as Farley does outside the precincts of a sociology of knowledge inquiry.

Minimalist as it is, this interest suffices to permit a proximate identification of the historicality of a determinate social world in terms of four parameters. A determinate social world is a multidimensional complex of meaningful (*sinnhaft*) relations of typified particularity, circumscribed diversity, extensible situationality, and transient durability. My account of these terms will be by way of illustration — brief and overly simple allusions to Christianity's faith world, the matrix of Christian theology. As a world of meaning(s), the faith world is a complex made up of typifications of particularities and the circumscription of these diverse typifications into generalized wholes that are situated in some specific (narrow or broad) band of social space and endure for some (long or short) social time. Living and dying and everything *ad interim* transpire within this faith world through this networking of meanings, which amount to negotiated and renegotiated world-relations.

The Christian faith world first makes its appearance "in world history" in the days of the early Roman Empire. It emerges at that time *into* a determinate social world with a history of its own by reopening negotiations with regard to world-relations that had been already set (and at points disputed) within the faith world of Israel. This process involved reconfiguring a network of cointended meanings: the retypification of particulars, the recircumscribing of diverse typifications into generalized wholes, and readjustments with regard to social location. Into this nascent faith world came various elements, structures, and patterns that had pre-existed long before its rise, others that were comparatively recent, and still others that were novelties of its very own. The durability of these buildings blocks — their persistence, adaptability, and liability to decay — varies from case to case. The complex as a whole is itself a case at issue, hard-pressed as it was and is to maintain continuities amid changes sufficient for preserving an identity that is true to type. Its half-life is, to date, still undergoing the test of time. The inescapably uncertain status of each of the parameters of historicality is routinely concealed (in this faith world as in every determinate social world) by a natural attitude, an everydayness, in which sedimented meanings of words and deeds alike are taken for granted. Yet intimations of frangibility repeatedly surface. The questionability of the typification of particulars, for example, is as evident early on in the restive search for words (messianic titles, etc.) honoring the status of Jesus "of Nazareth" as it is today in debates over reserving those words for this figure alone. That of the circumscription of diverse typifications into a generalized whole is played out in irrepressible disputes over what belongs to *esse* and what belongs to the *bene esse* of the church. In which respects and to what extent this faith world extends beyond (each and every) one of its historically given social locations is an ever-open issue with no fixed answer except that the determinacy of the faith world is at odds with provinciality. The transient durability of the faith world comes to the fore in discussions of the development of dogma or doctrine, the absoluteness or finality of the Christian religion, and doleful or gladsome prophecies of a Christian-free future.

The citation of illustrations might go on and on. It is not to be thought, however, that there is — ever — a simple point-by-point correspondence between any one parameter of the faith world's historicality and some one specific *topos* or *Schwerpunkt* in the history of theology. The four parameters are equiprimordial and coconstitutive and concatenating: to operate on or with any one of them is to trigger a redetermination of the others along the line, and hence the function as a whole. Should this point call for exemplification, this one may serve.

Even as theological attempts to distinguish orthodoxy from heterodoxy and heresy "center" attention on the question of the adequacy of the hitherto taken for granted circumscription of diverse typifications into a generalized whole, they are also and at the same time exercises involving the retypification of already typified particulars according to some entrenched or revisionist classificatory schema. These exercises are by no means conducted by simply affixing pre-formed labels on unmistakably identifiable objects. Each is an experiment — or a *Putsch* — of discernment: an effort to determine which, when, and where certain elements of the faith world are to be "properly" considered discretionary rather than indispensable and inappropriate.

The term "properly" is a qualifier that has to be added, although a parenthesis is required because propriety in the sense of idealized faithfulness is — it seems in church history — always alleged regardless of the actual process of decision-making or its outcome. (The allegation is necessary even when it is a mistake or a lie, given that "faithfulness" is an ideal belonging to the *telos* of the faith world.) Properly considered or not, the act of discernment is not merely a recording but an agenda-driven reconstruing of what had been taken for granted. Features of the faith world that were once indistinct are differentiated; others once distant or disjointed are linked; this and that are revalued; the configuration of the whole is altered, kaleidoscope-like.

Once in place, the result (self-serving as it may be) encumbers anyone who nears or participates in the faith world thereafter. Its effect is not only to apportion this world like Caesar's Gaul into three parts, the realms of the indispensable, discretionary, and inappropriate. It is also to legitimate this map as the ancient but still-vital heritage of "we, the faithful" in distinction from those who, while having once been with us in faith, have since strayed into some other social space. In sum, orthodoxies gain their solidity by revisioning theology's history. Even so, both the positing and legitimizing of some such differentiated faith world remain contextually embedded — they are extensible only so far. Every presumptive claim to orthodoxy is socio-culturally situated, as those the self-avowed orthodox classify as heterodox and heretical unfailingly realize and even the least critical of theology's historians now commonly admit. Last but not least, these categories — and along with them the categorizers, the categorized, and the situational-specificity of the lot — persist over time for only so long. They make their entrance and take their leave in history; their durability is transient.

Oversimplified as they are, these illustrations should make it plain that to speak here of the parameters of the faith world's historicality is not to speak theologically at all, much less to identify a content or criteriology to which the material claims of faith, church, and theology are subject. The aim is "simply" to point out structures of the faith world as such. When they are at home in mathematics, parameters are constants or variables that go to make up a function. So, *mutatis mutandis,* in the case of the faith world the parameters of historicality are filled and operated upon and thereby "function" to constitute this world in its parts and in toto as the complex that it is. Within this complex, with its corporate memory, vehicles of social duration, and entelechial future-orientation, the manifold world transactions of "the faithful" are interpretively negotiated and renegotiated by means of the (re)typification of particulars, the (re)circumscription of diversities into generalized wholes, the (re)settlement of some (restricted or extended) socio-spatial territory, and throughout it all, the (more or less limited) capacity to persist over time.

These transactions occur in the faith world pre-reflectively, responsorially, that is, logically "before" and temporally in, under, and with the proceedings of thematization that issue in the everyday, or first-order, language (and action) of Christian witness. And this is to say that they have first occurred "twice before" critical and self-critical theological reflection on them — "ordered learning," as Farley might call it[4] — is undertaken. It comes as no surprise, then, that the phrase "the problem of theology's history" is shorthand not for one problem but for a many-faced, indeed hydra-headed, challenger to the theological status quo. Faith's pre-reflective world transactions take place subject to the condition of belonging to history. So too does the first-order theological reflection that thematizes those transactions and in so doing renews or revises them. And so too does the critical and self-critical reflection of the second order, which reinterrogates both givens en bloc. The forms, terms, methods, pressure-points, and styles of each of these (re)appraisals are many and varied; their multiplicity, variety, inertia, and flux are indicative of the condition of belonging to history. All this, taken together and as it recurs over time, is the stuff of which theology's history is made. The most readily available term for this whole is "the Christian tradition," which embraces both the sum total of the faith world's material content and the perpetual process of its transmission over time.

And then there are histories of theology's history. That is, tradition itself — perforce some sectors of it more or rather than others — becomes as it were a story-to-be-told and as such an object of historical interest and (perhaps) historical research. Whether edificatory, celebrative, or revisionist, these always present themselves in the manner of Greeks bearing gifts.[5] Even when theology welcomes them, it is likely to do so warily. The sorts of explorations that pass or count as genuinely or respectably historical vary from time to time and place to place and social circle to social circle, as any historian of historiography or sociologist of knowledge who cares to can easily demonstrate. These variations too partake of historicality — that of historical inquiries and their findings.

That noted, haste must be made to stress that the moral of this story is not that theology's problem with its own history is at root historicality. Historicality means theology no harm; it is nothing other than part of (as Farley might say) "the way things are" or "what we are up against." Many if not most Christians are already prepared to contend that world-structures like historicality are aspects of the "order" created by God and, as such, not the cause but the setting and occasion for human problems, errors, evils, and sins — in brief, for idolatry and flight. Yet there is no doubt that theology has all too often throughout its history typified historicality as enemy, recoiling or lashing out in frustration when history, historians, historiography, and the condition of belonging to history fail to support its claims, or contest them, or (*horribile dictu!*) expose their historical relativity. These protests and refusals and tantrums may afford theology some temporary relief. But they are at length futile. They are also fake, and deceitful — at least, that is, when

they come from theologians who cannot plausibly deny any awareness
of the historicality of theology's history.

At the bottom line, then, the problem of theology and its own history
is not historicality per se but how human beings — Christians, theologians — respond to their awareness of it. The point can be posed in the
form of a question: will theology deal with its own history historically,
that is, with circumspection born of an awareness that faith, church, and
theology are in the condition of belonging to history? Even the most
daring of the theological responses to this question prominent in the
first and middle third of this century, e.g., those of Troeltsch, Bultmann,
Tillich, and Rahner (and Barth in his own way, especially early Barth)
have now yielded the field to a new corps of volunteers. Among them
Farley is to be numbered. So too is an energetic band of self-declared
radicals and a-theologians.

With precious few exceptions, the professionally and professorially
accredited historians of Christianity, church, and theology seem to prefer
to take the historicality of their work and its subject matter unthema-
tized, thank you. And no wonder, one might say. There are stories to be
retold and others to be recovered, methods and strategies of interpretation to be tried out, horrific injustices to be exposed and noble causes
to be defended. All this and more can go on by operating upon, and
within, the parameters of historicality — without thematizing them at
all. Yet if much is gained in this way, something is also in danger of loss.
The capacity of historians of theology to prove that they are not "really"
theologians but historians whose works are strictly historical has the un-
toward effect of contributing to the further marginalization of rigorous
historical inquiry in the study of theology as a whole. (Ironically, it also
fosters the illusion that the task[s] of theology per se can be met by re-
telling stories of some "historic" individual or group.) To anyone even
dimly aware of the historicality of theology's history, honesty demands
searching out some better way.

Reckoning with Theology's History
by Historical Theology

The consciousness-raising that roused theology from its "dogmatic
slumbers" to wide-awake attention to the condition of belonging to
history came about as part of the birth of modernity in the era of Enlightenment. It seems to have appeared first more as a foggy sensing of
a family resemblance among newly emergent possibilities for attacking
or reforming the status quo of church theology than by premeditated
plan. And what seemed, or now seems, at first to have distinguished
these possibilities as new (as modern) from other and in many respects

similar possibilities of the past (the traditional, the premodern) was their common association with canons of "enlightened" reasoning. It is now generally acknowledged, thanks to hindsight, that history was not the forte of the Enlightenment, Gibbon and pioneers of "the historical-critical method" notwithstanding. Awareness of historicality itself was incipient and played a secondary and mainly polemical role in the formation of the Enlightenment paradigm of critical knowledge. Yet the recognition that present knowledge always arises as criticism — a criticism of inherited knowledge "pressing for the establishment of the basis, evidence, and assumptions of any claim" — altered longstanding assumptions regarding relations among faith, theology, and history.[6] And so in this epoch the question of whether theology will deal with its own history historically surfaced and was addressed, if only by proxy, that is, inasmuch as theology set about to deal with its history in keeping with terms, methods, and standards of judgment honored by Enlightenment historiography.

Keeping abreast of changing historiographical fashions, however, has proved to be the least of challenges posed by the rise of modern historical consciousness. That this was to be so became evident even before the end of the eighteenth century in the works of Lessing, Hamann, and Herder. In the wake of subsequent developments — which Farley has termed the romantic, theological, and radicalized (social scientific and praxis-oriented) correctives to the Enlightenment paradigm of critical reasoning — the task of dealing with the historicality of theology has become ever more daunting.[7]

It was Schleiermacher who first tipped off early nineteenth-century theological colleagues to the impact that a decision to accept the challenge might have on the study of theology as a whole. In his theological encyclopedia, philosophical analysis was denied the role of "proving" or "founding" the truth of the Christian religion and assigned instead the task of determining the constitutive features of Christianity's self-identity as one of many historically determinate corporate faiths. The field of historical theology was expanded to encompass nothing short of tradition's full historical sweep. Embraced in it were studies of antecedents and origins (biblical history and literature), the history of the church and its thought, and reports on the current state of the Christian religion, including its sociological profile (church statistics) and its doctrinal teachings of faith (*Glaubenslehre*) and morals (*Sittenlehre*). What is projected here for historical theology is, in effect, a thoroughgoing survey and appraisal of the historical determinacy of the Christian religion.[8]

Schleiermacher's dream of a historical theology of such grand scale never came true. Farley's exposé of the history of theological encyclopedia has helped historians and theologians alike better understand why.[9] To his remarks one other might be added. As Schleiermacher conceived

it, historical theology is not only aligned to the historical determinacy
of faith, church, and theology but for that very reason disclosive of the
irremediable historicality of the theological enterprise itself. It thereby
mandated any future theology (under threat of indictment for deceit) to
respect the reality of belonging to history. The thought of this reality was
discomforting to many, and still is — no doubt and above all because
to think of it is to concede that the question of Christianity's truth(s)
is settled neither by the wisdom of tradition alone (within theology's
historic house of authority) nor without it (by trading the historical determinacy of this religion for some more general wisdom of the world).
Flaws, missteps, and situation-specific limitations of Schleiermacher's encyclopedic conception of theological study must be granted, but just and
honestly so only if his base-line concern to grapple with the historicality
of theological inquiry is taken to heart.

For the most resolute responses to the peculiar problematic that
Schleiermacher grappled with, attention is drawn to those who recognized that a contemporary critical account of the Christian faith
(viz., dogmatic, doctrinal, systematic, or constructive theology) cannot
be given "in conscience" without also giving, implicitly if not explicitly, a critical account of the history of such accounts. This alone is
reason, even if there were no other, for a few dead white European
males such as Baur, Newman, von Harnack, Loisy, and Troeltsch —
and yes, Kierkegaard too, the once-lonely Dane — to figure still in
histories of theology. (By the same token, histories of theology that
blithely ignore Hegel, Feuerbach, Marx, Nietzsche, and *Religionswissen-
schaftler* certify that they somehow "just don't get it.") In the works of
the most ambitious *fin de siècle* historical theologians the outcome of
the task of theology was understood to turn on rigorously historical-
critical research into the development of doctrine and the essence of
Christianity.

Following Farley, who follows Troeltsch in this respect, the Achilles'
heel of the quest for *das Wesen des Christentums* can be readily identified: "we have here an intellectual enterprise whose only method and
therefore type of evidence is *historical,* but whose motivation and expectation is *theological.* 'Essence of Christianity' is therefore both whatever
historical method procures about Christianity and whatever is fundamental and indispensable to faith." This odd-coupling of history and
theology leads, inescapably, to historical-theological dilemmas so in-
tractable that in the final analysis Farley's conclusion is also inescapable:
"the historian's attempt to describe 'Christianity' can never itself *be*
theology."[10]

That Farley's critical comment betokens tough love rather than anger,
fear, or disdain will become evident later on. It suffices at the moment
to say only that the criticism does not signify, as it has done for so many

others, allegiance to some dogmatic rather than historical method of theology or a yearning to return to rooms under the cover of theology's (historic) house of authority. In any case, the glory days of questing for the essence of Christianity have long since passed. The term "historical-critical" has lost the specificity and with it the cash-in value it held in the days of Mommsen and von Ranke and even Dilthey. History has spawned a welter of competitive historical methods and hermeneutical strategies to be used on tradition. The gain, here and now, is that something more and increasingly "different" about Christianity's past is constantly being procured. The downside is that what if anything of its own history *commands* theology's attention is altogether up for grabs and all too often treated less an issue to be settled by painstaking inquiry and reasoned public debate than as preferential option or an opportunity to assert a point of personal or group privilege.

Considering that piecemeal handlings of tradition — from "neo-Reformation theologies" on — are so common among historians and theologians, the scope of the five-volume panoramic history of the Christian tradition by Jaroslav Pelikan makes it especially worthy of late twentieth-century note.[11] It also builds upon an exceptionally prolonged examination of historical theology's uncertain sense of its own disciplinary self-identity. The Pelikan history owes much to Newman, but beggars comparison with von Harnack, and in terms of sheer erudition it fares tolerably well. The revisionist self-definition of doctrine that emerges lays claim to a field of inquiry far broader than that of old-style *Dogmengeschichte* and yet more confined than that of modish histories of Christian thought. The study aims at focusing with hawk-eyed concentration on the history of *doctrine:* "what the church of Jesus Christ believes, teaches, and confesses on the basis of the Word of God."[12]

Much acclaimed and much criticized, and in both instances for a variety of good reasons, the Pelikan history is beyond doubt immensely informative. Yet its responsivity to theology's historicality cannot be said to represent a signal advance beyond its scholarly antecedents. The point might be put this time in this way: a historical theology that aims at *what* the church believes, teaches, and confesses falls short of its target when it proceeds to itemize, sort, collate, and (re)count continuity and change evident in church-historical variations on theological themes.

The shortfall is due to the ambiguity of the word "what." Harbored there are no less than three objects: (1) the *topoi* of church-historical statements of belief, teaching materials, and confessions of faith; (2) the sense of those *topoi,* which taken together make up a distinct(ive) set — perhaps even an array or system — of (co)intended meant-objects; and (3) the referents or realities (if any) that are intended by and with the sense of those *topoi.* From the *History* itself one is hard-pressed to decide which of these "whats" is or is supposed to be historical theology's ultimate target. This undecidability is hardly like that of Derrida's, even though Pelikan's rehearsal of variations on theological themes certainly has the (unanticipated?) effect of illustrating intertextuality: see here how much the history of theology is a recycling of the same ole' well-worn words. In any case, the ambiguity here has its rewards. One reader may come away satisfied with having been informed about the *topoi* of theology; another, the grammar of faith; a third, the very body of divinity; a fourth (perhaps), the ceaseless cross-referencing of entries within the church's dictionary of theological terms.

Historical Theology as Theological Portraiture

From Farley come repeated warnings that grasping *what* the church believes, teaches, and confesses is not to be equated with or reduced to reporting on church-historical statements of belief, teaching, and confession, even when to those statements are added the deeds that allegedly speak more loudly than words. It is not hard to understand why. The Christian churches should be the first rather than the last to admit, for example, that they themselves are not yet — and in that respect something less and so other than — the one, holy, catholic, and apostolic church that is believed, taught, and confessed. Such asymmetries are, if I read Farley rightly, either disclosive of ideal, telic aspects of the faith world or distortions and corruptions of that world. It is up to theology to determine which it is.

But there is also another reason that theology's efforts to deal with its own history must take due note of the difference(s) as well as the presumed identity between what Christians believe, teach, and confess and that to which their beliefs, teachings, and confessions (are supposed to) bear witness. It is not a doctrine of God but God, not a soteriology but a redemption, and not a christology but a Redeemer that constitute the "objects of faith" of which theology has sought to give account throughout its history. Thus inquiring theologians want to know (even as non-inquiring theologians think they already know), how matters stand with respect both to the distinctive character and to the reality-status, the truth-status, of theology's church-historical claims. These twin questions (that of Christianness and that of truthfulness) are logically separable; each is perplexing enough to engage the full-time interest of any given historian or theologian. They are also in actuality so entwined throughout the history of faith, church, and theology that accounts that focus on one to the exclusion of the other and so ignore the problematic relationship of the two are invariably underestimations of the burden of theology's history.

Theological rather than strictly or merely historical interests drive

Farley's attempts to think through the connection and differentiation between the two questions, and to do so by marshalling resources other
than those provided by language analysis or social scientific analysis
alone and pressing beyond (more widely and more deeply) the literature
of theology alone. Among the outcomes of this thinking is a proposed
reordering of the study of theology in which a round of historical-
theological inquiry is designated the indispensable first step along a
route that leads to fully deliberative theological judgments. The name
given to this undertaking is theological portraiture.[13]

To the chagrin or relief of academic specialists in the history of
church, Christianity, theology, or thought, the task of theological portraiture is neither identical to any of these disciplines nor a replacement
for them. They remain at liberty to cultivate their gardens and to trans-
port and hawk their wares on the open market. Now and again — more
often than not, one might hope — theological portraitists may be buyers.
Yet Farley's construal of what historical theology is and what it could
and should provide theology is clearly an alternative (part rebuke, part
corrective, part opportunity) to business as usual conducted by Christianity's historians and theologians. How and why this is deserves brief
comment.

Farley himself sets his proposal within the history of theology's history by referring to it as a "step-child" of the questers for the essence of
Christianity. Like that quest, the task of theological portraiture undertakes to survey the entire historical course of the Christian religion, to
descry there the clustering(s) of elements constitutive of this religion's
faith, and to draw up a historical-theological sketch of what has been
descried. In several other, decisive respects, however, the task of portraiture is to be distinguished from the old quest for the essence of
Christianity.

Although portraiture takes into its purview the whole of Christianity,
its aim is not to inventory every detail of this historical phenomenon.
What is to be focused on is the pattern of elements and their interrelations constitutive of Christian identity as a historically determinate
type of corporate human existence. Farley calls this type "ecclesiality"
or "ecclesial existence." Inasmuch as this distinctive type of historical
corporate existence is at once partly embodied and partly aimed at by
the socio-institutional communities known as the Christian churches, so
"the configured totality of those aspects of the church which carry this
type of corporate existence" is termed "ecclesia."

The effort to portray the ecclesiality of tradition is an extension of
the "traditional" critical and self-critical task of theology. There is always found along with all that churches and their members are and
say and do some elemental sensing, a synthetic grasp, of Christian identity, "the Christian thing." This is, as Farley puts it, a picturing, "less a

photograph than an impressionistic painting."[14] The production of such
pictures — wordcuts, as it were — is an integral task of theology. To
set out upon this task with even minimal regard for the historicality of
the faith world and the fragility of knowledge is to engage in historical-
theological labor, and in critical and self-critical fashion. The pictures
on display in the gallery of theology's history are subjected to analysis
and assessment for clues to the constitutive features of ecclesial existence. The result of the labor is a fresh sketch, and so a re-view, of
that "object." Theological portraiture is bound to focus on and contend
with tradition because it is the only route of access to the historically
determinate object to be portrayed. For the same reason, no aspect of
tradition — not even tradition's traditional authorities (the Scriptures,
magisterium, dogma, books of confessions, et al.) — are exempt from
searching examination.

The key question then becomes what it is about tradition, and where
in tradition, that ecclesiality comes into view. In *Ecclesial Reflection,*
Farley points to three primary avenues of access to the type of corporate existence for which tradition is the field of evidence: the transition
from antecedent types of corporate existence to the new type; the overall mythos and symbolic universe of the faith, and the depth sociality
of the faith world. In addition, disclosures of aspects of ecclesia are
potentially available by attending to the community's process of ongoing, living interpretation of its environing world and to the perpetual
roiling and settling of its sedimented self-interpretations over time. Of
special interest are those moments of its history swept up into its corporate memory as "historic" ordeals of self-survival. These struggles may
afford glimpses not only of ecclesia's gestalt but its *telos.*

Farley is aware that the metaphor of portraiture is, like every other,
limited. Preferable as it is to the kernel-and-husk metaphor so familiar
in essence of Christianity literature, the term "portraiture" may lead at
least some to mistake ecclesia for an immutable something hidden behind or beyond the veil of history. To this easily anticipated mistake,
it is to be emphasized that the sort of portrait Farley calls for is dou-
bly historical. Both ecclesiality itself and depictions of it are in time
and subject to change over time. To be sure, the pattern of elements
and interrelations constitutive of ecclesia as a type of corporate existence changes at a pace all its own, far more slowly than that of the
comings and goings of everyday church life and yet far more quickly
than the birth and death of a solar system. Re-depictions of ecclesiality
(should anyone other than Farley seek to attempt one) are to be expected to come at a trot. In this respect at least the rule of thumb that
historical theology, like theology and history generally, is rewritten in
every generation may well hold and occasion no alarm. More likely to
be alarming to perhaps some historians and theologians these days is the

fact that Farley takes theological portrait-painters to be under obligation to aspire to adequation with respect to the relationship between the portrait and its object. My own best reading of this point is this. There is a certain givenness and a durability and hence an over-againstness to ecclesiality that theological portraitists *will* themselves to respect — insofar as their aim is to portray ecclesiality rather than something else.

This obligation in no way inhibits or condemns what is now celebrated as methodological pluralism. On the contrary, diverse approaches and resources are called for in order to penetrate from tradition's ever-shifting surface crust and reach the levels of deep structure, depth linguistics, and depth sociality of ecclesial existence. Still others are necessary to probe those levels and map the pattern of elements and interrelations that are constitutive of this particular type of corporate historical existence. And no one who reads Farley at any length and with any care will confuse the respect for reality appropriate to portraiture with a naive realism, a mirroring of nature, a neoclassical correspondence theory of truth, or another logocentric ploy.[15] The "postmodernity" of theological portraiture need not be debated here. Yet this much about Farley's account of it should be noted: it is because of and in order to respect the historicality of theology that theological portraitists are self-mandated to acknowledge the givenness and the durability and hence the over-againstness of the ecclesial existence they (claim to) portray. After all, the historicality of theology means not only that theology's vaunted claims to "timeless truth" sooner or later break under the burden of history but also that elements and interrelations constitutive of the ecclesiality of the faith world are capable of enduring as "a unity" that remains true to type amid and by means of — and in this sense alone despite — changes over time.

Farley's inspection of the three primary fields of evidence for ecclesia — the original transition to ecclesial existence, depth symbolics, and depth sociality — as well as his suggestions regarding tradition's vehicles and processes of social duration are ample surety, but not yet payment in full, of the yield to be gained from a construal of historical theology as theological portraiture.[16] From them (to date), this much is clear: it reopens old lines of inquiry, reorders others already underway, and generates a host of new issues to pursue.

Remarks on the Complexification of Historical Theology

At this juncture it is tempting to leave the matter at that, with an open invitation to historians of faith, church, and theology as well as theologians of whatever camp to try their hand at theological portraiture.

Farley has pointed out that ecclesial existence is "there." (Lest anyone think it goes too far to say that it is there in the sense of Edmund Hilary's Everest, let us say instead that it is there in the sense that Gertrude Stein's Oakland is not.) Hence some scholars may take interest in portraying it. Dispersed as it is, the study of theology as a whole is a mansion with many rooms. All comers may be welcomed, among them up-and-coming theological portraitists. Their labors would do no theology great harm and, depending on their skill, a great deal of good.

But a somewhat stronger claim than this is in order, as early reference to the "necessity" of Farley's prolegomena for any future historical theology indicated. It was playful, and admittedly un-Farley-like sport. But it was and is serious play nevertheless and altogether in keeping with Farley's reminder that whether or not faith apprehends any realities at all is the problem beneath the problem of theological method. A full-strength claim would go far too far. It is not the case that theological scholars "must" abandon what they are doing in favor of theological portraiture. The obligation has mid-range force: since Farley has pointed out that ecclesial existence is "there," and that it is historical, those who callously disregard it can no longer honestly claim to have owned up to the historicality of theology's history.

Farley sets the construal of historical theology as theological portraiture within the context of a thoroughgoing reassessment and reform of the state of the study of theology as a whole. To his statements, nothing need be added here: since these reflections are expressly *fachgemäss,* they are limited here to no more than a few comments about how Farley's construal of historical theology impinges on historical-theological business as usual. Four suggestions along these lines come readily to mind as propaedeutic for future historical theology.

1. Neither the disciplinary dispersal of the study of theology nor the fragmentation of the church into divers denominations is cause to forget that theology's history is a "whole" to be reckoned with. Pace Farley, the whole is the faith world's tradition, which is a totality of material content and a perpetual process. Here are to be found whatever evidentiary clues there are for ascertaining the distinctive(ness of the) type of corporate historical existence that is usually called "Christian identity" but that Farley calls — acknowledging the sociality of the faith world and its telic orientation — ecclesiality. The historian qua historian may bristle at the Graeco-Latinism. Yet historians can hardly deny that in proffering their histories of theology (or "thought"), they are ipso facto tracking the thinking associated with a human community through its history. Nor can they deny that to track this "object" is to typify this community, along with its thought, as a (diverse and mutating) whole in which a distinct type of corporate human existence is partly embodied and partly envisioned.

2. With the recognition of the (historically and socially determinate) inclusivity of tradition comes a call to dismantle and reassemble, if not discard, a number of the customary categories within which the study of theology's history has labored since the rise of the fourfold paradigm of theological encyclopedia. Chief among those which collapse with the thematization of ecclesial existence as a whole are the markers that effect a substantive and unsurpassable distinction between "Scripture and tradition." It is the case that a distinctive type of corporate historical existence emerged with "the birth of Christianity," that a corporate memory (or inner history) of originative events is sustenance for the faith world thereafter, and that the formation of the biblical canon is a fateful external carrier of the story of origins. Yet it is not the case that the distinction between "founding" and "following" is coterminous with the list, age, scope, and/or content of the books of canonical literature. (Von Harnack knew this; why Pelikan did not follow him in this regard is puzzling.)

By the same token, "the rest" of tradition becomes at least potentially of greater consequence for the study of theology's history than ordinarily recognized. To oversimplify, the most customary handlings of the history of church and theology are those that cast rays of light — in celebrative or reproachful fashion — on some portion(s) of "heritage" rather than some other(s) and those that, taking the long view, emplot the whole as either an epic or an episodic hermeneutical adventure. In the former instances, the choice of the portion(s) of heritage for the privilege of praise or condemnation is arbitrary. In the latter instances, the tendency is to identify Christianness itself as either something changeless amid and despite all change or something recurrently (re)invented with and by each change.

If Farley is right, the study of epochs and regions of ecclesial existence has a constitutive role to play in forming a historical-theological understanding of the ecclesiality of church history. In this field is to be found whatever evidence there is disclosive of previously unrecognized but genuinely constitutive features of the ecclesial type of corporate historical existence. Passions of church-historical conflict would seem to indicate that nothing other is (understood to be) the root theological issue between advocates of the status quo versus advocates of reform. The claim, for example, that justification by grace through faith is the article upon which the church stands or falls can be cited by way of illustration. Whether this or any such claim can withstand historical-theological scrutiny is another matter. It may well be that here or elsewhere the historically relative context of some has granted them "eyes to see" certain aspects of ecclesiality that others before missed and others afterward must acknowledge. Theology has not rightly reckoned with the historicality of its own history without critically assessing if and when such claims are in order.

Also in the field of tradition is found whatever evidence there is disclosive of adaptations that have been undergone or undertaken so that ecclesial existence might remain true to type over time. Even though as a *type* of corporate existence, certain features of ecclesiality endure throughout and despite countless variabilities of history, the type itself is neither timeless nor impassible. Adaptive development, Farley notes, takes place in ecclesial existence, as it does in every other recognizable type of corporate historical existence: endurance in history requires actualizing some possibilities rather than others. In the case of ecclesiality, such adaptive developments are to be understood as "true to type" to the extent they are in accord with (in the sense of not contrary to) its own inherent *teloi*. Hence, e.g., efforts to forswear racist provinciality — however tardy and fitful they may be — are true to ecclesia's type.

Displaying the variability, adaptability, and contextuality of theology is a hallmark of contemporary "critical" accounts of the history of theology. This is as it should be, as Farley construes historical theology. With this construal, however, comes a corrective to historicism. Historical theology is a normative as well as a descriptive inquiry; it seeks not merely to record theology's dialectic of inertia and innovation but to ascertain if those dialectical turns are disclosive or distortive of ecclesia's self-identity.

3. Ecclesial existence, enduring over time through the vehicles and activities of tradition(ing), is a multidimensional complex of interrelated elements, processes, and teleological impulses. To the historical-theological study of the Christian tradition, which now finds the appeal to unity-amid-diversity a center that will not hold and now struggles to cope with conflict of interpretations on every side, Farley calls attention to still other complicating factors. Perhaps the most important — and helpful — of these complexifications has to with the multiple layers of tradition, its stratification. This notion is by no means without precedent, as references to axial existence, the *communio sanctorum,* the kerygma behind the kerygmata or the deep grammar of the language of faith, and the *sensus fidelium* (to cite just a few) attest. Farley's findings, however, are a decided advance over conventional wisdom on the matter, at once more extensive and more calibrated. Taken together, *Ecclesial Man* and *Ecclesial Reflection* offer instructions regarding the sort of differentiations to be made within tradition: e.g., the level of institutionality (and with it "literature" as well), that of typifications and depth symbolics, and that of the base-level intersubjective cointentionalities of depth sociality. What these discussions yield are core-samplings of hidden masses, fissures, and tectonic forces or (to shift metaphors) first-found artifacts of hermeneutically expeditionary digging. Enough

has been turned up to show that theology's history is a problem no more or no longer adequately dealt with by reference to surface (literary or institutional) continuities and changes than the problem of the age of the earth can be dealt with by reference to Bishop Ussher's arithmetic on biblical genealogies. Farley's probes show that the strata of tradition have not yet been mapped much less carefully sounded, that the attempt to do so is arduous, and above all that nothing other than such an attempt can credibly claim to have faced up to "the problem" of theology's own history.

4. Last but not least, Farley's work offers counsel with regard to the limits of historical-theological inquiry. Two of them, very much bound up with the fragility of knowledge, are worth brief highlighting. There is nothing about historical theology — neither its aspirations nor its rigor nor its subject matter — that propels it beyond the gravitational force of historicality. Theology's history as well as studies of that history are historically determinate, and in this sense at least "historically relative." Were this alone the counsel to be drawn from Farley's work, however, it surely could and so probably should go without saying: at this late (post)modern date, it is stale news. What distinguishes Farley's account of historical-theological dealings with the relativities of history from those that are commonplace is its respect for the reality of the historicality of theology's history. Historical theology asks of tradition neither more nor less than it is prepared — however grudgingly — to deliver: evidentiary clues that, placed in the hands of a skilled sketch-artist, result in a portrait of one distinct(ive) type of corporate historical existence among others.

To respect the reality of tradition to this extent, no more and no less, calls to mind once again the admonition that "the historian's attempt to describe Christianity can never itself be theology." This is as true of theological portraiture as of any other construal of historical theology. Portraiture is history in that it examines theology's history by historical means; it is theological in that the examination aims at the ecclesiality of this history. Its results, however, can never themselves (alone) be theology. They are only (as yet) putative reality-intentions, now expressed in doctrinal form and duly certified as ecclesial. The work of historical theology might be likened to a qualifying heat. Further tests are required before what is ecclesial can rightly be called "true" as well. Describing this second battery of tests that Farley asks doctrines to withstand is, as it were, another story for another time.[17] As for reckoning with the question(ability) of theology's own history by way of historical theology, the force of the admonition is significant in its own right: history does not *overcome* history. This of course means (as critical historians and theologians should be prepared to admit in any case) that being traditional does not ipso facto make a theological doctrine either ecclesial or true. It also means that the only *truth*-claims that theology must and should make in the name of the (socially determinate) faith of Christians are those that have withstood historical-theological testing. There is no shortcut by which to identify and formulate these claims: they emerge only from reckoning with the historicality of theology's history at least as long and as hard and as carefully — in sum, at least as well — as a post-Farley theological portraitist.

NOTES

1. Paul Carus, ed., *Kant's Prolegomena to Any Future Metaphysics* (La Salle, Ill.: Open Court Publishing Company, 1947), title and 21.
2. Edward Farley, *Requiem for a Lost Piety: The Contemporary Search for the Christian Life* (Philadelphia: Westminster Press, 1966).
3. Friedrich Nietzsche, *The Antichrist,* in *The Portable Nietzsche,* trans. Walter Kaufmann (New York, Viking Press), 526; quoted by Edward Farley, *Ecclesial Man: A Social Phenomenology of Faith and Reality* (Philadelphia: Fortress Press, 1975), 3.
4. Edward Farley, *The Fragility of Knowledge: Theological Education in the Church and the University* (Philadelphia: Fortress Press, 1988), especially chapter 5.
5. This terminology seems especially apt in light of the market appeal of church histories and histories of theology from, say, Eusebius if not Luke-Acts on. But the threefold schema is surely less provincial and arbitrary than it may at first appear: cf., e.g., Friedrich Nietzsche, *The Use and Abuse of History,* trans. Adrian Collins (New York: Liberal Arts Press, 1957), and Martin Heidegger, *Being and Time,* trans. John Macquarrie and Edward Robinson (New York: Harper and Row, 1962), 448.
6. Ibid., 4–5.
7. Ibid., chapter 1.
8. Friedrich D. E. Schleiermacher, *Brief Outline of the Study of Theology,* trans. Terrence N. Tice (Richmond: John Knox Press, 1966).
9. Edward Farley, *Theologia: The Fragmentation and Unity of Theological Education* (Philadelphia: Fortress Press, 1983), chapters 4–5.
10. Edward Farley, *Ecclesial Reflection: An Anatomy of Theological Method* (Philadelphia: Fortress Press, 1982), 203–4.
11. Jaroslav Pelikan, *The Christian Tradition: A History of the Development of Doctrine,* 5 vols. (Chicago: University of Chicago Press, 1971–89).
12. Ibid., 1:x.
13. Farley, *Ecclesial Reflection,* chapter 9.
14. Ibid., 196.
15. See especially with regard to logocentricity, Edward Farley, *Good and Evil: Interpreting a Human Condition* (Minneapolis: Fortress Press, 1990), Introduction.
16. Farley, *Ecclesial Reflection,* chapters 10–12, and Appendix.
17. Ibid., chapters 13–14.

⇒· 8 ·⇐

A Historical Theologian in Ed Farley's Court

JACK FORSTMAN

The metaphor in the title of this essay has two allusions. One is to tennis. Having known Ed Farley as a friend for forty years, having enjoyed him as a colleague for twenty-five years, and having been astonished from the beginning and ever more strongly through the years at his mental powers, I am more than ready to stand with him on his side of the net. Our games are not identical, but in our different ways we move together for the most part and like to try to handle any shot that comes across the net.

The other allusion is to Mark Twain. Like the Connecticut Yankee in King Arthur's court, I have the sense of being an alien in Ed Farley's court. But also like the Yankee, after familiarizing myself at least to some degree with the terrain, I find myself wanting to make a few suggestions.

— I —

Why should I want to stand on the same side of the net with Ed Farley? Our games, indeed, are not identical. His partner discipline as a Christian theologian is philosophy. Mine is history. Although one cannot pursue the vocation of a historical theologian — or "historian-theologian," as he prefers to put it (*ER* 209 et passim)[1] — without more than just a familiarity with the philosophical texts and traditions, a historical theologian does not normally "do" philosophy. Philosophy is Ed Farley's milieu, not mine. I am not "at home" as he is with the inclination to abstraction and the terms that characteristically go with it. In this and other ways our games are quite different.

Moreover, there are direct statements and overtones in his work that one might well think would give pause to a historian. He seems convinced that the work of a historian is of necessity provincial because it cannot deal with universalities, and the role he grants to the historian-theologian in contributing to the "portraiture" of "ecclesiality" is rather limited and not in any thorough sense normative. The historian's contribution to the portrait has "a certain status, if not that of a norm, at least that of an indispensable source" for further "dimensions" or stages of theological reflection (*ER* 216). The historical study of Christian faith appears to be, in his judgment, a helping discipline.

This assessment of the role of the historian-theologian is caused not just by Farley's rejection of authority and his observation that historian-theologians tend either to live within the "house of authority" or implicitly to assume that at least a corner of it is intact. More substantively it has to do with his conviction about what theology is. For Farley theology is the exploration of the meaning and implications of Christian faith (ecclesiality) and the display of its truth. He points out that a historian as historian cannot deal with the question of truth. Thus, in his view, a historian can be a theologian only in a limited sense of the term.

These judgments about historical work do not, however, lead me to assume that vocational interests necessitate standing over against Farley, on the other side of the net, so to speak. In the judgments I have mentioned he is, I think, right. The studies in which a historian engages are provincial in his use of the term. The historian deals always with specific human constructs and acts of other sorts. To be sure, there are human constructs — like Farley's — that point to what is universally the case or make claims to universal truth, but the historian can only analyze, interpret, and present coherencies and incoherencies in what others have done. The historian might be so bold and comprehensive as to make a case for what Christian faith is, but in Farley's sense that yield would not yet be itself a claim to universal truth, and that apparently is what he means by provincial.

The substance of this judgment and others about the historian's work is simply that the historian cannot make and defend a universal claim to truth. She or he can only deal with specific understandings and claims of the past. Farley is right. The historian, like a newspaper reporter, cannot speak, for example, about what God has done but only about what others have claimed that God has done. Farley's occasional comments about the limitations in the work of the historian-theologian do not lead me to be wary of him as a partner.

On the contrary, there are solid reasons for the historical theologian to want Farley as a partner in theological work. First of all is his competence. His keen analytic powers are buttressed and funded by an astonishing range and depth of knowledge. These talents and accomplishments are evident not only in his varied publications but even in faculty meetings — at least on those rare occasions when theological faculties talk about substantive issues — and invariably in conversations.

But it is more than his competence that leads me to want Ed Farley as a partner.

For me the basic question of historical theology is whether and, if so, how one pursues historical studies of texts and artifacts pertinent to Christian faith in such a way that the yield is theological.[2] By theological I mean insight into the meaning of Christian faith and its implications for human life, the church, and the world. This understanding is more modest than the role Farley assigns to theology. Later in this essay I will comment at some length on this difference. Let it suffice here to note the difference and to observe with Farley that so long as theology remains historical it cannot deal with the question of truth but only with explicit or implicit intentions to speak truth and with the coherence or incoherence of such intentions.

This is the case not only for the reason, given above, that the historian is like a reporter and thus able to speak only indirectly about God (i.e., about what others have had to say) but also for a more substantive reason that seems to me implicit in this more superficial observation. History, as Vico argued, deals with human thoughts and deeds. It is governed by the historical sense, that is, by sensitivity to change and difference, to continuities and discontinuities, to appropriations and creativities, etc. Historical study uses the informed historical imagination to try to discover not only the meaning another person had in mind but also the foundation or base that brought forth this intended meaning. The task is not essentially different from the impulse and effort to understand another person in a substantive conversation, although, of course, different languages and contexts require more careful and conscious attention. Because there is an infinite diversity among human beings the task is never-ending, but because there is a commonality in humanity the effort can succeed, at least in part.

I do not see how one can undertake historical studies without the premise of humanity. That premise in turn requires that such studies be as thoroughly critical as possible. The premise for such criticism is self-criticism. If one's intention is to understand the other, then one must be open to what is different from oneself and must struggle against the inevitable tendency to impose one's own thinking and context on the other. This self-criticism, though it is never complete, not only permits but requires as thorough a critical analysis, interpretation, and judgment of the other as one can muster. The intent is historical understanding.

Given these considerations I do not see how it is possible to undertake historical studies presuming authority with respect to any text, set of texts, institution, or whatever. Schleiermacher was insightful on this issue with regard to the authority his church held most firmly, the Bible. In his lectures on hermeneutics he pointed out that even if the texts of the Bible have God as their author, they were written for the purpose of communicating to human beings and thus have to be understood by us in the same ways by which we understand other texts.[3] This view contains a brilliant insight with important implications not only for the study of biblical texts but for hermeneutics as such, and in principle it breaks the premise of authority. However, in a way that is relatively easy to understand in an early nineteenth-century German theologian and minister, it finesses the question of canonical authority. Farley is for the most part right when he observes that in Schleiermacher's hands the inspiration of Scripture has little in common with the "classical criteriology" Farley associates with the premise of authority in Christian theology (ER 171), but the authority of the canon continues to preside in evident ways not only over Schleiermacher's preaching but over his theology as well.

A particularly interesting example of a variation on Schleiermacher's position that more strongly states the implications of historical understanding and the historical sense for the issue of biblical authority is found in a thesis proposed by Walther von Loewenich for defense in his Habilitation examination before the theological faculty at Erlangen. Loewenich, one of the finest historical theologians of the mid-twentieth century, had been a member of the Karl Barth circle at Göttingen in 1924–25, and his first book (on Luther's theology of the cross) reflects Barth's influence, but in his further study and reflection about the historical sense he distanced himself from Barth. Loewenich reports that when Barth saw the thesis to which I refer he exclaimed, "Ganz übel, ganz übel" (very bad, very bad).[4] The thesis was equally alien to the prevailing theological orientation in Erlangen. It states: "In exegesis the concept of the canonical may not be introduced as the point of departure but only as a point at the end."[5] Although we do not have an account of how Loewenich defended his thesis, it is clear from his memoirs and other works that reflection about the historical sense and its implications led him to construct it. It is not sufficient in theological work merely to bracket the question of biblical authority. One must simply and straightforwardly surrender it not only for the purpose of historical interpretation and understanding but for the work of theology as such.

Loewenich, of course, is not alone in defending this position, and he certainly was not the first. What makes his thesis particularly interesting is the movement in it toward an affirmation of the Bible as Word of God, though not as a premise for theology. What he means is that when theology has explored the meaning and implications of Christian faith such that the character of redemptive ecclesial existence — to use a formulation of Ed Farley — becomes clear, it finds itself led to speak of the texts assembled by the church as embodying the original expression of and witness to its faith as the Word of God, God's gift, revelation. Being led to speak in this way is something like a confession whose warrant is its "fit" with what the work of theology has yielded. It is obvious, however, that this "fitting" statement or confession is not in any normal sense a straightforward claim to truth. If it were it could then stand alone — that is, it could be separated from the line of theological description and explication that preceded it and that gave it its character as "fitting." It could then be employed by theology as a truth on the basis of which further theological work could be developed. That is, it would become a norm, criterion, or basic premise for theology. Loewenich's thesis cannot permit such a movement because to permit it would be to violate the first part of the thesis, the part that is the condition for the second part.

We will return later to this mode of interpretation, analysis, or thinking. It strikes me as different from the various modes Farley has considered. For the present I wish only to point to what seems to me a flaw in Loewenich's thesis even if for the moment we grant him the mode of thinking that led him to connect the two parts. The flaw resides in the way he put the second part. One may be able to understand why people of Christian faith, those who participate in redemptive ecclesial existence, might want to stand in awe of what they receive as original and originating expressions of this common faith, but the identity of those expressions with the twenty-seven books of the "New Testament" or the sixty-six (or seventy-three) books of the Bible as a whole is a non-sequitur. The original or originating expressions may indeed appear in some of these texts, but to move from these statements and texts to a whole set of texts is to make what Lessing called a *metabasis eis allo genos*, a leap or transformation into another class.

The allusion to Loewenich is illuminating because it leads reflection about the historical sense as it pertains to Christian faith (ecclesiastical existence) to set aside not only the premise of biblical authority but the premise of the Bible as a unified set of books as well. The problems these recognitions present to historical theology are immense (and I shall want to allude to them in some detail later), but it seems to me that thinking through the implications of putting historical and theological together such that the thoroughly critical historical study of Christian faith is also and as such theological in its yield requires that these premises be set aside not only in principle but in the actual work as well. Thus, for me, the first question that presents itself to the one who wants to be a historical theologian is "whether and, if so, how." Is it possible to proceed with no premise of authority?

These comments point to at least one basic reason for wanting to play on the same side of the net with Ed Farley. I know of no one who more carefully and thoroughly has analyzed the structure of authority as it has operated in Christian theology and who has shown how that structure has collapsed. Careful readers of Farley may want to argue with him on this or that point of his "archaeology" and critique, but the force of his argument as a whole is so strong that I suspect rejections of it to come in the form of assertions and in that sense to be provincial (i.e., they claim something on grounds the likes of which they do not grant to others who make claims that are formally similar but substantively different). The "house of authority" has collapsed, or, as Farley occasionally says, changing the metaphor, it has eroded, implying that it was like a house of sand.

The argument against the premise of authority in *Ecclesial Reflection* extends over 166 pages. In *Ecclesial Man* Farley has another argument in support of the same conclusion. It is elegant in its brevity, though it is in part a summation. He begins by pointing out that the realities intended by faith "are not present in a direct or originary way" (*EM* 216). The crucifixion is not directly grasped by those who were not there, and the creation of the world is directly present to no one. He states that the traditional way of defending these affirmations of faith has been to construct arguments in support of authorities in which the affirmations may be found. He finds this mode unacceptable and gives two reasons. The first is more or less the point I have tried to make about historical consciousness. That consciousness has relativized authoritative sources of all sorts. The second is that the act of faith and what he calls the apprehensions that go with it are not essentially different for those who were first and for those who come later. If faith's convictions, for example, about Jesus as historical or the cosmos as not ultimate are not present by mediation, to hold that access to them is available only through authoritative declarations "only pushes the question back one step to those prophets and apostles whose testimonies and formulations comprise the cited authority" (*EM* 216). That is, one has to deal with the question of how faith originated. Farley is convinced that "the way of authority presupposes a pre-authority mode of apprehending these indirectly present realities" (*EM* 216). Such a difference is untenable to Farley, and he concludes that the act of faith together with its convictions about the realities surrounding the life-world of ecclesiastical existence cannot have been different for the "prophets and apostles" than it is for later believers.

This argument, as Farley knows, is not persuasive to those who continue to find their home in the house of authority. Even so, it makes clear, directly and indirectly, some discomfiting consequences of staying within the house: in one's understanding of faith one must account for the difference between the act of faith in its originators and in those that come after; one must be aware of the provincialism in making universal claims for one's own faith on the basis of authority while not granting other sets of universal claims based on sources others hold to be authoritative; one must live with a bifurcation, understanding many things through the historical sense while exempting that sense from the matters most pertinent to faith. These points with their implications draw me ineluctably to Farley's side of the net.

Farley's view that we cannot differentiate the act of faith in faith's original witnesses from the act of faith in subsequent persons connects with the bulk of his argument in *Ecclesial Man* and is a substantive part of his theological foundation. It has to do with his inventive appropriation of Husserl and his combination of that appropriation with the principle of positivity in faith, at least one of whose sources is Schleiermacher's fifth speech. Within the principle of positivity he argues — in my judgment persuasively — that the apprehensions of faith include simultaneously and, I should like to add, immediately, convictions (truth intentions) not only about anthropology (human being) but also about what is beyond experience (in the plainest and broadest sense). Farley, following Husserl's analysis of other matters, distinguishes these perceptions as presentations and appresentations.

What faith perceives is everything that goes with what Farley calls the "transition toward redemption" in "ecclesia." Directly present to faith is the shaping of one's consciousness toward freedom and obligation and social participation in these realities as co-intentionalities. He speaks of this modification of existence as redemption, and because in its pure form it is what he calls an "ideality" and *telos* he speaks of the new mode of being in its actuality as a transition. At the same time, however, the act of faith necessarily perceives indirectly, so to speak, realities that are not directly present but are inseparably connected with what is directly present. These are appresentations to faith, and they are cognitive in intention just as are the direct presentations of faith. He gives examples of historical cosmological and transcendent appresentations that are immediately joined with faith's presentations. They are the historical reality of the redeemer, Jesus Christ, the cosmos as creation, and God. Showing the necessity of these appresentations in their immediate connection with faith's direct perceptions (presentations) is not to give proofs for their reality, but it is to display them as truth intentions (realities) that are "not coincident with human subjectivity" (*EM* 223). Also it serves to explain "faith's seeming indifference to evidence" (*EM* 216).

It seems to me that these "appresentations" — or something like them — bear their own clear marks of necessity as simultaneous accompaniments of faith's "presentations." The connection in faith between certain anthropological statements that are known directly and certain theological statements that are known indirectly (and thus intended as true) is clear, and they constitute a coherent unity that is available not only to those who participate in ecclesial existence but to those outside as well. From within, the coherence of these "truth intentions" is grasped spontaneously. From the outside a viewer should be able to understand that given these presentations their appresentations — or

something like them — must follow. This clarification is not a proof because it does not exclude explanations of the entire phenomenon from
perspectives alien to it. In this sense Feuerbach, contrary to Farley, is
not overcome (*EM* 227), but the internal "logic" that is by no means
private or subjective holds.

With this logic of presentation and appresentation goes another
"logic." In ecclesial existence (transition toward redemption) what
Farley calls "the power of self-serving" is broken (*EM* 225), and participation in the new sociality gives one a new identity. Out of the new
consciousness of "what one is" and its matrix, Farley writes, the person
of faith "pursues activities of gratification, sacrifice, and competition,
and . . . exists in determinate ways in a family (or out of it), as a citizen (or revolutionary) and in relation to a career (or rejection of one)"
(*EM* 211). The sentence, to be sure, is sketchy, but it points to what
might be called a descriptive logic in explanation of the implications of
Christian faith for human life (and for theological statements as well?).
This mode of explication is utterly different from the way of authority,
and it helps to clarify changes and varieties in modes of Christian life
in different times, cultures, and social configurations with their different
mores and perceptions and to clarify the continuities (with disruptions)
between these varieties. It provides at the same time the handle by means
of which one might discuss with others what is appropriate and exercise
both self-criticism and criticism of others. Farley is talking about what
follows from what is. It reminds me of Martin Luther's illustration of a
similar point by reference to a man and woman who "love each other,
have pleasure in each other, and thoroughly believe in their love." He
asks, "Who teaches them how they are to behave one to another, what
they are to do or not to do, say or not to say, what they are to think?"
Confidence alone, he states, is their teacher. They do "the great and the
important as gladly as the small and the unimportant, and vice versa."[6]
The presiding mode is the indicative, the mode Farley uses in the citation. The imperative mode is absent. Thus the "logic" that displays the
mode of life between the man and the woman or the modes of life of
Christian faith in the world is descriptive. Farley's use of the indicative
mode runs throughout his explication of the presentations and appresentations of ecclesial existence and elsewhere where his discussion reaches
back to the foundation of faith (cf. *EM* 217ff. et passim). This indicative
or descriptive "logic," just as the "logic" of presentation and appresentation, is available not only to those who live within ecclesial existence
but to those outside as well.

What I find so engaging in Farley's philosophical analysis of these
matters is its close parallel to a not just occasional yield of historical interpretation as one applies it to the texts of Christian traditions.
Historical interpretation strives for an understanding not only of what

another has written but of what it is that stands beneath what the author wrote, consequently displays more fundamentally why the author wrote such and such, that is, what founds it, and thus can also serve as a handle to make judgments about its coherence and incoherence. Something comparable to what Farley finds in his analysis and exposition of ecclesial existence is by no means present in all the texts of the Christian traditions, neither in the texts that originated those traditions nor in subsequent texts. However, it is evident in more texts of the traditions than one might think, and there are substantial points of contact with still others.

I have by no means settled for myself the question that presents itself to me as the fundamental question of historical theology (whether and, if so, how?), and I am not certain I ever shall. However, insofar as I have been able historically to understand the traditions that claim to be Christian and the sources that have funded them I find something like Farley's analysis of the simultaneous presentations and appresentations and something like the descriptive "logic" that displays their implications as both substantively and formally distinctive. I find them here and there in the earliest sources, though usually expressed in ways that are foreign to our modes of expression and though distorted in ways that go beyond the differences in world-view and language. I find them here and there in the wealth of subsequent sources though always expressed in modes and reflecting issues of the time and distorted in ways that try to accommodate faith to one or another generic mode of religion.

If the reader has begun to think that I am enthusiastic about the work of Ed Farley as he has thus far presented it to us, then the reader has understood me and understands why I, as one who wants to be a historical theologian, am eager to stand on the same side of the net with him.

— II —

The basic difference between us remains. Farley is at home in philosophical, ontological analysis; I am at home in historical analysis and interpretation. To find myself standing in Farley's court is to feel somewhat like the Connecticut Yankee Mark Twain transposed into King Arthur's court. It is not only that the mode of dress, the way of speaking, and the rules of the court are different. After I have accustomed myself to the mode of dress, developed some confidence that I can understand the way of speaking, and learned at least the basic rules of the court, I find myself wanting to raise some questions and make some suggestions. In doing so I am aware that I may not have properly construed the landscape.

I.

Farley's use of presentation and appresentation with respect to faith, as I have noted, is insightful and suggestive to me. However, one of his illustrations in the important chapter 6 of *Ecclesial Man* ("Presence and Appresence") puzzles me. In this discussion he picks up on an objection that has often been raised against theologians. Critics have pointed out that Christians tend to disregard the premise of object-evidence correspondence. Farley, drawing on his lengthy discussion and appropriation of phenomenological analysis, uses the correlation of presentation and appresentation to explain how ecclesia perceives realities in a way that evades the problem of object-evidence correspondence. He states that there are three areas in which ecclesia "appresents" realities: the historical, the cosmological, and the transcendent. He gives three examples that he claims are "dramatic indications of faith's seeming indifference to evidence" (*EM* 216).

I understand how the consciousness of redemption in ecclesiastical existence "appresents" the reality of God (the category or sphere of the transcendent) and the finitude of the world (the category or sphere of cosmology). To speak of the reality of redemption is at the same time and necessarily to speak of the reality of God and of the world as finite. It seems to me, however, that there is a point of confusion in the contention that the consciousness of redemption in ecclesiastical existence appresents Jesus of Nazareth as a historical figure.

As stated this assertion seems to be intended to answer the challenge to the historicity of Jesus as was raised by Arthur Drews and others in the first decade of this century. That challenge did not succeed. The arguments were not weighty. However, the question could appropriately be brought again into the historical discussion in the unlikely event that the paucity of evidence is overcome. Even so, it is at least imaginable that the issue could be raised again on historical grounds. If so, historians could deal with it because it is a question of history. When Farley contends that faith appresents Jesus of Nazareth as a historical figure, he surely does not mean that the ecclesial community could not be disturbed in its apprehension that Jesus was historical even if it were shown convincingly and with broad consensus that Jesus of Nazareth was a mythical figure. My point is only that faith's apprehensions cannot settle questions pertaining to the past that are genuinely historical questions on the order of "Bill Clinton was declared the elected president of the U.S.A. in the 1992 election." If historians showed convincingly and with broad consensus that Jesus was a mythical figure and if ecclesia could not make the case for the contrary on historical grounds, ecclesia would be affected root and branch.

Although Farley affirms that "bare" historical event as an appresentation of faith I am not at all sure he means it that way. In his discussion he refers to "the redeemer, Jesus of Nazareth." He writes, "What replaces bounded conditions of redemption is simply a testimony to one whose death and resurrection was the occasion of this negation and the creation of ecclesia" (*EM* 219). The allusions here go beyond what can properly be called a historical question. History as a mode of inquiry about the past cannot deal with whether Jesus was the redeemer or rose from the dead. It can, of course, deal with the question whether Jesus was crucified, but that "bare" historical question is not what faith says about it. Faith wants to say something like, "The Jesus who died on the cross is the redeemer."

Two key sentences in Farley's argument are:

> Because redemptive existence is a displacement of flight by obligation, the past presents itself historically, that is, as comprised of significant, even decisive events which establish the conditions of obligation. Because redemptive existence is existence in a community which negates provincialist conditions of divine presence, the beginning of that community presents itself as involving an event powerful enough to accomplish this negation. (*EM* 219)

It is not, then, the "bare" event that faith "appresents." It is the event as decisive, and that is not, strictly speaking, an issue the discipline of history can deal with.

Farley, I think, is misleading, but he is not entirely wrong in his claim that faith has an apprehension (or something like it) in the sphere of history, but what he means is history as a sphere that is not available to historians. The "history" to which he refers — in distinction from "history" as it is normally understood — is, after all, parallel to the appresentations in the spheres of cosmology and the transcendent. It is a "history" that is not available to historians just as the appresented cosmology and transcendence are not available to scientists. Thus the claim that his discussion of the matter "suggests why faith does not wait for the judgment of the professional historian before claiming that its redeemer is a historical figure" (*EM* 220) is, I think, misleading. Appresentations of faith do not settle the kinds of questions that historians properly can deal with. If, on the other hand, the emphasis is on assertions about the past that historians cannot properly treat (what some German theologians have called *Geschichte,* overdoing a nuanced distinction of the term in contrast to *Historie*) — most strikingly the claim that Jesus rose from the dead — then Farley needs to tell us more. In the case of resurrection we need to know on the basis of what persons of faith rightly, in his judgment, make the claim and what it means and does not mean. Treating that and related issues would surely lead to a nuanced discussion, and one or another form of historical understanding might be illuminating.

2.

My uneasiness about Farley's orientation to history grows when I note the contrast between the care, subtlety, and profundity with which he develops his own constructive themes and the apparent ease with which he treats difficult historical issues.

Here are two examples:

1. In the course of his discussion of historical appresentations of faith he writes, "Empirically speaking it can be argued that the processes of testimony, corporate memory, oral tradition, and written records all functioned to preserve the ministry and teachings of this man [Jesus]" (*EM* 219). It is empirically the case that this point of view has been argued, and it is the case that it can be and has been argued on empirical (i.e., historical) grounds. Even so, the issue is not settled because of those facts, and it seems to me that those historians who apply the critical principle in their work as rigorously as Farley applies it in his thinking about and analyses of most other things would find this statement questionable.

2. In laying the foundation for his "archaeology and critique of the house of authority" at the beginning of *Ecclesial Reflection* Farley gives what he takes to be "a summary of the convictions taken for granted by the authors and compilers of the New Testament collection" (19), and he refers to it as kerygma. He lists five assertions: (1) the kingdom announced by Jesus has arrived, inaugurated by Jesus' life, death, and resurrection; (2) this kingdom is the fulfillment of Israelite prophecies and of Israel's aim and promise; (3) with the kingdom has come the community (ecclesia), the instrument of the fulfillment of Israel; (4) Jesus is God's agent in the inauguration of the kingdom; (5) to be saved means to participate in God's eschatological act, to be free from God's punishment, to be forgiven and to have the higher righteousness, and to be prepared for death or the Parousia. "Participating in the community of the kingdom (thus believing in its cultic Lord and what God offers through him) is the only necessary condition for salvation" (20). Farley observes that writers used different summary phrases and themes in expressing this gospel, and in a footnote he acknowledges that his summary is "historically simplistic and misleading." In that same note, however, he states, "Yet it does seem legitimate to ask for whatever unity these writers do share," and he adds, "I am using gospel as the term for whatever unity we discover among them that expresses the distinctiveness of the new corporate existence, ecclesiality" (19).

This summary and the claims for it puzzle me, above all, because of a contrast between it and Farley's own description and analysis of redemption and ecclesiality. What he writes in developing his own thinking is invariably careful and nuanced. In contrast this summary seems flat, and the mode of coming to it strikes me as facile and questionable. I think he would consider it bizarre, for example, if a critic declared him to be in unity with all those in this extended generation who say at least that redemption involves both obligation and freedom. The reason, of course, is that it is not just the terms that are important but their meaning and grounding.

To find a unity among the earliest Christian writers by excerpting affirmations they (perhaps) hold in common is a flawed procedure with possible damaging consequences. It overlooks the question whether, in the case of any given writer, the five assertions properly represent what the author was trying to say, and consequently it bypasses the question whether there are substantive differences among the earliest writers with respect to what constitutes the gospel, redemption, participation in ecclesiality, etc. Moreover, it suggests implicitly a principle of interpretation of the texts in which prominence is given to those texts that more nearly yield such a summary with the result that those that do not are understood in the light of those that do. One striking illustration of this principle would be the tendency to identify Paul with Luke-Acts, where the sermons of Peter, Stephen, and Paul more nearly yield the kerygma as Farley summarizes it. In my judgment it is a misconstrual of Paul to try to understand him in conformity with Luke's view of salvation history or of redemption (*ER* 32 et passim). The summary tends as well to level the substantive differences, for example, between Mark and Matthew, Paul and Colossians/Ephesians, on the one side, and the Pastorals, on the other. It seems to me that if one is going to try to do the work of theology without the premise of authority and if, for whatever reason, one considers it important to say what one can about Christian origins, then the better procedure is to try to understand what each particular writer says and why, and only then to raise the question about similarity and difference and the significance of both.

The work of historical interpretation involves an uneasy oscillation between an exploration of differences and a tendency to recognize similarities. When the oscillation gets stuck on minor differences the danger is triviality. When it gets stuck on comprehensive similarities and typifications the danger is the violation of distinctive understandings. Historical understanding is certainly not an exact science. It limps, and it knows that it limps not only because it is aware (or should be) that the historian as such never stands outside of history but also because if one maintains the oscillation one can never be fully satisfied with a photo taken at one point.

3.

These comments pertain also to Farley's proposals for theological portraiture. As one of three dimensions of "theological reflection," theological portraiture is clearly important to his enterprise. It is the place in his
program where the work of historical theology is most pertinent.

The image of portraiture is attractive to Farley because it doesn't
suggest a snapshot or clear picture representing the object (Christianity, the tradition, ecclesial existence) in exact detail but rather a display
of major themes and their interconnections. Also, the term at least tolerates the suggestion of a never-ending act. Portraiture continues as a
dimension of theological reflection. The purpose of portraiture is "to
capture the unity, the interrelation of features. The result, if successful — the face staring out of the portrait — is ecclesiality" (ER 205).
Given this purpose aiming at this result, the work of the "historian-
theologian" is twofold: to grasp that to which the proclamation of the
ecclesial community has attributed its existence and to trace how it has
survived and endured. Consistently in all of his work Farley emphasizes
that ecclesial existence is an ideality and *telos* and thus is never fully
realized in actuality. Even so, he asserts that there is a tradition that
bears it in history. "Theological portraiture is a theology of tradition"
(ER 200).

Portraiture may be as good a word as any for the work of historical
theology. The work surely is always unfinished and continuing. However, Farley's section on theological portraiture makes me uneasy for
reasons related to those I set forth above. He seems to presume that
there is a unity of themes in earliest Christianity and that one can speak
historically in a substantive way about a single tradition. To be sure, he
acknowledges that there are differences in earliest Christianity and that
one speaks rightly about traditions, but apparently he does not consider
these differences and this plurality of traditions substantive with respect
to the successful completion of portraiture in displaying ecclesiality. He
continues to speak at critical points in the singular. In describing the first
task of the historian-theologian, he writes:

> First, the historian-theologian will attempt to grasp that to which
> *the* proclamation of *the* ecclesial community has attributed *its* ex
> istence.... It [origins-oriented theological portraiture] inquires into
> the ministry of that figure [Jesus] with special attention to the qual
> ities of the figure that initiated a sequence of events the end of
> which is universalized redemptive existence.... The enterprise of
> describing Jesus includes not only Jesus' own activity and teaching
> insofar as they are accessible but also *the* response to that activity
> and *the* historical effect thereof. (ER 209, italics mine)

I am confident Farley did not intend this statement to be prescriptive for the work of the historical theologian. On the contrary, I think he meant that what he chooses to call "redemption" and its occurrence in "ecclesial existence" was introduced into history in the events centered around Jesus and that its imperfect embodiment (including in its origins) has endured. Thus, by definition, this singular reality is what the historian-theologian will display.

The use of the singular, however, overlooks difficult and complex historical problems. Moreover, I think Farley's work would be enhanced — and perhaps altered here and there — by dealing with these problems. Here are two illustrations though they only point in the direction of the more difficult and complex historical problems.

The first has to do with Farley's certainty that the portrait will discern ecclesiastical existence as a theodicy (*ER* 198). He writes:

Insofar as every religious faith presents a vision of the relation of human beings in their fragility, misery, and evil to the sacred, giving some account of the activity [?] of the sacred toward those things, theological portraiture has the character of theodicy. In this comprehensive sense the Adamic myth is a theodicy even as the Gospel is a theodicy. Drawing the portrait is thus discerning ecclesial existence as a theodicy.

I think this declaration also was not intended as a prescription for the work of theological portraiture but rather as a description of what by definition theological portraiture will do. But this definition needs to be supported, not so much with respect to "every religious faith," which is not the subject of this section, but with respect to the theological portraiture of Christian faith or ecclesial existence.

Farley explains what he means by "theodicy" in a footnote:

Theodicy as used here should not be taken in the narrow and rationalistic sense of a set of arguments which address or "solve" the problem of God and evil. It is rather the attempt to discern how the symbolic universe of the religious faith "makes sense of," addresses, alleviates the human experience of chaos, misery, mortality, and evil. (*ER* 198)

Certainly there are texts from early Christianity that address and try to make sense of the human experiences Farley mentions. What is not settled is (1) whether all the texts deal with the issue as Farley defines it, and (2) whether, if they do, they give it the priority and thus the meaning Farley assigns to it. In illustration of the complex problem we meet on this issue, one could ask, if (or when) one finds texts in the Hebrew writings or those of earliest Christianity that do not "make sense of" chaos, misery, mortality, and evil or do not address the issue with the priority that Farley gives to it, what are the implications, if any, for Farley's formulation?

My second illustration pertains to what Farley calls the second prominent task that attends the study of ecclesial origins as a dimension of ecclesial reflection. He writes:

> Even if a messiah figure had such an impact as to bring into existence a gathering of followers resulting in a new sect of Judaism, this does not show how it was that this new sect survived and maintained itself over generations. To endure over time, the new sect had to solve certain problems, equipping itself with generation-bridging features such as a sedimented language of new primary symbols and new forms of institutionalization. (*ER* 209)

Putting the important problem of institutional duration in this way seems to me to assume a positive assessment of the transitions in early Christianity and a predominantly "level" movement in the early generations. If so, one would be led to understand earlier texts in the light of later ones, at least to the point of assuming that the new themes and developments in the later texts were in substantial continuity with the earlier ones. One may overlook Luke's leveling of serious and divisive issues in the early years in his second volume, Acts, because the issues were apparently no longer issues of contention, but to take his presentation as a reliable account would be a mistake. It would be more serious to interpret Paul in the light of Luke (and one could add, in the light of Colossians/Ephesians or the Pastorals, where issues of sedimentation and institutional duration are quite prominent).

My point is that Farley's use of the singular with respect to gospel and tradition in early Christianity bypasses historical problems that, if treated, would complicate and possibly enrich theological reflection in all its dimensions. It is puzzling to me that he does not suggest the importance of dealing with substantive diversity in early Christianity and, related to that, with the employment of criticism on the early texts with respect to the question of the adequacy of the representations of faith, gospel, ecclesial existence, etc. in those several texts.

Clearly he exercises critical judgment on contemporary forms of Christianity. "It is my conviction that contemporary branches of Christendom have at best a highly tenuous relation to ecclesial existence" (*ER* 277, note 6). In his judgment not only is ecclesial existence, as an ideal and *telos*, never fully embodied in history but it also is never perfectly expressed. That, we must assume, is also the case with its earliest expressions.

At this point the problems mount. If one finds a diversity of expressions of gospel and faith, how is one to judge which are "better" than others. What criteria shall be applied to make judgments about expressions of something that comes into history only with these expressions? The question of the character (or characters) of early Christianity and of its courses through the centuries is important to theological reflection. When the work of historical understanding points to substantive differences, one must choose. To choose is not different from what has actually been the case among those in ecclesiastical history who, in one way or another, have lived in the house of authority. It does seem better, however, to be self-conscious about what one is doing and to support it as best one can with whatever arguments one can muster on the basis of historical investigation, coherence, or whatever. To undertake all this is no more to move back into the house of authority or a piece of it than affirming Farley's summaries would be. It also seems necessary that one undertake the task with a sense of irony — that is, with utter seriousness and a sheepish smile.

4.

Finally — and more briefly than I would like it to be and than it should be — I have the uneasy feeling of an alien in Ed Farley's court because I do not share his confidence in using analogy as a means of knowing something about God and God's relation to the world and to humankind or in the cognitive (or beyond cognition?) experience of reality itself.

Farley states his conviction about the latter most eloquently in *Good and Evil.* Here are some statements from one place:

> Wonder then is not just openness but empathetic participation in whatever is to be known and experienced.... And the agent yearns for participative knowledge of whatever is to be known.... And it is this vulnerable and pathetic beauty of things that evokes participative knowledge.... It is what happens ... when natural egocentrism is taken to another plane. The passion for reality as a freedom is an openness beyond the pragmatic predetermination of reality to reality itself in all of its surprises. It is also a desire to participate in ... what is understood. This two-fold passion of openness and participation is the freedom of wonder. Wonder is the passion for reality transformed by being-founded in the sacred. (208)

The language is as beautiful and enticing as any one can find in Farley's corpus, and that person is poor in spirit and unimaginative who does not feel the tug of it. In these statements and others like them Farley establishes points of contact with certain religious traditions all over the world and at all times. But however deep and self-attesting the experience may seem to be, it is closed to me because it requires a leap I consider arbitrary in a sense at least comparable to living within the house of authority. *Credo ut intelligam.*

As for analogy, Farley repeatedly uses the phrase, "in some sense," with respect to what one says about the cognitions that go with faith or ecclesial existence. For example, "If the symbol does bring to expression realities, how the world is, it is inevitable that these realities are linked in some way with the world structure and therefore with the universalities discerned in science, history, and ontology. But it is also the very nature of the symbol to hide this linkage" (*ER* 317). It is the essence of analogy to show something but not everything. Perhaps better, in asking about the relation of generic universals to ecclesial universals and noting that "general features undergo modification in their instantiation in the faith-world," he states, "This means that the most general characteristic of the relation is that of analogy, because the generic feature, being present by modification, resembles but is not identical with itself in its generic sense" (*ER* 339).

The base of analogy is the confidence that transcendent reality is being at least in some sense comparable to being as we know it within the limits of our own world. It seems to me that that confidence is arbitrary in a way at least analogous to the arbitrary act of living in the house of authority. I cannot make that leap of confidence, but I have to add that neither can I make what seems to me an identically arbitrary leap, namely, to assert the contrary. In this respect I have to remain agnostic, in the literal sense of the term, about the analogy of being, neither a believer nor a disbeliever.

Is there an alternative? I can conceive of none except to consider the language we use to speak about the transcendent and its "relations" and "actions" to the world and humankind as metaphors and to find the base and "authorization" for these metaphors in something like what Farley so carefully lays out as the presentations and appresentations of faith, which, as he says repeatedly, are not challenged by the further steps of applying theological criteria and judgment.

However, I think I understand by metaphor something different from what Farley understands. At any number of points he seems to hold that metaphor yields theory without respect to what gave birth to the metaphor. The most striking example of this is his preoccupation with the treatment of the royal metaphor as a theory by Orthodox Protestant theologians. In that discussion he sometimes refers to the kingship of God as a metaphor and sometimes as a theory and sometimes as both at the same time. Apparently it did not occur to him that the theologians might have committed a fundamental misconstrual in treating a metaphor as a basis for theory.

My understanding of metaphor is simple-minded but closely related to linguistic usage. It is a figure of speech in which one transfers a word from its normal and clearly understood sphere to another sphere with a point of contact that gives it its descriptive and illustrative power. But its meaning is tied to the one point of contact such that to separate it from that point is to violate the metaphor. Thus "redemption" is a metaphor taken from the practice of buying back what was one's own but is held by another party, for example, a pawnbroker. Thus "sacrifice" is a meta-phor taken from cultic practice. If one could genuinely participate in the cult one felt that one's purity or relation to the divine had been restored. In the same way, "reconciliation" is a metaphor drawing on the image of a mediator standing between two alienated parties with a hand on each shoulder and bringing the two once again together. In the same way the "Christus Victor" story is a metaphor in which the power of evil is over-come in a dramatic battle. Clearly these metaphors are contradictory if they imply theories. But if the point of contact is the connection with what happens in faith, they are all legitimate and illuminating within the cultures and ways of speaking in which they arose.

The key to metaphor in this simple sense is that what one wants to describe calls forth a multiplication of metaphors with no implication of theory about how things work. In this sense there is no such thing as a "deep" or "root" metaphor — symbol, perhaps, but symbols and metaphors are not the same. It seems to me that to think of metaphors with respect to the transcendent reality in this sense is in no way an abdication of claims to truth though it is an abdication of the attempt to demonstrate truth. But then Farley makes no claim to demonstration.

My theological problem — at least one of them — is that I cannot get beyond something like what Farley means by the presentations and ap-presentations of faith and that it seems to me that what we say about the appresentations of faith (or however they are best named) can be nothing other than a limping human way of pointing to the unfath-omable. And since I have no confidence that human language can be used analogically to gain knowledge of God's "relation" to or "actions" toward this world and humankind, I must, at least for now, be content to take the words we use, including "relation" and "action" as meta-phors, the substantive thrust of which we cannot fathom. One can make judgments about these metaphors on the basis of their coherence with and rightness in relation to the "presentations" of faith and the source faith necessarily apprehends.

I wish I could know more, but I take heart in Farley's clear insistence that the success or failure of theological judgments that claim to know more does not affect the authenticity of faith or the realities it appre-sents. Thus, I am an alien in Ed Farley's court, and like Mark Twain's Yankee I cannot live indefinitely in the alien land. But I am attracted to its landscape and most especially to the person who designed it. As an outsider I wish him and those who find their home in that land well. I stand on the sidelines as an agnostic cheerleader.

NOTES

1. I will refer to Farley's works by abbreviated titles followed by page references. Thus *EM* refers to *Ecclesial Man* and *ER* to *Ecclesial Reflection*. The reference to *Good and Evil* will be clear.

2. I have set forth my understanding of historical theology a bit more expansively, though not exhaustively, in "On the State and Future of Historical Theology," David W. Lotz, ed., *In Memory of Wilhelm Pauck (1901–1981)*, Union Papers No. 2 (New York: Union Theological Seminary, 1982), 41–45. See also "On the History of Christian Doctrine: A Demurral to Jaroslav Pelikan," *Journal of Religion*, January 1975.

3. Friedrich Schleiermacher, *Hermeneutics: The Handwritten Manuscripts*, ed. Heinz Kimmerle and trans. James Duke and Jack Forstman (Missoula, Mont.: Scholars Press, 1977), 67.

4. Walther Von Loewenich, *Erlebte Theologie* (Munich: Claudius Verlag, 1979), 89.

5. Ibid., 231.

6. "Treatise on Good Works," in *Luther's Works* (Philadelphia: Fortress Press, 1966), 44:27.

PART THREE

Essays on
Practical Theology

≫· 9 ·≪

Speaking between Times

Homiletics in a Postmodern World

DAVID BUTTRICK

Back in the 1960s, there was a catchword that showed up in theological school catalogues again and again. Faculty members were teaching the same old courses, yes, but they were adding the phrase "a revolutionary age" to their titles: Christian Missions in a Revolutionary Age, Introduction to Homiletics for a Revolutionary Age, The Gospel of Mark in a Revolutionary Age. Well, the term of choice nowadays is "postmodern." Use of the slogan "postmodern" has reached flood stage, for by now the term has seeped into every school's academic catalogue. So, lest homiletics be lagging, here is an essay on "Homiletics in a Postmodern World."

Matters of Definition

At the outset, let us be candid. Though the term is overused, "postmodern" is still ill-defined.[1] What on earth does the word "postmodern" mean? In some ivy-league circles, the word seems to be synonymous with "postliberal." Here the notion is that social liberalism and theological liberalism are both products of Enlightenment and, with the demise of Enlightenment, we are justified in clinging as fervently as ever to Karl Barth and/or literal readings of biblical narrative.[2] In other circles the term points to a collapse of objective reason and therefore seems to condone a turn toward romantic subjectivity, rationalism's sticky other self.[3] Some critics sense that we live between the ages and that while the age of Enlightenment is over,[4] something new is beginning to form. They label the "something-new-beginning-to-form" in the mind of the age as postmodern. The only point of agreement in all the definitions is *change*. So, at the outset, let us admit that "postmodern" is a slippery term for a dramatic cultural change that now agitates the world in

147

which we live. Obviously the four-hundred-year period running from the Renaissance/Reformation until mid-twentieth century is over, an epoch that some cultural historians label "Enlightenment," but which theologian Paul Tillich named the "Protestant Era."[5] So if nothing else, for us, postmodern means an end to the Protestant Era.

When you plow through the literature on postmodernism[6] you can sense why definitions seem to split. If we agree that the Enlightenment — an epoch characterized by objective reason, individual focus, and an entrepreneurial spirit — is over, and that we live now in the midst of cultural breakdown not dissimilar to the collapse of the Greco-Roman world or the fragmentation of the medieval synthesis, then "postmodern" requires a descriptive decision: Is postmodern a label for the void left behind by a failed rationalism? Or is postmodern an attempt to discern inchoate strands of thought that may be trying to come together in some new cultural mind. The literature on postmodernism cuts both ways. Of course, the literature also subdivides into different fields — postmodern art, postmodern architecture, postmodern literature, politics, religion, science, and so forth.[7] And why not? In the shift between the medieval world and the Renaissance, feudal principalities gave way to national states, Gothic cathedrals eventually turned into corporate skyscrapers, and the Catholic Church splintered into Protestant clans that, regrettably, are still splitting. So though it may be tempting to predict our political future, our post-industrial prospects, or the institutional shape of a new church, we will constrain the topic. We will try to get at postmodern both as (1) something we must leave behind, and as (2) something forming to which the field of homiletics must attend.

Anatomy of a Failure

Let us begin by looking at postmodern as something we are leaving behind. Here we will be looking back at the "modern" in post*modern*. If church and salvation ordered the medieval world, reason, science and individual well-being have been the impulse in Enlightenment. Luther's phrase "Here I stand" ushered in an epoch of personal religion, and Descartes's "cogito ergo sum" — "I think therefore I am" — announced the triumph of objective reason. Descartes's bold logic objectified the world and located reason out of the world looking at the world — very much like Deism's God! If the world is an object to reason then the world is "out there," something to be studied, tamed, catalogued, ordered, and above all used. What's more, Descartes's "cogito" was defined as skeptical reason, installing personal judgment as a tacit authority for all things. And Descartes's "sum," while not exactly a threat to the voice from the burning bush, nevertheless asserted the free force of the enlightened individual.[8] So at the outset, let us suppose that in Descartes's famous phrase the modern world was born. But then, with Luther's "Here I stand," so was personal Bible-believing religion. The Protestant Era has been a peculiar synthesis between a personal biblical religion and Enlightenment rationality.

Why has the cultural edifice of Enlightenment come tumbling down? We could argue that it has been shattered by the split between objective and subjective, between reason and feeling, but such a diagnosis is probably too simple.[9] Albert Borgmann views Enlightenment as a system built on Francis Bacon's impulse to control nature and build a New Atlantis, Descartes's rational investigative method, and John Locke's *Second Treatise on Civil Government*, which championed the notion of government as a contract among individuals to further individual well-being. The results, he argues, are a despoiled ecology, depersonalizing corporations, and the contending projects of individualism. Borgmann describes the culture as "sullen."[10] We live in systems that no longer work: a politics of gridlock, an economy based on four million homeless people, an educational network that is now entered through metal detectors, and churches that isolate lonely-for-God members in their own subjectivities. Though we live trapped in systems that no longer work, we are as yet without other options. So we are sullen. Of course, there are people still dedicated to trying to preserve modernity, but they have become hyperactive.[11] They try to make corporations work by more and more management or keep churches going by multimedia worship and Lyle Schaller promotions. But the verdict is inescapable: rationalism has objectified neighbors, alienated us from the natural world, and split selves. In a word, modernity has *failed*.

Underlying the deflation of the age is what might be termed a loss of correspondence. The so-called "great ages" of Western culture all have been dominated by some structural sense of correspondence. Thus in every major epoch people have had the notion of "something out there like us" — a correspondence between the seen and unseen, between the earthly and the transcendent. Greeks affirmed Platonic "forms" along with their reflected images flickering in the encaved understanding of the human world. And medieval folk truly believed that for hierarchies on earth there were hierarchies of heaven, if there was a churchly city of earth surely there was a City of God. What's more they drew *imago* analogies between human being and the Being of God. Likewise, in the Enlightenment, there was an analogy of reason — what Carl Becker long ago labeled *The Heavenly City of the Eighteenth Century Philosophers*.[12] There was God's rationality, which ordered the world of nature, and there was divine reason given to us all by which we could comprehend the world. Today, rather obviously, the sense of correspondence has broken down, so that contemporary notions of human being do not seem to project into a beyond. Though we may have ventured past the flat-out negative correspondence of late 1950s existentialism, at present there is little sense of anything "out there like us." The "sacred canopy" of Christian myth has tumbled and, as deconstructionist philosopher Lyotard would put it, we have no "metanarratives" to give life meaning. We have no agreed canons of beauty or virtue either.[13] At best, we have small, partial meanings within glades of temporality[14] and ad-lib pragmatic strategies adjusted to the several "models" in which we move and have our being. We seem to be left with little more than psychology and management to guide our lives unless you want to count a host of Bible-lesson sermons. The postmodern world is at a loss, baffled, tentative, groping, fragmented, and emphatically secular.[15]

As a kind of footnote, please acknowledge homiletics' involvement in rationalism. Notice the point-making sermons that objectify and categorically discuss subject matters, sermons that rationally point at ideas. Notice as well the tendency in our sermons to third-person objective language, a looking-at language, that is characteristic of rationalism; even when we turn to regard our own religious experience, we do so employing the language of objectivity. See the origins of sermon structure during the time of the Protestant scholastics — *subtilitas intelligendi, subtilitas explicandi,* and *subtilitas applicandi* — which became a parody of rational, scientific method; a text was isolated for study, a hypothesis was drawn, and applications formed. What about the custom of distilling topics from texts that, as Hans Frei demonstrated, derives from rationalism's dismay with the embarrassments of biblical narrative.[16] And, recently, hasn't Neil Postman observed the linear "book logic" that dominated oratory during the eighteenth and nineteenth centuries but has dissolved in our odd multimedia world.[17] Homiletics during the Enlightenment was ordered by rational deductive systems and, later, with the rise of a contrapuntal romanticism, by added appeals to subjective religious experience. There is an old gag about two signs, one reading "This way to God," and the other, "This way to lectures about God for proper Bostonians." A homiletic method that objectified truth and then talked about it rationally may have separated the presence of God from listeners.[18] Of course, we may also have confused the gospel message itself with entrepreneurial bravado and, obviously, with blatant all-American individualism, both of which may underlie the notions of personal salvation we preach.

Shattering a Boxed World

Can we stop now and take a look at what may have happened to shake the mind of our age? What has shattered our confidence in objective reason? If you look at paintings done, let us say, toward the end of the eighteenth century, you are astonished at how many compositions seem to be boxed in. Even if the paintings are landscapes, usually there will be a line of trees, a hedge of hills, a fence, something to box the scene. Of course, all the paintings are painted from a third-person objective stance. Thus, though the paintings may be labeled "descriptive realism," you have an odd sense that they are objectively ordered and firmly boxed. (Perhaps they were busy fencing out the angels and the demons that had edged into medieval art.) But if you wander an art gallery these days you suddenly sense you are dealing with a very different kind of art.[19] In a single painting you may discover several angled perspectives layered on top of one another. You may also find symbols, fused multiple-scenes, and strange uses of color that seem to disturb traditional notions of "harmony." Now artists, in spite of Beaux Arts balls and other off-beat friskiness, are usually interested in helping us to see reality anew.[20] So let us conclude that what has changed in our contemporary world is an understanding of reality. Reality is less boxed in because it is no longer defined by its objective "thereness." No, the reality of any scene will not only be sights and sounds that can be recorded in some objective fashion, but realities in consciousness — sights, sounds, feelings, day-dreams, past memories, future anticipations, fantasies, desirings, social symbols, hoary myths, and so forth. And any artist, film-maker, novelist, or poet who tries to get at complex reality will no longer do anything like the eighteenth-century representations. The world has changed or, more precisely, a world in consciousness has changed. Art historians claim that it took hundreds of years for human beings to see dimen-sion. Now contemporary art is struggling to express the complexities of synonymous reality in fields of human consciousness. Our world has widened spectacularly.

But we have also had to face up to the demonic lurking in the ration-alist enterprise. In Eugène Ionesco's play *The Killer,* his hero Bérenger tours a "Radiant City" with a rationalist architect. He is captivated by the vision — "this neighborhood beyond compare, with its sunny streets and avenues bathed in light...this radiant city within a city...a tech-nical marvel!" — until he discovers a fountain filled with throat-cut corpses and realizes that there is a maniac killer loose in the city of light.[21] So the eighteenth-century dream of a "heavenly city" on earth has been undercut by world wars and economic depression and, of course, absolutely destroyed by the huge hard fact of the Holocaust. So in Arthur Miller's astonishing *After the Fall,* a character stands beside a tower of skulls piled up from a German concentration camp and confesses,

> And what's the cure? Who can be innocent again on this mountain of skulls? ...We meet unblessed; not in some garden of wax fruit and painted trees, that lie of Eden, but after, after the Fall, after many, many deaths.[22]

Enlightenment has produced sanitary bathrooms but also B-1 bombers; nuclear medicine, yes, but derived from a rain of death on Hiroshima. What Enlightenment could not do was to exorcise evil, a killer loose in the human world that sometimes theologians politely label "the problem of theodicy."[23] During the Holocaust, our rational "radiant city" turned into a tower of skulls.

A Glance toward the Future

Can we turn around and begin to trace some of the strands of thought that may yet twine together in common cultural meaning? Can we catch a glimpse of some new understanding trying to form in the mind of our age? Of course, the future is forming largely in countercultural groups, those peoples whose lives have been obscured by parading power structures or hidden in poverty that enlightenment often confused with ignorance. Obviously social structure will be reconstructed by the rise of so-called third and fourth world peoples. Their voices are beginning to be heard and their hermeneutic orientations may well shape new ways of looking at and being in the world.[24] There is a hard truth to the voices of poverty that will not distance the world with reason or succumb to the converse rationalism of romanticism. The future may be forming in the excluded mind of counterculture as well as in half-forgotten fringes of truth omitted from the tacit convictions our age has embraced. We speak of pluralism as if current diversity is an absolute. But there may be unifying myths forming even now in the broken heart of our world.

At the outset, let us guess that the movement of thought begun in Immanuel Kant will be fulfilled. If the Enlightenment was based on an analogy of reason, the future may well be ordered by the term "consciousness." Should some structure of correspondence emerge again, it may feature shared human consciousness and Consciousness, capital C, a Consciousness that is conscious of us. Though Karl Barth denied any "natural theology," that is, any notion of a general revelation to human reason, nevertheless the word "God" shows up in most languages, and, presumably, the word has some sort of social meaning. When wide-ranging human consciousness is suddenly conscious of its own finitude, then human beings are able to suppose the possibility of a free, *unlimited* consciousness under the linguistic symbol "God." So let us argue that a postmodern world will be conceived by consciousness, quite beyond categories of objective and subjective. If scholars have labeled the eighteenth century as "The Age of Reason," cultural historians in centuries to come may refer to our future as "The Age of Consciousness."

What about the world of nature? Borgmann is probably correct in arguing that Descartes's observational stance led to an alienation of society from its natural setting and that Bacon's utopian optimism endorsed a "conquest" mentality that despoiled nature in the name of progress.[25] The result of our alienation from nature is well described by H. G. Wells, who admitted:

> There was a time when my little soul shone and was uplifted by the starry enigma of the sky. . . . Now I go out and look at the stars as I look at the pattern of wallpaper on a railroad station waiting room."[26]

In spite of backpacking enthusiasts and trail-mix provisions, nature, though soulful and sometimes even awesome, does not seem to offer religious uplift. Sometimes nature may even produce an eerie sense of orphaned aloneness.[27] If rationalism investigated the world "out there," a new era may investigate the world as it is phenomenally structured in consciousness. When nature is objectified, the self is separated from context and from any sense of God's presence impinging on creation. But suppose the natural world is relocated as a project in consciousness. Perhaps then mystery will return and, with mystery, some renewed form of awe that can be basis for a venturing "natural theology."

Another gambit: With the breakdown of third-person objective and the realization that perspective may order reality, a new age will probably define truth in relation to perspectives and models in consciousness. Ultimate truth, transcendent truth, will be conceived as a model that in some way embraces our many human perspectival meanings.[28] At the same time, a new age will view everyday truth as interactionally discovered or inferred. Truth will not be deduced, but rather may be something that emerges from multiperspectival human discussion.[29] Thus logic will change. In addition to standard philosophical or mathematical logic, "a = b, because . . . ," there will be something like a visual, or associational logic, something that can best be described as a logic of consciousness.[30] We may begin to analyze reasons behind conjunctions of images in consciousness, a mode of metaphorical logic. Logic will move closer to the rationale for shifting visual fields in filmmaking than in our usual tautologies.[31]

Obviously, we are moving into an age of communal values and communal meanings. If John Locke established individual well-being as an ultimate social goal, the future will probably regard interpersonal well-being as a more appropriate social goal. As playwright Tony Kushner observes:

> We pay high prices for the maintenance of the myth of the Individual: we have no system of universal health care, we don't educate our children, we can't pass sane gun control laws, we elect presidents like Reagan, we hate and fear inevitable processes like aging and death, and on and on.

But Kushner begins to see a different order forming in the midst of our broken society:

> Together we organize the world for ourselves, or at least we organize our understanding of it; we reflect it, refract it, criticize it, grieve over its savagery; and we help each other to discern, amidst the gathering dark, paths of resistance, pockets of peace, and places from whence hope may be plausibly expected. Marx was right: The smallest divisible human unit is two people, not one; one is a fiction. From such nets of souls societies, the social world, human life springs.[32]

Presumably, there are signs that a postmodern world may be turning toward communal understandings of human life. Are we finally beginning to realize that, as Kushner says, "one is a fiction"?

Homiletics and the Postmodern Mind

The task of moving out of the rationalist model and into a new paradigm for preaching is a rather frightening prospect. During mid-twentieth century, homiletics has been captive to a biblical theology movement that is now passé. As a result, we have studied biblical forms and biblical meanings (as if they were sufficient in themselves) but have paid little attention to theology, to hermeneutic questions, or to the changing mind of our age. But now, as postmodernity seems to be signaling, we will have to reconsider the task of homiletics:

1. If we are moving into an age defined by analogies of consciousness rather than by objective rationality, then we must attend to how language forms in consciousness. Such a task will lead us into a renewed alliance with rhetoric. In the 1960s when homiletic classes were fed Dietrich Ritschl's *Theology of Proclamation* or perhaps Jean-Jacques von Allmen's *Preaching and Congregation,* both Barthian bulwarks of biblical theology, it was a matter of honor to reject rhetoric.[33] In those days we supposed we could derive homiletic strategies from the biblical page alone, shunning all forms of human sophistry. But rhetoric at

best is descriptive of how meaning forms in human beings and is strategic insofar as it demonstrates modes of argumentation that are generally
persuasive and are connected, therefore, with believing. Homiletics and
rhetoric have interacted through the centuries.[34] Thus the attempt to
deny rhetoric during the 1960s and 1970s consigned preaching to un-
tutored improvisation because, bluntly, the Bible does not tell us a
homiletic methodology for the twentieth century. Now homiletics must
once more turn to rhetoric and begin to study how religious meaning
does form in contemporary consciousness.[35] Thus we will be joining
with rhetoric in searching new forms of logic, ways in which perspective orders meaning, alternatives to third-person objective language, and
the like. Homiletics will describe the "hows" of preaching in a new way.

2. We will seek to recast the gospel promises in communal modes
of thought. We speak of "American individualism" and, while individualism does seem to be a peculiarly American proclivity, it is actually a
byproduct of Enlightenment. Of course, there is virtually no support in
Scripture for the personalism of our preaching; the "you" on Bible pages
is almost always a "you all." The postmodern world will turn toward a
renewed interest in the interpersonal. Please note, we did *not* say "a renewed interest in the social." No, the individual/social dialectic that has
hampered our thinking must give way to a study of the interpersonal
as something quite other than a common mind or a mere assemblage of
individuals.[36] The gospel we have been preaching has promised personal
salvation — often described in psychological terms, personal survival —
guaranteed on Easter Day, and, often, something called "a personal relationship with Jesus" that sounds positively sweaty. Personalism will
have to be revised not by a return to the so-called social gospel, but to a
reconceiving of the promises of God interpersonally.

3. We will join with theologians in the search for a new way of ar-
ticulating the gospel message: How can Christianity be imaged in a new
disclosive language? Must we not admit that the agenda of the biblical
theology movement has been a failure. We have preached more Bible in
mid-twentieth century than ever before, and yet people are still biblically
illiterate — after all, lectionary preaching is piecemeal at best[37] — and
mainline churches are still emptying. An untranslated biblicism is simply
insufficient for the living of life; people need meaning. What we have
done is to hand out Bible-lesson sermons but left our people without
any solid basis for theological thinking. As a result we have produced
people who have a scattering of biblical ideas amid secular meanings in
which they actually live. The task that faces pulpits now is the forming
of theological meaning in a twenty-first-century consciousness. Lately,
theologians have begun to underscore the role of imagination in the
constructing of a doctrine of God.[38] Through the language of preaching, narration, and naming, we are called to build a theological world

in which people may live and move and indeed have their being.[39] The task is not merely trading in one vocabulary for another. No, we must seek metaphor and image that can open the reality of God to contemporary consciousness. Preaching will have to be as much interested in invocation as in redefinition.

The term "postmodern," we have argued, cuts both ways. So preaching will have to disengage from Enlightenment Christianity and quite deliberately seed itself in a forming new world beyond modernity, a world that is being shaped largely in countercultural communities, among the socially disenfranchised and in the liberation movements of the "other world."

NOTES

1. Margaret Rose in her *The Post-modern and the Post-industrial* (Cambridge: Cambridge University Press, 1991) attempts to sort out the many different definitions.

2. For example, George A. Lindbeck, *The Nature of Doctrine: Religion and Theology in a Postliberal Age* (Philadelphia: Westminster Press, 1984) or, more recently, William C. Placher, *Unapologetic Theology: A Christian Voice in a Pluralistic Conversation* (Louisville: Westminster John Knox Press, 1989).

3. Some writers urge preachers to express feelings, unleash bodily movement, and tell their personal stories — all justified on the basis of being the opposite of a restrictive rationalism. Nineteenth-century romanticism was prompted by rationalism and, therefore, still lived within a rationalist paradigm. Twentieth-century homiletic romanticism may be an odd form of nostalgia.

4. For the notion of Enlightenment, see Peter Gay's awesome study, *The Enlightenment: An Interpretation,* vols. 1 and 2 (New York: Alfred A. Knopf, 1966 and 1969). But see also Crane Brinton's critical *A History of Western Morals* (New York: Harcourt, Brace and Co., 1959), and, for a strangely positive assessment, Richard Tarnas, *The Passion of the Western Mind* (New York: Harmony Books, 1991).

5. Paul Tillich, *The Protestant Era,* trans. James Luther Adams (Chicago: University of Chicago Press, 1948), especially chapter 15.

6. A few of the more helpful works: Albert Borgmann, *Crossing the Postmodern Divide* (Chicago: University of Chicago, 1992); Hal Foster, ed., *The Anti-Aesthetic: Essays on Postmodern Culture* (Port Townsend, Wash.: Bay Press, 1983), with essays by Baudrillard, Jameson, and Habermas; David R. Griffin, *God and Religion in the Postmodern World: Essays in Postmodern Theology* (New York: SUNY Press, 1989); David Harvey, *The Condition of Postmodernism: An Inquiry into the Origins of Cultural Change* (New York: Cambridge, 1989); Ihab Hassan, *The Postmodern Turn: Essays in Postmodern Theory and Culture* (Columbus: Ohio State University, 1987); Frederic Jameson, *Post-Modern Culture: The Logic of Late Capitalism* (Durham, N.C.:

Duke University Press, 1991), an important work; Charles Jencks, *What Is Postmodernism?* (New York: St. Martin's Press, 1987), and *The Language of Postmodernism* (New York: Rizzoli, 1987); Jean-François Lyotard, *The Post-modern Condition: A Report on Knowledge*, trans. Geoff Bennington and Brian Massumi (Minneapolis: University of Minnesota Press, 1984); Rose, *The Post-modern and the Post-Industrial*; Barry Smart, *Modern Conditions, Postmodern Controversies* (London: Routledge, 1992), and *Postmodernity* (London: Routledge, 1993).

7. See Charles Jencks, ed., *The Postmodernism Reader* (New York: St. Martin's Press, 1992) for a broad survey.

8. On Descartes as the source of the modern secular age, see Franklin L. Baumer, *Religion and the Rise of Skepticism* (New York: Harcourt, Brace and Co., 1960).

9. But please note the shape of American religious life, now torn by an objective fundamentalism and a subjective "habits of the heart" religion. The split between objective biblical truth and the so-called "inward testimony of the Spirit" was built into the Protestant enterprise from the start.

10. Albert Borgmann, *Crossing the Postmodern Divide* (Chicago: University of Chicago, 1992), chapters 1 and 2.

11. Ibid., *Crossing*, 12–19.

12. Carl L. Becker, *The Heavenly City of the Eighteenth Century Philosophers* (New Haven, Conn.: Yale University Press, 1932).

13. Lyotard, *The Postmodern Condition*, 71–82.

14. For helpful discussions of the temporality and relativity of modern thought, see Langdon Gilkey, *Naming the Whirlwind: The Renewal of God-Language* (New York: Bobbs-Merrill, 1969), chapters 2 and 3.

15. Though secularity may have been a byproduct of the Protestant Reformation as well as Cartesian skepticism, in 1851, under the leadership of freethinker George Jacob Holyoake, it became an "ism." He urged contemporary people to cast off the constrictions of religious meaning and be natural selves. A half-century later, when Marcel Proust used the host on the tongue as metaphor for a french kiss, secularism had obviously triumphed! Now we live in what Stephen Carter has described as "the culture of disbelief"; see his *The Culture of Disbelief: How American Law and Politics Trivialize Religious Devotion* (New York: Basic Books, 1993).

16. Hans W. Frei, *The Eclipse of Biblical Narrative: A Study in Eighteenth and Nineteenth Century Hermeneutics* (New Haven, Conn.: Yale University Press, 1974), especially chapters 5, 6, and 7.

17. Neil Postman, *Amusing Ourselves to Death: Public Discourse in the Age of Show Business* (New York: Viking Penguin, 1985), part 1.

18. Fred B. Craddock, writing out of the "New Hermeneutic," was an early critic of rationalist, deductive homiletics in his, *As One without Authority: Essays on Inductive Preaching* (Enid, Okla.: Phillips University Press, 1971), chapters 1 and 2.

19. For an earlier study of twentieth-century culture and art, see Paul Tillich's essay, "The World Situation," in Paul Tillich et al., *The Christian Answer*, ed. Henry P. Van Dusen (New York: Charles Scribner's Sons, 1945), 1–44.

20. So argues Denis de Rougemont, "Religion and the Mission of the Artist," *The New Orpheus: Essays toward a Christian Poetic,* ed. Nathan A. Scott, Jr. (New York: Sheed and Ward, 1964), 59–73.

21. Eugène Ionesco, *The Killer and Other Plays,* trans. Donald Watson (New York: Grove Press, 1960), 11–12.

22. Arthur Miller, *After the Fall* (New York: Bantam Books, 1965), 162.

23. Some years ago a television cartoon pictured a scientist lecturing about an ape. Dressed in a white lab coat, armed with a pointer, he was objectively describing the ape's anatomy. But as the scientist spoke, the ape grabbed him and twisted him into a painful knot. Throughout the pummeling, the scientist kept on "pointing out" aspects of the ape dispassionately. Clearly, the cartoon announced the end of a rationalist era.

24. For the issue of hermeneutics and social location, see Fernando F. Segovia and Mary Ann Tolbert, eds., *Reading from This Place* (Minneapolis: Fortress Press, 1994), the first of a three-volume study.

25. Borgmann, *Crossing,* chapter 2.

26. See a similar discussion in my *Preaching Jesus Christ* (Philadelphia: Fortress Press, 1988), 18.

27. For example, see Antoine de Saint-Exupéry, *Wind, Sand, and Stars* (London: William Heinemann, 1939), 91–95.

28. Edward Albee saw such a possibility in his peculiar play *Tiny Alice* (New York: Pocket Books, 1966).

29. Jürgen Habermas seems to suggest something of the sort with his confidence in dialogue and discourse. For a critical analysis of Habermas, see Richard J. Bernstein, *Beyond Objectivism and Relativism: Science, Hermeneutics, and Praxis* (Philadelphia: University of Pennsylvania Press, 1985), part 4.

30. See my *Homiletic* (Philadelphia: Fortress Press, 1987), 71–73.

31. Chaim Perelman has recognized the change in logic; see his *The Realm of Rhetoric* (Notre Dame, Ind.: University of Notre Dame Press, 1982), as well as C. Perelman and L. Olbrechts-Tyteca, *The New Rhetoric: A Treatise on Argumentation,* trans. J. Wilkinson and P. Weaver (Notre Dame, Ind.: University of Notre Dame Press, 1969).

32. Tony Kushner, *Angels in America: A Gay Fantasia on National Themes,* part 2: *Perestroika* (New York: Theatre Communications Group, 1994), 150, 158.

33. Dietrich Ritschl, *A Theology of Proclamation* (Richmond, Va.: John Knox Press, 1960), and Jean-Jacques von Allmen, *Preaching and Congregation* (Richmond, Va.: John Knox Press, 1962). See also Thomas G. Long, "The Distance We Have Traveled: Changing Trends in Preaching," *Reformed Liturgy and Music* 17, no. 1 (Winter 1983): 11–15.

34. George A. Kennedy, *Classical Rhetoric and Its Christian and Secular Tradition from Ancient to Modern Times* (Chapel Hill: University of North Carolina Press, 1980) as well as *Greek Rhetoric under Christian Emperors* (Princeton, N.J.: Princeton University Press, 1983).

35. Such a project was gestured years ago by the astonishing Kenneth

Burke in his *Rhetoric of Religion: Studies in Logology* (Berkeley: University of California Press, 1970).

36. See the important essay by Edward Farley, "Praxis and Piety: Hermeneutics beyond the New Dualism," *Justice and the Holy: Essays in Honor of Walter Harrelson,* ed. Douglas A. Knight and Peter J. Paris (Atlanta: Scholars Press, 1989), 241–55.

37. See Edward Farley, "Preaching the Bible and Preaching the Gospel," *Theology Today* 51, no. 1 (April 1994), and also my article, "Preaching the Lectionary: Two Cheers and Some Questions," *Reformed Liturgy and Music* 28, no. 2 (Spring 1994).

38. For example, see Gordon D. Kaufman, *In the Face of Mystery: A Constructive Theology* (Cambridge, Mass.: Harvard University Press, 1993), chapter 3, as well as *Essay on Theological Method* (Atlanta: Scholars Press, 1979), and *The Theological Imagination: Constructing the Concept of God* (Philadelphia: Westminster Press, 1985). Also see Sallie McFague, *Models of God: Theology for an Ecological, Nuclear Age* (Philadelphia: Fortress Press, 1987). For a somewhat more conservative treatment, Garrett Green, *Imagining God: Theology and the Religious Imagination* (San Francisco: Harper and Row, 1989).

39. Thomas H. Troeger presciently saw the shape of the homiletic task in his articles, "Homiletics as Imaginative Theology," *Homiletic* 12, no. 1 (1987): 27–30, and "The Shape of Post-Modern Homiletics," *Homiletic* 13, no. 1 (1988): 28–32.

⇛· 10 ·⇚

Theologia as a Liberation *Habitus*
Thoughts toward Christian Formation for Resistance

MARY McCLINTOCK FULKERSON

When a sufficient number of specialists are assembled on a (divinity/seminary) college faculty, the subject of which each knows only a small part is said to be covered, and the academic department to which they all belong is regarded as fully manned. In ancient Ireland, if legend is to be trusted, there was a tower so high that it took two persons to see to the top of it. One would begin at the bottom and look up as far as sight could reach, the other would begin where the first left off, and see the rest of the way.
— John Erskine

The Tower Problem in Theological Education

It is not difficult to identify with John Erskine's comments for many of us in theological education. The parable of a pseudo-cooperative venture in seeing reminds us of the practice of defining faculties by "manning" slots for a fixed number of field subjects. It can be translated further into pedagogical terms as the "field coverage principle," which also resonates with our problems in the study of divinity.[1] Although Edward Farley has never described the situation of theological education quite this way, I feel sure he would agree that the story strikes a familiar chord. We have Farley to thank for some sense of how the anomalies behind the divinity "tower problem" came about. His investigation of the history of theology/*theologia* exposed the foundations for this problematic principle in the academic setting of many seminary and divinity schools.[2]

Farley's critique of the fourfold disciplines that accompany residual institutional compromises of the last two centuries can be summarized

160

in terms of the field coverage principle. It would go something like this: Requisite for the well-being of a theological institution are faculty trained in each of the four "fields" (Bible, church history, theology, and practical theology); a student who has taken a predetermined allotment of courses in each of these requisite fields is adequately prepared for the work of Christian ministry. Farley has shown us that the subject of "divinity" simply is not "covered" by this assemblage of specialities.

An alternative accompanies Farley's criticism of contemporary theological institutions. With the intriguing notion of theology as a *habitus*, he offers a proposal for rethinking the fourfold division and its reduction of theology to the study of texts and systematics. By connecting theology to *habitus* (to habit, or disposition) Farley argues that theological education is a *paideia* — an enculturing or forming of dispositions in persons. To make *theologia* the unifying goal of education is to prioritize theology in the limited sense of the study of theologians' works, and it displaces the clericalism that conceives of preparation of clergy for parish work as its organizing goal. To resolve the problems of fragmentation, Farley commends capacities for *theologia*, the process that orders the reflective *habitus* of Christian faith. To define the process he outlines modes of understanding that order the capacitating of the cognitive aspects of this *habitus*.[3]

As a life-formative pursuit, *theologia* is a kind of wisdom that (ideally) joins knowledge of God as *scientia*, the rigorous study of earthly things, with the transformative affective knowledge that is *sapientia*. *Theologia* reunites the noetic and soteriological dimensions of God-knowledge, falsely separated by the disciplines of *Wissenschaft*. It signals the way life practice is a necessary part of the successful intellectual appropriation of the "divine things." *Theologia* is related to life practice because it is gained as a *habitus*, the habits and practices that form the dispositions of a believer. Although Farley's description of *habitus* focuses on the matrix of theological education of clergy, and, thus, is primarily cognitive, the idea has the potential to encompass a much broader sense of dispositions and formation.

If *theologia* is our goal, education is neither the passing on of information nor apprenticeship in the task of research. It is, one might say, the forming or disciplining of Christians in the *habitus* of transformative reflective modes of God-knowledge, or what David Kelsey calls the practices of "understanding God truly."[4] Thus in the most basic sense the answer Farley offers to the problematic field coverage paradigm is that the formation of Christians — of lives faithful to the gospel — is the subject of the education. A *paideia*, or training of persons, in God-knowledge provides the conditions for its unity and, by implication, an institution is fully "staffed" less by virtue of field coverage than by some judgment of the faculty's ability to enable this formation.

As a challenge to problematic Enlightenment legacies in theological study, even in fledgling form *theologia* suggests an attractive (if ideal) answer to the "tower" problem.[5] When concern for forming certain kinds of subjects and communities replaces the current practice of combining (incoherent) methods and knowledges that ignore the status of the subject, an excellence is produced that either enables subjects to *scale* high towers (by doing something practical like standing on each other's shoulders) or redefines what would be a desirable task altogether.

There is, however, a second problem associated with the field coverage principle, and it is fruitful to ask how *theologia* might address this dilemma as well. That problem is the challenge of liberationist perspectives. For Gerald Graff, critic of the field coverage principle in literature, this comes from the questioning of the literary canon by feminist, African-American, gay, and non-Western writers.[6] In theological education there are parallel critiques from analogous marginalized groups that challenge the notion that there is such a thing as "the tradition."

One does not have to look as far as the problems created by the fourfold division for liberation perspectives to see that the questions posed by marginalized voices exacerbate the inadequacy of field coverage. Marginalized communities call into question the settled character of the world-views that make up the tradition and its guardians, literary and theological alike. These oppositional voices can be *added* to a curriculum, but they simply become more territorial pieces. The already fragmented "field" of divinity remains — a compromise from a time long before liberation theological discussions. This add-on strategy does not resolve the dilemma imaged by Erskine's story. Adding marginalized perspectives is like solving the problem of the tower by adding persons distinguished by gender, race, and class to help the committee see further.

Although Farley has not developed it in this direction, the ideal of *theologia* has implications for liberationist concerns as well. The idea that there will be "enough" marginalized perspectives covered to gain "objectivity" is as problematic as the same model for the fourfold — that the proper amount of knowledge from fields of Bible, church history, theology, and "practical" disciplines constitutes theological wisdom. If theological formation is for the formation of redemptive wisdom, the real question on Farley's terms is the role of marginalized perspectives in Christian *formation*.

To formulate the issue in the spirit of Farley's proposal, let us say that the question at hand is the proposal of a liberation *paideia*. In addition to the cognitive *habitus* needed for *theologia* and the ideology critique that can be provided by the reflective aspects of *Wissenschaft*, adequate formation must take account of a posture from the margins in the creation of a liberation *paideia* and habituation. This does not mean that only marginalized populations can be trained at theological schools, nor does it mean we simply include books about them in courses. It requires a different way of thinking about taking liberationist concerns seriously — one that takes the formation of subjects as its starting point.

Central to most liberation theological thinking is the conviction that resistance to the State or other apparatuses of the social formation (including legislative, military, cultural processes, and their intersection with a capitalist mode of production) is integral to Christian practice. It is as logical that resistance, peaceful or otherwise, be considered a core practice of being Christian as it is that worship be deemed a central Christian practice.[7] This is not only because sin rather than ignorance (the need for "Enlightenment") is the problem that should be addressed by *theologia* as formation, but because sin is not just something initiated by individuals. As a social phenomenon, theological formation to resist sin must address relationships to such social entities as institutions. It requires the formation of individuals through concrete social practices.

In the spirit of Farley's critique, not only is a turn to *theologia* a correction of *Wissenschaft* as it distorted the soteriological character of theological knowledge; it produces insights into the realities of marginalized voices. (And I depart here from the way Farley would introduce the topic, as part of the contextualizing of theological reflection.) Liberation formation will be aimed at the worst effects of *Wissenschaft* — like the schooling that creates docile citizens for the social order. Although discourse critical of the social order does happen in theological institutions, as long as its dominant form is still shaped by Enlightenment modes of education rather than soteriological wisdom, it is not likely to produce practitioners able to stand against the forces and apparatuses of the State. At worst research-oriented criticism is likely to produce docility, at best no protection against it.[8] The notion of *theologia* can help us think about a liberation formation that could guard against intellectually formed docility by habituating subjects into *liberation dispositions*.

Theologia as Liberation *Habitus:*
Virtues and Formation for Resistance

To sketch the outlines of a liberationist extension of *theologia*, I will argue the following thesis: a liberationist perspective can be developed with the terms of *paideia* and "habituation" in the virtues. Only when the community of learning can create or form subjects habituated into practices that resist the social order can thinking about Christian *paideia* that supports rather than contradicts Christian visions of radical criticism even begin to happen. To make suggestions toward such a possibility, I will bypass Farley's proposal for a unified cognitive structure of *theologia* and pursue his idea of the formative practices of *habitus*. To work from an account of *habitus*, I will borrow from the definition of practice developed by Alasdair MacIntyre. The terms from the popular MacIntyrean account of a virtue tradition are not problem-free, however, and must be expanded. I will argue that the set of dispositions that constitute the activities of social change qualify as a socially established practice. It is a practice generated out of a thick tradition of hospitality to the stranger, which is part of the good of Christian life. A liberation account will differ from MacIntyre's version of the Good and from his choice of the narratives that constitute a tradition. It will need to correct his failure to recognize that any narrative is co-constituted by those it excludes — accounts of "the Christian story" not excepted. The goal of habituation into such practice and the goods that adhere to it are not dependent upon the possession and policing of the "right" story. Rather it depends upon enabling communities with the humility to have their own stories criticized. It is this latter virtue and formation that add-on strategies or Enlightenment *Wissenschaft* cannot be trusted to create.

First I turn to a definition of practice, the creation of goods internal to its execution, and the provision of narratives and traditions that point to a unifying good for Christian practice of social change.

Social Change as a Practice: Reasons, Gaps, and Narratives

Alasdair MacIntyre's helpful definition for "practice" is already in use for thinking about Christian *paideia* after Farley. Developed out of the tradition of *habitus*, his account offers us the mediating social forms through which transformative habituation occurs.[9] Recuperated from the Thomist appropriation of the Aristotelian notion of *eudaimonia* (happiness, well-being) and the virtues of excellences (*arete*) necessary to that good life, his notion of practice makes it possible to identify particular activities in light of their corresponding dispositions and goods. With it we can ask about habits that correspond to actions that are commensurate with the Good of a liberation theological vision.[10]

Practice is a notion considered central to an adequate account of virtue, argues MacIntyre. It is defined as "any coherent and complex form of socially established cooperative human activity through which goods internal to that form of activity are realized in the course of trying to achieve those standards of excellence that are appropriate to, and partially definitive of, that form of activity, with the result that human powers to achieve excellence, and human conceptions of the ends and goods so involved, are systematically extended."[11] By identifying these socially established activities and their goods, we will have "the arena in which the virtues are exhibited and in terms of which they are to receive their primary if incomplete, definition."[12] Integral to this account are two other concepts, the narrative ordering of a life and a fuller moral tradition that offers us an account of the good. By taking up these three — practice, narrative, and moral tradition — I will propose an outline for a liberation *paideia*.

The first qualification of a practice is easily met by a liberationist case for *paideia*. Social activism, Christian or otherwise, is a socially established human activity.[13] Social protest movements are as old as social life itself. What may be less obvious, but no less true, is that they inevitably include traditions — ways of telling about the practices, about the "saints," the failures and victories of a struggle for justice or emancipation that enable the passing on of concrete wisdoms. The oral history of slave traditions for African Americans is an example of movements in the U.S. that are crucial to our formation as a people, although they are only in the initial stages of being recorded and widely acknowledged. Christian participation in the contemporary Civil Rights movement, the second wave of feminism, and gay rights movements are other examples of organized activities for social change. They target legislative, cultural, and economic aspects of the social formation, employing varieties of strategies and tactics for change — from boycotting, protests, sit-ins, countrywide consciousness-raising, to the slower-going production of popular and expert literatures.

Although social activism for change qualifies as a practice simply by being an activity that is socially established — something we are all familiar with and associate with certain groups — the argument for the central nature of resistance to Christian practice and formation is not advanced dramatically by fulfillment of this criterion. Recognition of social activism as a practice allows us to focus a basic assumption of MacIntyre's definition, however, namely, what it means for something to be an *act*. The answer to this question is not as obvious as may appear. The implications of MacIntyre's answer come into some conflict with their assumption in liberation theologies (and my examples) that the social order itself is implicated in agency. Let us consider these issues by first taking up the requirement that action be an intentional category.

The definition of *habitus* assumes that agency is central to human being and identifies that agency as purposeful. It comes from the belief in "the special nature of human action as a task."[14] In order to qualify as an act, however, a behavior must be intelligible. That is to say that it must be intended by an agent and, ultimately, be established as a socially significant activity with goods internal to its accomplishment. "There is no such thing as 'behavior,' to be identified prior to and independently of intentions, beliefs and settings," says MacIntyre.[15]

The feature of intentionality disqualifies involuntary bodily movements from being acts and lays the groundwork for a view of accountability. What makes behavior action is that *reasons* can be given for it. The point of this privileging of reasons in MacIntyre's view is that intention must be transparent. Too Wittgensteinian to mean that intent is a transparent window to some private Cartesian realm of subjectivity, MacIntyre may be understood to say that an intention is only real or available in an act, where it becomes public. As available or public, intention becomes a socially established phenomenon, as Stanley Hauerwas points out.[16]

Intention is a complex phenomenon in this view. MacIntyre concedes that despite its public character the intentional nature of an act may not be immediately transparent. An act can have double intentionality. (I take my child for a stroller ride in the park, intending both that she be stimulated and that I get exercise beneficial to my health.) Setting places an action in a socio-historical context; thus context is also crucial to the meaning of intention and therefore to an act. By virtue of causal factors and diachronic order in both the agent's story and in the story of the setting itself, context is the web of narratives that multiplies the category "reasons" beyond the agent's personal narrative. Our intentions and the stories that place them are always embedded in other narratives, many of which we are unaware. We are, at best, always "co-authors of our own narratives."[17] As a consequence of its contextual setting, access to the intention that is primary in an act is never simple, for a judgment about the reasons for an act can be shifted in relation to the number of stories admitted into consideration.

Despite this complexity of content, intentions and, therefore, reasons *may* be ascribed to individuals in MacIntyre's account. What is more, the agent's reason for a behavior is the privileged description of that behavior. This does not mean that the interpreter must agree with a reason to say that an intention is intelligible, only that a reason must be defensible. Thus a man who, upon arriving at a bus stop, makes nonsense comments about a duck is judged to be engaging in an unintelligible act, barring his ability to supply a reason for such behavior. Such behavior becomes action (namely, intelligible) if we find out that it is a secret coded message intended for another secret agent in the vicinity.[18]

Although reasons can be placed in more complex discursive webs as we test their intelligibility, the litmus test of that intelligibility is keyed in to the agents' accounts. Thus, a life must be readable as a unity so that blame and credit can be assigned. To say this another way, once reasons are given, one is led to look for broader (synchronic) and longer (diachronic) frames for that life in light of which those reasons and intentions may be interpreted. Thus extended, reasons take shape out of narratives of a life, a family, a country, and so on. A dialectic between the agents' reasons and these more complex discourses creates the matrix for accountability.

Understood this way, discernment of the intelligibility of the bus stop scene is discovery of a narrative that gives it sense. Clearly the odd movements in question remain simply behaviors until some narrative such as the secret agent encounter is provided. We also see that intelligibility is inevitably broadened by placing this narrative in a personal life history, a national history, and so on, from which we discern whether the agent was a brave and heroic patriot or simply duplicitous. The broader narratives are more than "context," we should note; they are crucial to the definition of intelligibility.

With the move from the concept of intention to narrative, the teleological logic that stretches out an agent's aim into a full-blown historical event, a very important concept is at stake. Accountability is grounded by the move that ties a practice to an act, where the reason for an event is thought to initiate. Even though he admits that a "piece of behavior can belong to more than one setting," MacIntyre wants to discover which aim is primary, which intent is "causally effective," and thereby enable us to situate the perpetrator in a complex of effects.[19] In short, the agent's reason is primary.[20]

Yet we need something else to display the kind of accountability that matters. That something else is the category of *character.* To have accountability, it is obviously necessary to have an agent to interrogate. More precisely, to deal with the problem of change, we must have a point of continuity in that agent. For MacIntyre, the inevitability of change in human life is its temporality — a feature displayed by the diachronicity of narrative. The *problematic* nature of incessant change for notions of accountability is resolved by the concept of a unified self.[21]

The self serves as a point of reference; it constitutes the possibility for reasons that make actions intelligible, and does so as a temporally thick self. This unified consciousness has the capacity to accrue, to collect, to be counted "the same" in some fashion, and thereby grounds a notion of character. Not only must there be an "I" to measure the flow of temporal change, but it is an "I" to which integrity and steadfastness or failure and blame can be attributed. MacIntyre says that "all attempts to elucidate the notion of narrative, intelligibility, and accountability are bound to fail."[22] It is the problematic aspects of this first qualification that we must consider for a liberationist *habitus.*

At one level MacIntyre's account of an act is adequate for analyzing practices of resistance. Let us take, for example, interracial work at a place like Highlander Center — a southern grass-roots community that provides training for justice work around class and race issues. Surely there are excellences of character pertinent to the good of racial reconciliation, excellences that can accumulate over time for the partic-

ipants. Working-class folks, black and white alike, are habituated into
the virtues needed to persevere in acts for which they can give reasons,
e.g., the need to challenge unfair labor policies and state tolerance for
devastating strip-mining practices. The participants can be said to be the
source of their actions — their intentions are primary indicators of the
meaning of their acts. With MacIntyre's definition of accountability we
can describe such a situation as character-building, based upon assessments of persons' histories as truth-tellers, as subjects whose capacities
for perseverance are enhanced. We can say that other goods will accrue
to their efforts to change laws that allow their health and well-being to
be continually destroyed if pursued with integrity, and we can say that
their reasons, even if multiple, are the source of the intelligibility (and
even virtuous nature) of their acts.

The point here is not to say that there are no intentions that are trans-
However, there are potential lacunae in MacIntyre's account. If Christian social change practices entail the view that the social order, not
simply individual subjects, is seriously flawed or corrupted, then two
potential complications arise. If they do not come from some private
Cartesian realm, reasons and intentions are constructed out of a stock
of social discourses that construct subjects — those of contemporary culture, a religious tradition such as presented in contemporary Christian
communities, *and* the tradition as a normative past. Residual patriarchal, classicist, heterosexist and racist meanings embedded in the social
formation deform that stock of discourses. The languages of society are
not neutral. They are scored with biases — from images of the ideal
(white male) citizen to legislative biases for certain kinds of families and
sexualities. Even those who define themselves *against* the social order
are constructed by this stock. Discursive grids for reality do not simply shape, but reach into the very "soul" of agents, including agents in
Christian communities.[23]

The point here is not to say that there are no intentions that are transparent to some sort of "intelligible reasons" in such cases as I describe.
In that case one would be prevented completely from making judgments
about character. The point is that reasons connect their subjects to social discourses, often to stories of oppression and violence. Consequently
they may be reasons that cannot be seen in their full dimensions by their
owners. We cannot, in short, treat a category of intelligibility from a liberation perspective prior to the social narratives that give it a sense and
that distort or blind the agent as the primary source of intelligibility.
Let me illustrate. A formal notion of an agent's intention is problematic because practices of social change typically emerge in response to
oppressions that are barely recognizable or of little concern to many
publics, those of the civil, legislative apparatuses, as well as the processes of the mode of reproduction. When these oppressions constitute
real subjects, such as poor women or victims of sexual abuse, claims

about the wrongfulness of a situation are rarely heard (regardless of who makes them) and always contested, often for quite some time. (The work of the Highlander Center on racial justice in the 1940s was greatly resented and persecuted by the locals.) One has only to note that the claim that rape victims are not suspects has only recently become intelligible in the courts and (to some extent) part of a broader public perception in order to see vividly how relative "intelligible reasons" are to a social consciousness. There are always "agents" who are invisible to the state *and to the church* as a result of these corruptions. Consequently their "reasons" and the intelligibility of their underlying character may be simply invisible in the public forum and in light of the canons of "objective" reasons.

Everything depends upon *who is* narrating the terms of intelligibility. Although MacIntyre argues that reasons come from communities and their narratives, his own narrative is an anti-Enlightenment story that attempts to correct the liberal legacy of moral bankruptcy resulting from tradition-less and community-less commitment. It is a legacy he wants to replace with a recuperated Aristotelian-Thomist tradition for virtuous communities. Remarkably silent with regard to an *actual community* capable of living by this narrative, MacIntyre fails to provide a piece of information that is vital, namely, how the shifting fate of the "unintelligible" might be dealt with.

Although the remaining elements of "practice" that specify the good and the concrete narrative of a practice will deal with some of this, the problem here is a model built on a certain kind of self — a unified one that is capable of giving reasons. Since social change practices will involve advocacy work by those with more visibility and credibility than those for whom they advocate, the question of how one counts "character" and accountability becomes very tricky. Work at Highlander is done by persons with some skills who enable grass-roots change — poor and working-class folks take action for their own communities.[24] Other examples expose the problem more explicitly. Take the child victim of sexual abuse who is incapable of giving reasons for her own behavior, much less reasons that can be placed in narratives of any sort. Does she simply fall off the map of the intelligible life? Does her drift into a life of self-abuse disqualify her for accountability?[25] These terms — intelligibility as unity of self, narrative, and tradition — can be extremely problematic for numbers of those around whom social change practices develop.

While *someone else* — the social worker, the activist, the theologian — may tell a story for this victim of sexual abuse and make a unity of her life out of the "causes" of her destruction, we cannot ignore the question about where unity can be legitimately identified for this life: who should narrate? There are countless subjects who do not have unitary selves or who do not have a tradition in which they are named as human. If nothing else, such subjects must cause us to place a question mark by the bounding and defining of the unitary self and its narratively constructed life as *the* primary unit of accountability.

My questions suggest that the MacIntyrean definition of accountability may be incomplete. If we are to take seriously the kinds of situations that constitute the need for social change practice, we must depart from MacIntyre's account of this issue and make it more complex. The fact that "a piece of behavior can belong to more than one setting" has more serious ramifications for character formation and ascription of accountability than his model allows. Conditions for character building in the abused child, as for many other subjects, cannot depend solely upon her having reasons or intentions for which she is accountable. Everything depends upon what other narrative hers is placed in. While a hope may exist for the child to have some kind of MacIntyrean accountability in the future (although that would need debating), it cannot be the condition of her humanity. (And there is a sense in which humanity is at stake with the definition of character.[26])

I propose that such subjects as this child are markers of the absent, the voiceless, the unseen, and as such they must constitute the here, the said, and the seen. To mark these gaps, the unity of a self and the capacity to have one must be formulated in relation to the social order that both prevents and makes that possible.

Liberation *Paideia:*
Goods, Narratives, Gaps, and Virtues

The next step in determining if social dissent qualifies as a transformative practice is to show how it differs from a host of other activities that are socially recognized, based on reasons, and yet still are not candidates. The second characteristic of a practice is that it has goods internal to it and virtues or excellences that enable those goods.

A lot of activities might seem to be practices. MacIntyre's examples include tiddly-winks and brick laying. Although these qualify on the first characteristic, tiddly-winks is not a practice in the MacIntyrean sense, nor is planting turnips or laying bricks. Chess, farming, and architecture, however, are practices. What makes the difference is that practices have traditions of excellence associated with them, as do chess, farming, and architecture. Those traditions of excellence (*arete*) are defined by goods that accrue to those who achieve standards of excellence associated with their right practice. Most importantly, practices of chess, farming, and architecture produce internally achieved goods that are themselves sufficient for the practice themselves.

Can the category of Christian social change activities — resistance to established social evils and advocacy for marginalized peoples, with the conflict and protest that accompany these activities — qualify in this last important sense? Is resistance conceivable as practices that habituate into forms of existence that Christians should sponsor? It seems that social change activities do qualify. I have already suggested this in the case of the work of the Highlander Center. But let us return to the MacIntyrean criteria again to demonstrate this. In the first place there is a set of goods that are internal to the practices that characterize social change movements. It would be easy to claim that the objects of social change are goal-oriented, so it is important to clarify the nature of internal goods and their virtues in order to see that having goals is not the whole story.

In the virtue tradition of Aristotle, happiness is defined as a good in itself in distinction from something that is a means to the good, as Hauerwas says. This is to suggest that true well-being is of longstanding durability not easily taken away.[27] It is in this sense that work with and for battered women, work against racism, or work for any social change all have goods internal to the practices. It matters how persons are formed if these goods are to be achieved.

It is not difficult to see social activism in this way, e.g., as requiring enduring capacities for its accomplishment. Women who work with battered women find the excellences attained to be increased capacities to understand and support women so that they can take their lives into their own hands — capacities coming from patience, persistence, and openness to empathy, capacities to rid oneself of class and cultural prejudices. Theologically speaking, we can say that the good in such practices is participation in the increase of God's reign, in the form of a diminishing of violence. It is a good that comes with or is internal to the work and is not attainable outside of the doing. Nor is the good an achieved state of social harmony, as the movement out of one state of deprivation or oppression is emancipatory. At best it is a move into empowerment for the next unexpected ill. *This* is what prevents the account from separating formation from the good. The practice and the "end" are very much related.[28]

The goods in these cases involve the diminishing of the violence of sexist domination and racist relationships through the emergence of situations of safety, well-being, and regard. For the Highlander Center — or its founder — these particular "goods" would come from a vision of justice as the good end of God's creation.[29] We can further specify the practices for such an end as participation in the kingdom, or realm, of the God of Israel and the community of Jesus the Christ. As a God-centered form of existence, that participation is a life of dependence upon God. It develops in the form of participation in the ongoing redemption of a tragic and sinfully corrupted creation.

Since the Good is sufficient in itself and is of such longstanding value that it is not a means to some other good, we must be clear on how such goods as racial reconciliation qualify. By defining a liberationist vision with such specificity — with resistance to particular forms of social oppression — I do suggest that some goods may be transient. It is conceivable that the historical end of certain kinds of racial prejudice may occur. However, by insisting that these goods are available for Christians within the frame of God's reign, I claim that such goods as racial reconciliation or gender justice are not simply dispensable means. If racial reconciliation is achieved by means of practices of God-dependence, a certain kind of life is necessary for it to happen. The dispositions toward such goods will come out of specific socially located narratives, and they must last. Capacities for racial justice work are capacities that endure, and they require God-dependence. This is to say that the fight against racism itself partakes in the Good that is God's reign.[30]

Liberation *Paideia:*
A Braided Tradition of the Stranger

There is one final step in the assessment of social change activities as a Christian practice. Such goods require narratives that form a moral tradition of Christian social change. To correct for MacIntyre's inadequate version of accountability/agency, however, we must mark the narratives. I will do that by insisting upon the intersection of biblical narratives with the co-constituting "subject" of the invisible history, the as-yet-untold story of the outsider. The mistake in MacIntyre's account of tradition is similar to his treatment of the agent's intention. It allows signifying processes to be defined apart from their creation by multiple discourses, including the "unsaid." There is no biblical text or narrative that is not defined by means of the stories of the communities that construe that text or narrative, as well as the stories that do not.

Given the gaps and multiplicity of discourses, can there be "a story" in a liberation *paideia?* I think there can, but it is a strange story. MacIntyre is right that a narrative of liberal democratic freedom is not appropriate here. However, I disagree with his contention that the story needed is *a* tradition. It is not even adequate to say it is a tradition of arguments. Subjects are constructed by multiple discourses — the story of the social formation about who you are as an African-American woman — as much as by who you are as a Christian. The so-called main story — the Christian story — *appears* to have boundaries, to be a tradition. However, a liberation reading of that story insists that its silent, invisible, and absent subjects mark it as well. There is no telling of the Christian story that is not marked by gaps — the refusals of large populations of human beings. That telling is always a tradition co-constituted by other discourses, a tradition that must be constantly braided together in new ways.

To be sure, we can tell pieces of a story about the Good or the good life. That good in a Christian community is defined in terms of a relation to the one God of Abraham, Sarah, Isaac, and Rebecca, decisively present in Jesus of Nazareth called the Christ. Loyalty to this God provides the parameters of the good life. As a liberation narrative, however, those parameters must allow us to organize such pieces without ignoring the gaps and elisions in historical versions of the story. This is not the same as defining *a* tradition, unless we define a tradition in a new way: as a set of narratives that can never be fixed — a story that must constantly be newly told, not simply re-told, a braid that must constantly be remade. And that is the strangeness of the story.

Farley offers a narration of Christian faith consonant with such gaps and elisions and refuses a closed narrative or notion of the self.[31] A narrative-without-closure that can shape a liberation *paideia* reads the Jesus events as a transition into a gracious posture toward the stranger. There is, of course, nothing particularly Christian about the centrality of the stranger. For a tradition of social activism, however, we read in Jesus the paradigmatic story of faithful response to the stranger. Circumcision is the first of a continuing litany of conditions on membership in the community of God's people which are done away with by the Christian community. In Christ Jesus, one does not have to become a Jew to be a part of God's redemptive community; one does not have to be a man, or Caucasian, or educated. We can tell a story about Jesus as the contradiction to false generic humanisms by connecting faithfulness to the stranger with the history of shifting boundaries for the human: the Gentile, the woman, the poor, the homosexual, the African American. The narrative continually expands its account of the Stranger as the community reconfigures its boundaries by exposure and rejection of the new conditions put on membership.

Thus the narrative that creates a tradition and its Good for workers against racism is a braided story or stories. It is a narrative about Jesus of Nazareth and the community of Yahweh out of which he came, ministered, was crucified, and raised from the dead. But this narrative is co-constituted by the stories of the United States (or wherever they are) as a story of a Christian nation that struggled to define blackness as human and to define femaleness or Nativeness as fully human and is only now contemplating definitions of gay and lesbian subjects as human. Arguments about the nature of the human are the constitutive pieces of this "tradition of arguments." (Not insignificantly, they were not necessarily arguments in which their primary subjects were participants, at least for some time.)

To tell this story is to shape communities into the good of loyalty to the one God. The central impetus to loyalty to this God is the posture toward the "outsider." The stranger to the land in Israel was to be treated justly; the poor were to be given surplus. To take up the position of the stranger now is to ask about the invisible subject, the one for whose life no unity or explanation can be given. It is this broken, open, and complex set of traditions that need to shape theological education as a *paideia* for social change. It is only artificially called "*the* narrative" that forms Christian practices. It will be "biblical" but will always change, as the effects of the co-constituting "invisible" stories will change through time.

To identify the tasks that are conducive to a *paideia* for Christian faith we must know something about the virtues that characterize the Christian life. These virtues come from our notion of the Good, its end, or aim. The sensibilities and desires are shaped by right practices, and the actor is created in the process. While I cannot complete such a task in this essay, three observations point toward the dispositions a liberation *paideia* needs to nurture.

The skills for social change practices must come from attention to the continual tendency of the nation-state and the church *not-to-see* things. It is just such skills or capacities that a Christian story can nurture as it shapes dispositions to ask "Who is the stranger?" and "Who is 'unintelligible' now?" The liberation narrative that fills out the definition of a practice is a clue to the unanswered question in MacIntyre's position, namely, how is the as-yet-unnamed stranger to fare? Its highlighting themes must convey the centrality of the progress of the stranger, the politically oppressed — the slave, the pariah population, the invisible "outsider," the hungry, the poor, the homeless.

A second observation reflects the situated nature of theological education as it might influence such a *paideia*. Hauerwas suggests that learning a virtue is like learning a craft. One puts oneself under the authority of a master at the craft, learning the ins and outs of bricklaying, for example, by doing and making mistakes. One learns the "feel" of a task that is a craft, one comes to be habituated to it, and (hopefully) to do it well.[32] Yet one of the problems for us as theological educators is that we who are "masters" are as liable as anyone to be shaped by the blinders and gaps of our shared stories as North Americans. The shaping and production of academic success may very well be antithetical to the production of virtues necessary to the dispositions to receive from the subjects produced in very different social locations.

A theological *paideia* must be devised for a liberation *habitus* that takes account of the institutionalities of our contemporary situation. A history of gender relations, definitions of private-public and correlated gendered spheres have characterized the dominant institutions of our national life. Racial and class alienations characterize us. They are not secondary attributes of some a priori real subjectivities: our shaping by these national bad habits is as much a part of our agency as are our commitments to Christian faithfulness.[33] Thus to say we are habituated is to speak of us as already shaped by gendered, racial, and class dispositions.

A third and connected issue arises because narratives are always marked by silences, intertwined with recognized or obscured narratives of the social order. The question of who is to define the virtues necessary to Christian practices is again an issue. We would not expect that all activities of variously constituted subjects will be recognizable as dispositions for the good by those whose stories dominate. Katie Cannon identifies the virtues of African-American women; "unshouted courage," "functional prudence" are habits of African-American women whose struggles for survival called from them the necessity to develop dispositions for "the often unacknowledged inner conviction that keeps one's appetite whet for freedom."[34]

The dispositions described by Cannon as virtues may be experienced differently by subjects who are shaped by social/cultural discourses of the dominant (white) race or class. The virtues she describes are inseparable from the situation of chattel slavery. The significance of this fact must be marked in a proposal for liberation *paideia*. Although from a contemporary place we have begun to appreciate the dispositions of African-American women, it is unlikely that the plantation owners recognized these dispositions as virtues. We must respect the differences that result from being located differently with regard to power, without being content with incommensurable virtues. To that end a liberation *paideia* must shape us to have capacities to receive from the Other when our constitution as subjects is rendered manifestly different by race, gender, class, and sexual preference.

What does it mean to habituate Anglo women, African-American women and men, upper-middle-class white men, into a coherent tradition? It does *not* mean only getting the appropriate intellectual virtues or learning womanist or feminist theological positions. It requires the formation of subjects who can recognize culturally alien practices as possible displays of virtues and develop dispositions for self-criticism in relation to such recognitions. While the description of steadfastness Cannon offers for African-American women may have some overlap with a disposition for steadfastness in another community, it is not the same; it is stamina that comes from dealing with total unpredictability — "the quality of steadfastness, ... [like] fortitude, in the face of formidable oppression."[35] It requires the development of dispositions for anger and conflict that come with the practices of long-term work. As activists remind us, that work always requires failures. For those of us in different subject positions, dispositions to receive from new "masters" must be formed.

Development of a special sensibility for the invisible fractures, the silent cries, is essential to the forming of Christian character. This means playing the non-dominant stories out of which a student is formed for all they are worth. Our goal is not simply to confirm these stories; we hope for transformations. However, we look to where the contradictions between the promise of Christian narratives and social stories are for the openings for new critiques and possibilities. We seek to learn where the habits for courage and for receiving gifts from others have come from. The virtue for receiving from the stranger is a presiding one for this *paideia*.

•

I have only begun to develop a liberation alternative to the field coverage principle. If nothing else, an adequate liberation *paideia* must offer an alternative to (or a radicalizing of) the "add-on" of perspectives and courses in order to avoid the continual "cafeteria counter" curriculum, that Graff calls "a product of democratic expansion of traditions and perspectives" that represents political deals and (sometimes) the refusal to face the conflictual nature of different perspectives. If *theologia* is formation, we must form a liberation character to replace a *Wissenschaft* approach to the marginalized as a subject matter, which only increases the course requirements of an education.

It is true that different perspectives and increasing numbers of marginalized representatives are crucial to move theological education toward liberationist ends. The kind of habituation I am suggesting could not happen without some diverse student-faculty population. However, the site of theological education is *not* that of politics, where social change is accomplished merely by representatives. A theological proposal regarding marginalized population cannot be made in the same terms as democratic, representation issues. More to the point, the kind of pluralism that seeks balance of perspectives is distortive of a theological vision. Balance is an ideal that ignores the very theological reason for attending to the marginal. The preferability of transformation as a model for theological learning over *Wissenschaft* is the reason that *theologia* has potential for liberationist pedagogy. In my view, such judgments can only be relative. Since one is never free of cultural production, one can only be habituated into better postures toward the Other, never final positions.

I have argued for a kind of vision, or a part of a vision, of theological formation. I have not offered the pedagogical strategy that might put such a liberation *paideia* into place in any particular institution. I have offered hints — the formation of capacities for conflict and courage, receiving from the "Other" when the other is constructed out of a class, race, or gendered story quite differently from one's own. Current field education programs or special "third world experiences" may appear to get at what I am describing, but not completely.

If students' habituation into the virtues necessary for hearing into speech the "Other" or of receiving from the Other and taking on the lifelong struggles with power structures were serious qualification for excellence in our current theological institutions, grade sheets would look quite different, that is, if grade sheets were capable of registering such excellences at all.

NOTES

1. Gerald Graff, *Professing Literature: An Institutional History* (Chicago: University of Chicago Press, 1987), 1–15; for the opening quote, see ibid., 1. Also his "Teach the Conflicts," *South Atlantic Quarterly* 89, no. 1 (Winter 1990): 51–67.

2. Beginning with his widely respected book *Theologia: The Fragmentation and Unity of Theological Education* (Philadelphia: Fortress Press, 1983) and later with *The Fragility of Knowledge: Theological Education in the Church and the University* (Philadelphia: Fortress Press, 1988), Farley initiated a lively conversation about theological education that has resulted in a number of consultations and books. A few of those include Charles Wood, *Vision and Discernment* (Atlanta: Scholars Press, 1985); Joseph C. Hough, Jr., and Barbara G. Wheeler, eds., *Beyond Clericalism: The Congregation as a Focus for Theological Education* (Atlanta: Scholars Press, 1988); Joseph C. Hough, Jr., and John Cobb, *Christian Identity and Theological Education* (Chico, Calif.: Scholars Press, 1985); David Kelsey, *Between Athens and Berlin: The Theological Education Debate* (Grand Rapids Mich.: William B. Eerdmans, 1993), and *To Understand God Truly: What's Theological about a Theological School?* (Louisville: Westminster John Knox Press, 1992).

3. See *Theologia*, 151–203. For the modes of understanding, see *Fragility of Knowledge*, 135–62. As Hough and Wheeler point out, there has been a notable enthusiasm for a number of Farley's claims, such as the critique of the clerical paradigm. See Hough, Wheeler, *Beyond Clericalism*. Some criticisms of Farley's proposal are simply complaints about the book he has not written. David Kelsey's very careful critique of his proposal asks if Farley's privileging of a kind of critical dialectical thinking is finally integrated clearly enough with an account of the soteriological nature of *theologia* and the sense in which it is a formative *habitus*, disposition to *do* something. I will not treat his proposal in such a nuanced way. See *Between Athens and Berlin*, 101–34.

4. Kelsey, *To Understand God Truly.* This description may be closer to Kelsey's ideal than what Farley actually says. I take its inspiration to be from Farley, however.

178

MARY McCLINTOCK FULKERSON

5. There is much enthusiasm for viewing theological education as a "form of Christian practice." See Ellen T. Charry, "Academic Theology in Pastoral Perspective," *Theology Today* 50, no. 1 (April 1993): 90–104. Also Randy L. Maddox, "The Recovery of Theology as a Practical Discipline," *Theological Studies* 51 (1990): 650–72.

6. Graff discusses the problem with regard to the challenge to "the canon" in the field of literature. See "Teaching the Conflicts."

7. Some form of the practice of social criticism or change is recognized by Farley, Kelsey, and Dykstra. It is clearly not the formation of capacities for resistance. See Kelsey, *To Understand God Truly*, 118–30. Dykstra lists social criticism, among others: "Reconceiving Practice," in *Shifting Boundaries: Contextual Approaches to the Structure of Theological Education*, ed. Barbara Wheeler and Edward Farley (Louisville: Westminster John Knox Press, 1991), 48. See Farley, *Ecclesial Reflections: An Anatomy of Theological Method* (Philadelphia: Fortress Press, 1982), 248–58.

8. In other words, I do not take Farley's focus on the cognitive structure of *theologia* to be the most promising aspect of his work for the creation of a liberation *paideia*. See my criticism of the problematic unity of *theologia* in "Theological Education and the Problem of Identity," *Modern Theology* 7, no. 5 (October 1991): 465–82.

9. Kelsey and Dykstra use MacIntyre's definition to develop *theologia* as habituation. See Kelsey, *To Understand God*, 118–24; Dykstra, "Reconceiving Practice." Also MacIntyre, *After Virtue: A Study in Moral Theory*, 2d ed. (Notre Dame, Ind.: University of Notre Dame Press, 1984), 181–225.

10. In contemporary Christian ethics *habitus* has been developed in terms of the formation of Christian character — a subject associated with ethicists like Stanley Hauerwas. An alternative to decisionist and principled ethics, the turn to virtue and character formation resonates with a strong contemporary mood in theology to resist modernity and liberalism and reclaim community, tradition, and identity.

11. MacIntyre, *After Virtue*, 187–88.

12. Ibid.

13. See Frances Fox Piven and Richard A. Cloward, *Poor People's Movements: Why They Succeed and How They Fail* (New York: Vintage Books, 1979). Forms of social protest are found in grass-roots organizations that work on issues of global injustice from a local angle. Some are Christian, some are not or marginally so; some are more explicitly adversarial toward the state, some are only implicit with their politics.

14. Oswald Schwemmer, "Habitus," *Sacramentum Mundi*, 3:1.9

15. *After Virtue*, 208.

16. Thus defined, intelligible action is a category that requires the linguistic construal of human behavior, for to have reasons is to be able to communicate. Hauerwas makes the point that this is distinctively linguistic to prevent the primacy of the agent's perspective from producing a subjectivist or individualist account of character and responsibility. See his *Vision and Virtue: Essays in Christian Ethical Reflection* (Notre Dame: University of Notre Dame Press, 1981), 56–57; and *Character and the Christian Life: A Study in Theological*

Ethics, Trinity University Monograph Series in Religion (San Antonio: Trinity University Press, 1985), xxiii.

17. *After Virtue,* 208, 213. Hauerwas agrees with MacIntyre on this. Consciousness is the skill or "ability to place our action within an intelligible narrative" (*Character,* xx, xxii).

18. This is MacIntyre's example (*After Virtue,* 210). Although a tradition, on his terms, is a history of *arguments,* MacIntyre does think it has boundaries for acceptable (intelligible) questions.

19. *After Virtue,* 207–8. Hauerwas refuses the notion of a self standing free from or prior to its actions. The agent is a basically social self, and a moral self is such because it is linguistically and corporately produced (*Character and the Christian Life,* 29–34), although he also says with regard to Aristotle's *Ethics,* "for Aristotle to be a man means that a person can be the source of his own actions, forming them in accordance with his own particular purposes" (ibid., 45).

20. Hauerwas distinguishes purpose and intention. Animals can be said to act purposefully; human beings do so and have intentions, reasons, for which they can be held accountable (*Vision and Virtue,* 56–58). The agent supplies the description and is necessary to it.

21. MacIntyre, *After Virtue,* 217. The unity of a self is found in the unity of a character (not on the "psychological continuity or discontinuity of the self").

22. *After Virtue,* 218. See Wesley Kort's quarrel with monothematic accounts of the features of narrative: *Bound to Differ: The Dynamics of Theological Discourse* (University Park: Pennsylvania State University Press, 1992), 125–34. For opposite accounts of a self postmodern images come to mind — the schizophrenic, the assemblages of Gilles Deleuze and Felix Guattari, or the "view from nowhere" of some poststructuralism.

23. Thus Hauerwas is right to reject too Kantian an approach to the subject and agrees that the intent may be complex and is socially constructed. See his new introductory reflections in *Character,* xiii–xxxiii.

24. See the work of Myles Horton, founder of Highlander Center, with Paulo Freire, *We Make the Road by Walking: Conversations on Education and Social Change* (Philadelphia: Temple University Press, 1990).

25. I draw this example from a story told by Kelly Jarrett about a young thirteen-year-old girl who was a victim of sexual abuse and the courts. Jarrett relates MacIntyre's definition of the primacy of intention and the narrative unity of a life to the broken life of this child victim of sexual abuse, who fell through the cracks of the judicial system and was tossed from one foster home to another ("The Act of Not-Seeing: Alasdair MacIntyre from the Margins," paper presented at the American Academy of Religion, November 1991).

26. I am pushing the question, which apparently Aristotle did not. Aristotle considered that a certain social status was necessary for one to be a candidate for a virtuous life. This self cannot be defined outside of a community and its discourses in their intersection with the social order.

27. Hauerwas, *Character and the Christian Life.*

28. To put it another way, those goods are not goods which are "external" to the activity. External goods such as money are rarely associated with social

activism. The Civil Rights movement resulted in risks and losses for those who participated. The Highlander Center is a minimally funded organization. Simple lifestyle is the order of the day and important to a way of being with the marginalized mountain people of Tennessee and the larger Appalachian region.

29. This is not a primarily religious organization. However, Myles Horton's commitment to social change was fueled by Christian faith. See his *We Make the Road*, and Horton, with Judith Kohl and Herbert Kohl, *The Long Haul: An Autobiography* (New York: Anchor Books, 1990).

30. The standard definition of virtue in the Aristotelian-Thomist tradition requires that a virtue be the kind of excellence determined by the end of human being, and an internal relationship exists between the acquisition of a virtue, and the good to which it habituates one. Virtue is "a quality which enables an individual to move towards the achievement of the specifically human *telos*, whether natural or supernatural" (*After Virtue*, 185). For the difference between internal goods, which I describe here, and external goods, see ibid., 187–99.

31. Farley, *Ecclesial Reflection: An Anatomy of Theological Method* (Philadelphia: Fortress Press, 1982). Thomas Ogletree uses "hospitality to the stranger" as the metaphor for the moral life. See his *Hospitality to the Stranger: Dimensions of Moral Understanding* (Philadelphia: Fortress Press, 1985).

32. Hauerwas, *After Christendom: How the Church Is to Behave if Freedom, Justice, and a Christian Nation Are Bad Ideas* (Nashville: Abingdon Press, 1991), 93–111.

33. How does an account of *habitus* for forming us come to terms with such realities as what Beverly Harrison calls the "theoretically conditioned ineptitude" that leaves women out? The habit of "not seeing" certain groups is culturally produced since birth in certain communities (Harrison, "Toward a Christian Feminist Liberation Hermeneutic for Demystifying Class Reality in Local Congregations," in *Beyond Clericalism*, 142, n. 16). These ineptitudes also characterize us with regard to race and class dispositions.

34. Katie G. Cannon speaks of the "functional prudence" of the slave woman, a sense of balance, "quiet grace," wisdom for survival, "unshouted courage" — "a virtue evolving from the forced responsibility of Black women." Such virtues are the "staying power of the Black community wherein individuals act, affirming their humanity, in spite of continued fear of institutionalized aggression." Cannon's position suggests that virtues produced in situations of marginality can alter classic definitions of virtue. She challenges the view that courage is a virtue only when it is not forced by fear, that one must have free will to be courageous. See Cannon, *Black Womanist Ethics* (Atlanta: Scholars Press, 1988), 127, 133, 143–44.

35. Ibid., 144.

⇉· II ·⇇

New Ground
The Foundations and Future
of the Theological Education Debate

DAVID H. KELSEY and BARBARA G. WHEELER

Edward Farley's 1983 book, *Theologia: The Fragmentation and Unity of Theological Education,* is a landmark in the history of North American theological education.[1] It inaugurated an unprecedented stream of essays and monographs on the nature, purpose, and organization of theological study and theological schools. In the decade since *Theologia's* publication, at least fifteen books and several dozen articles have addressed the questions that it introduced.[2]

Theologia provided the template for several features of this new literary subgenre.[3] It set the tone and established the form. Much of the previous writing and public debate about theological education in North America had been highly polemical; often the format was public speeches or articles of opinion in magazines.[4] Several ambitious sponsored studies of theological education were comprehensively reportorial,[5] but with perhaps the single exception of H. Richard Niebuhr's major work, *The Nature of the Church and Its Ministry,*[6] none could be described as scholarly or intellectually provocative.

Theologia is both. It undergirds its criticisms with a painstaking historical analysis of the assumptions that regulate contemporary theological education, and it proposes fundamentally different conceptions of theology and education than are currently in play. The works that have followed in the wake of *Theologia* have the same qualities: they take great analytical care with terms and concepts, and they make serious and sometimes radical constructive proposals, though often along quite different lines than Farley's own.

This shift in the mode of writing, from casual and descriptive treatments to the scholarly and intellectually constructive approach modeled in *Theologia,* has attracted a different group of participants — seminary faculty members — to the public discussion of theological education.

181

Theological scholars, including several distinguished ones, did take part in the periodic comprehensive studies of theological education, but most of the North American debate had been conducted by seminary presidents and church officials. In the recent spate of writing about theological education, that pattern has been reversed. Following the example of Farley, a philosophical theologian who took the time to write a scholarly book about theological education (and subsequently published a second one[7]), a sizable group of seminary professors — systematic and practical theologians, ethicists and historians — have published substantial works on the topic, using the methods of their disciplines. Church and seminary leaders have participated in the ensuing discussions, though more often as reviewers and commentators than as authors and protagonists.

Perhaps *Theologia*'s most important contribution to the form of the new literature on theological education was its definition of the kind of problem that theological education presents. The long North American tradition had been to assume that the nature and purposes of theological education have been established by consensus; the questions and problems that remain are matters of practical application and technique. Farley argues in *Theologia* that this approach is mistaken. The widely observed incoherence of theological education is the result not of a failure to find appropriate educational means but of a profound confusion about ends. The problem of theological education, he contends, is a *theological* one, deeply anchored at the level of assumptions and conceptual structures.

Virtually all the works published after *Theologia* share Farley's assessment: the problems of theological education are essentially theological ones. Like Farley, the writers view theological education as a practice of religious communities. As such it deserves (and because of longstanding neglect of the basic issues in theological education it acutely needs) the kind of theological attention that all religious practices require: scrutiny of basic premises, examination of historical foundations and the coherence of arguments, tests of truth claims, and judgment about what kinds of action are consistent with theological principles and appropriate for the setting in which they are carried out. The writers of the recent period, following the path first cut by *Theologia*, have produced such theological resources in abundance. Their work constitutes something never before available in North America: a body of practical theology focused on theological education.

Theologia redefines the core problem by making three moves. First, it digs down to expose the tangled historical roots of current conceptions of theological education. Then it displays theological education's contemporary incoherence, showing the connections between the jumbled history and perennial complaints and difficulties. Finally, it sketches an

alternative conception (which is further elaborated in sections of Farley's *Fragility of Knowledge*[8]) that is, Farley claims, theologically more
coherent.

Between them, *Theologia* and *Fragility of Knowledge* may be said
to transform the categories in which basic issues bedeviling theological education are commonly analyzed and debated. Not that Farley's
achievement has been to say the last word and end the discussion. On
the contrary, his proposal about how to reconceive theological education
has provoked plenty of disagreement. Nothing published so far, however, has challenged either Farley's explanation of the almost universal
experience of fragmentation or the terms he uses to analyze theological
education's malaise. Indeed, the entire continuing debate about the nature and purposes of theological education-as-such has simply assumed
the cogency and importance of Farley's explanations and categories.

As a result, the assumptions, terms, and categories of the current literature are radically different from those that dominated writing about
theological education before the publication of *Theologia*. The previous literature and much public exchange about theological education
was larded throughout with three slogans: "effective preparation for
the practice of ministry," "the integration of theory and practice," and
"contextual" or "experiential" learning. A wide range of texts — including the papers and reports that led to the establishment of the
new Doctor of Ministry degree, documents of committees of the Association of Theological Schools, standards for programs accreditation,
and evaluations of the numerous "field-based" program experiments
launched during the 1970s[9] — is pervaded by these formulas, which reflect the central themes and assumptions that had not, before Farley,
been seriously challenged.

Taken together and rarely if ever questioned, these themes and assumptions constituted a solid package of conventional wisdom about
theological education that, by and large, rested on three settled convictions: that "theological education" is by definition the education of
future clergy or professional ministers; that ministry is best understood
when analyzed into a set of "functions," such as counseling, preaching,
management, administration, and teaching; and that the movement or
dynamic of theological education is from mastering several bodies of
theory to applying that theory in the practice of ministry's several functions. "Theology," including the theologies of the several books of the
Bible, was assumed to be one of those bodies of theory. Together with
historical studies of the Bible and the church on the theoretical side and
"ministerial" studies on the other, the theological curriculum naturally
fell into four parts, three theoretical and one ministerial or practical.[10]

In this scheme, the solution to most problems, including the fragmentation so widely evident and the educational ineffectiveness so often

charged, was "the integration of theory and practice." As noted earlier, the general view was that this could be accomplished by a change in pedagogical techniques: require students to learn the bodies of theory, including theology, in the context of experience, that is, while actually practicing one or another of the ministerial functions. That way the "relevance" of the theories would be amply clear, the motivation to learn them heightened, and the learning itself deep enough to shape professionally competent performance of the functions.

Farley challenges every feature of this conventional view: the truth of its assumptions, the validity of its way of defining and solving the problem, and the appropriateness of the categories in which both the assumptions and the problem are framed. He shows how the goal of theological education has changed and become progressively less clear over time; he illustrates the confusions among and artificiality of the divisions into which theological study is usually partitioned. And he argues that the conceptual scheme that allows one to contrast "theory" and "practice" in such a way that they stand in need of "integration" is inappropriate to theological education. When the scheme is used, it both obscures and compounds theological education's real difficulties.

Because his critique rests heavily on an identification of the historical sources of the themes and concepts that make up the conventional view, Farley's critical contribution to the new literature on theological education is often characterized, following Foucault,[11] as an "archeology," a term that Farley himself favors. The metaphor serves to describe part of Farley's achievement: he has uncovered the original context of many conceptual "artifacts" of earlier periods that are still used in the current culture of theological education, and he has illuminated the incoherences that arise when those artifacts continue to be pressed into service outside the context of their original functions and meanings. But insofar as "archeology" suggests that what is laid bare is sedimented, compressed, impacted, dead, the image is inadequate. Farley looks not only back to past meanings but deeply into present ones. He shows that theological education may, like a living organism, experience as vague discomfort very serious underlying conditions that are hidden from ordinary view.

A better figure for this aspect of Farley's work is radiography. His examination of theological education discloses shadows and obscurities on its tissues, growths that obstruct important functions, and fragilities and fractures in its skeletal structure. The whole body of educational activities, he demonstrates, is weakened and compromised by previously undiagnosed anomalies and structural flaws.

One deep source of problems that Farley discovers is unrelated, even antagonistic conceptual systems that work side by side in theological education to the same ends, generating great confusion and incoherence. The fourfold structure of studies is, in Farley's account, a center of such confusion. Though Farley is not as dismissively critical of the fourfold structure as he is sometimes read to be (at least as a "formal apparatus," he says, it embodies "something of the natural movement of theological study"[12]), he does portray it as a holding tank for perspectives and systems that contradict each other.

For example, the structure holds in place the residue of the view of religious knowledge and authority that generated it in the first place, a linear pattern of theological movement through four moments: starting with biblical studies, one proceeds through historical studies of how Scripture's witness has been preserved or distorted century by century, to normative doctrinal study of how the witness ought rightly to be conveyed, to study of the church and its mission and in particular the responsibilities, authority, and roles of its ministerial leadership. This pattern of movement is, Farley notes, "pre-critical," and no longer dominant in most North American theological schools.[13] But something of its implicit order hangs on, even while the historical and critical perspectives have transformed the contents and methods of each of the divisions of study. So, for instance, "the texts of Scripture are still thought of as something exegetically interpreted and then applied," even though the results are now obtained by historical methods that do not support such a procedure.[14]

In other ways, however, the pre-critical order no longer operates to pull the pieces together. Theologians are handed exegetical results "like a hot potato," often dropping them to do their own philosophically grounded constructive work, with little reference to proceedings in the other fields. Similarly, historical studies have lost their apologetic character and been transformed by the priority assigned to them in the Enlightenment: because it has the highest standing outside the theological world, history has become the most independent field of the four fields.[15] Practical studies are also largely autonomous, not because their status is high but because their role is "self-evident" in a structure whose overall justification is the training of clergy.[16]

As the pattern for arranging virtually independent fields of study, then, the fourfold pattern is arbitrary. The fields are there simply because they are there and have developed that way. Yet at the same time they imply their earlier order. The result of this inconsistency — the fields are conceived both as related to each other and as unrelated — is deep confusion and educational incoherence.

The confusion is further compounded by another phenomenon that Farley's analysis of the fourfold structure has brought to light. Each of the divisions of the structure, floating to a considerable extent free of the others, is further isolated by a pattern of growths within it that take on a life of their own and impede the proper functioning of the larger processes to which they are supposed to be contributing. Farley calls these growths academic "specialties" or "subspecialties."[17] Specialties are not identical with the fields (Bible, history, theology, practical studies); in subject matter they tend to be subdivisions of those areas (not Bible, not New Testament, but Synoptic Gospel Studies). Nor are they to be identified with one or another of the several disciplines, if "disciplines" are understood as traditions of methods, heuristic models, technical terms, bodies of theory, and consensus about what counts as relevant data and strong argument in dealing with theoretical and practical problems. Rather, academic specializations often employ several different disciplines in academic study of a relatively narrow range of subject matter.

Academic specializations bring with them a series of difficulties. Though they may be interdisciplinary, they are intellectually insular, resisting generalizations that connect them to other inquiries. Thus they contribute to the isolation to the field areas in which they cluster. Even more troubling, they tend to take on a life of their own, generating unique criteria that determine both agendas for research and the status of scholars, quite apart from any criteria rooted outside the specialization in, say, the larger concerns of theological education. And because they determine research agendas and scholarly status, the specialty fields also shape teaching, orienting it to their own current scholarly agenda. Consequently, the specialty fields, though ostensibly present in theological education in the service of bringing resources for rigorous self-criticism to the studies that shape students' theological capacities, tend rather to obstruct that process by diverting attention to themselves.

The specializing process is most visible in the three fields usually labelled "academic" or "theoretical." It also operates in the practical field area, though in somewhat different form. Practical studies have been narrowed in the first instance by what Farley calls the clerical paradigm, which limits all concerns about practice to those of professional clergy.[18] The contemporary North American version of this paradigm further specifies the picture of clergy leadership as a functionalist one organized by ministerial tasks, each of which becomes the basis for a subspecialty, though on a rather different basis (function rather than subject matter) than the subspecialties in "academic" fields.[19] Many of the consequences are the same: the subspecialties further splinter the already fragmented fourfold arrangement of studies. One consequence, however, is especially damaging. Because clergy training is taken to be self-evidently the purpose of the whole of theological education as well as its practical field division, the activities of the other three fields are cast, in typical professionalist and functionalist fashion, as "theory" in relation to clerical practice. This is both a profound distortion of practical studies, which in their current form are laden with theories of all kinds, and an alarming reduction of the purposes of all kinds of theological studies to narrow clerical ends.

Farley's thorough probe under theological education's skin thus discloses very serious reasons for the symptom of fragmentation: a rigid structural arrangement, partly arbitrary, partly anachronistic, each division of which houses autonomous enterprises that usually ignore but sometimes distort the activities in the other divisions. Farley's contribution does not, however, end there. He further offers diagnosis at a deeper level and a constructive proposal related to it.

The deeper diagnosis is that, as a cognitive enterprise, theological education's skeletal structure is fragile. This is not the result of some earlier trauma. The structure of *all* efforts to know is inherently fragile.[20] Every inquiry must distort its object of knowledge by abstracting it from its concrete setting in order to focus just on it. This can be corrected by subsuming the results of specialized research under larger "perspectives" on all knowledge that offer synoptic interpretations in which the objects of knowledge are returned to their larger settings. But it is tragically easy to fail to do this, and the result is a deformity of knowing. Farley shows that under pressure theological education's fragile knowledge structure has in fact fractured.

The fracture happens like this. Theological education is genuinely *theological* only insofar as it aims at *theologia,* that wisdom that is achieved as faith seeks rigorous understanding. Using the medieval term for a character trait or disposition to act in a distinctive way that can be learned, Farley characterizes *theologia* as a *habitus.* "Faith" is the way in which human beings live "in and toward God and the world under the impact of redemption."[21] Faith is inherently cognitive in a prereflective way that seeks to become rigorously reflective understanding, i.e., *theologia.* The process of achieving this is theological education.

By Farley's constructive account in *Theologia,*[22] this process has a structure composed of four moments. First, the complex of images, stories, doctrines, and forms of communal life that mediate redemption to the person in faith — faith's mythos — must be identified ("thematized") so that they can be used to illumine the social and cultural situation in which the person lives. Second, the truth and possible ideological captivity of the dominant values and convictions of that very situation must be rigorously tested lest they be uncritically accepted as criteria of the intelligibility and truth of faith's mythos. Then, third, the mythos itself must also be rigorously tested for truth and ideological oppressiveness.

In each of these three moments, rigor is provided by use of appropriate academic disciplines. Thematization requires the resources of historical studies (including historically conducted biblical studies). Testing the mythos for truth and ideology calls into play the resources of theology and ethics. Testing the social and cultural situation for truth and ideology invokes the social sciences, many of which, it should be noted, are not present in curricula of most schools, because they have no assigned place in the fourfold scheme.

But even if all the disciplinary resources were at hand and the moments of rigor were to become the touchstones of a new, self-consciously theological structure such as Farley proposes, this movement from faith's pre-reflective cognition to *theologia*'s rigorously won wisdom would be a vicious circle, with the normative claims of the cultural and social situation and the central themes of faith's mythos relativizing each other. The specialized knowledge achieved in each of the first three moments is distorted until placed back into a more comprehensive interpretive context. What is needed is a fourth moment in the structure of theological education that discerns concerning faith's mythos how it expresses enduring truth about the presence of God and concerning the situation how "God undergirds it, pervades it, disposes it, lures it to its best possibilities."[23] This moment is achieved when movement through the entire structure is guided by the overarching goal of cultivating *theologia* in persons of faith.

But that is precisely what conventionally does not happen in theological education. In conventional practice, the movement of theological education is guided only by two much more limited goals that have little relation to each other: the goal of cultivating capacities for doing well the forms of disciplined inquiry that make each of the first three moments rigorous, and the goal of equipping people with a set of skills needed to fill clergy functions. In this way theological education, unbound by any overarching aim of cultivating the wisdom that faith inherently seeks, is fractured and experienced as fragmented.

The core difference that Farley has made here lies in the definition of "theological" in the phrase "theological education." Conventional wisdom assumed, as Farley made clear in his unmasking of the clerical paradigm, that "theology" is the revelation-based theory to be applied when engaged in professional ministry. Though Farley favors and advocates the preparation of professionally competent clergy[24] (a goal that, he argues, the clerical paradigm does not accomplish[25]), this reduction of theology is unacceptable to him. In its place he has retrieved the classical definition of theology by reference to God and knowledge of God.

The parties to the debates about theological education do not all agree with the material content of Farley's own ways of talking about God and theology. Far from it: the ensuing literature can be read as a series of competing proposals for how to specify what should be theological about theological education. But all seem to have accepted Farley's critical argument and constructive starting point. With him, they agree that it is a serious mistake to frame the basic issues of theological education in a way that defines "theological" by reference to clergy functions rather than to God. With him, they are convinced that it is a further mistake to consider theology a type of theory that needs to be applied to practice rather than a type of wisdom that forms persons' lives. By seeing more deeply into the structural fracture that underlies theological education's fragmentation, Farley has undercut conventional wisdom's view that the problem of fragmentation arises, and can be overcome, at the point at which theology is brought to ministerial functions as a body of theory to be applied to practice.

•

Despite the magnitude of Farley's critical and constructive achievement — an achievement compounded by a diverse group of other writers who build their own proposals on the foundation of redefined terms and reconceived categories that Farley has laid — the discussion of theological education outside the circle of writers and their critics has changed very little. It would be unrealistic, of course, to expect massive programmatic change in the short space of a decade, especially because most of the new proposals have not included specific suggestions about curriculum and other pragmatic educational topics. Recognizing the great differences among seminaries and thus the small chance that any specific educational design would fit any particular school, the writers have focused their criticisms of the present and recommendations for reform at the level of concepts and principles that are likely to be invoked in any local attempt at educational reform. Their goal has been to change the conceptual environment in which activities like curriculum revision are conducted, unraveling old conventions and offering new materials for the unique program-making work of particular schools. This effort has not, so far, been a success. When theological educators meet as faculties or denominational committees to discuss educational issues confronting their particular theological schools, they still employ the old binary rhetoric of theory/practice, academic/professional, head/heart, knowledge/skills — dualisms that Farley and other writers have shown to be sources of rather than solutions to theological education's perennial problems. There remains a stubborn gap between the theoretical literature about theological education and the terms and concepts that structure the discussions of theological educators who are engaged in evaluating or recasting important parts of their school's educational program.[26]

Why does this gap persist? Why do stale terms and notions that have been effectively demolished retain their power to dominate the debate? Why don't new terms and images that have the potential to refresh the discussion receive much attention? We suggest three reasons.

The recent literature on theological education has often been misunderstood. This body of work has proved difficult to read and digest.

Most of the authors are, like Farley, trained in historical and systematic theology, and their literary products are serious scholarship in that field. As we have noted, this is one of the cardinal virtues of the recent writing, but it is also a painful limitation, since the technical complexities of the scholarship seem to have obstructed communication across the lines of fields and disciplines and opened the way for several misconstruals.

Two common misreadings of the literature illustrate how difficult it is to reuse familiar terms, even if the new use is really a restoration of former meanings. The prominence of "theology" in this literature as the recommended goal of theological education has created the misimpression that these works advocate the hegemony of "academic" over "practical" studies. All the restructuring and the renaming of segments of the structure of studies (usually as one or another type of theology — "historical theology," "philosophical theology," "practical theology," etc.) are viewed by some as screens for a plot to privilege academic theology; and the theological reorientation of theological education as a whole prompts fear of a takeover by the fields that have traditionally been identified as "theoretical," because it is those fields that the term theology now colloquially designates.

The intent of Farley and most of the other writers seems to be quite different from — even contrary to — the motives some suspect. In their narratives of the fragmentation of theological education, contemporary academic theology, divided as it is into free-wheeling pedagogical fields that themselves are balkanized into independent subspecialties, is the villain, not the savior. As we have tried to show in our account of Farley's disclosure of theological education's deepest flaws, the new literature portrays theology in this sense as an impediment to *theologia,* which is theology defined again as it once was, as wisdom about God that should orient and lend its inherent structure to theological education.

The word "practice" creates a similar misapprehension. The term is pivotal in several proposals that reject Farley's contention that faith has an essential, inherent structure on which *theologia* can be modeled.[27] Instead, these proposals suggest, theological coherence — a truer understanding of God, in David Kelsey's phrase — can be achieved by inquiries into the practices of Christian communities. The emphasis on practice and practices in these proposals has created anxiety about whether the kind of theological education they describe is intellectually serious. Because "practice" has long been associated with the functionalist view of professional ministry and with clinical and field-based educational activities designed to teach "skills" for ministerial tasks, practice-oriented proposals raise fears that the kinds of intellectual rigor traditionally linked with studies in the "theoretical" fields of the curriculum will be slighted.

Again, the authors are being misread. The new literature on theo-

logical education is as deeply critical of the current conventional understanding of "practice" as it is of the current conventional understanding
of "theology." Like many other contemporary writers, the authors of
practice-oriented proposals deplore the technological, ahistorical and individualistic features of the conventional definition of practice. In its
place, they mount a picture of practices as the historically embedded,
theory-laden activities that are constitutive of communities. Theological
education in the practice-oriented proposals is learning practices in this
sense. Such learning does entail some kind of participation in practices,
but its focal point in all the proposals is rigorous critical inquiry, using
the resources of a wide range of disciplines, into the origins and truth of
practices and their appropriateness to their current context.[28] Far from
dispensing with rigorous intellectual proceedings, the practice-oriented
proposals bring them to bear on practice in ways that the reigning functional approach to practice, which locates "theory" and critical inquiry
elsewhere, systematically excludes.

   Another kind of misunderstanding attends the notion of structure.
Here the problem is not the persistence of older meanings but the fact
that the term has a double referent. The fourfold structure describes
the usual pattern of administrative units — fields or departments — into
which seminary faculties are divided. The structure also has a conceptual
dimension: it defines the constituent parts of an adequate theological
education.

   The new literature on theological education focuses on the structure
of studies in the second sense. Farley devoted most of *Theologia* to
demonstrating that the structure is an aggregate of conflicting systems
and concepts that has no unity or order. Other writers, convinced by
the demonstration, simply assume that a new conceptual structure of
theological education is required. Very often, however, criticisms of the
fourfold *conceptual* structure and the calls for its replacement have been
read as proposals for a new arrangement of fields and departments. The
administrative manifestation of the fourfold structure is more obvious
than the conceptual one; therefore it is often supplied by readers as the
referent for the term whenever the fourfold division is mentioned.

   Misinterpreted in this way, the critical dismantling of the fourfold
structure has created frustration and confusion among some readers,
who point out that prospects are dim for replacing the four fields with
some other departmental pattern in even a single school, let alone in
theological and religious studies as a whole. Most people are convinced
that it can't be done — certainly not all at once, and maybe ever. So
what, they ask, would these writers have us do? What is the point to
thoroughly undermining something that is unlikely to change?

   The critics of the fourfold structure would probably agree — indeed,
some have explicitly said — that the table of faculty organization is un-

likely to be modified any time soon.[29] Further, Farley suggests, the inherent fragility of all knowledge makes it likely that any new administrative arrangement, along with the new conceptual structure that justifies it, would shortly absolutize and thus distort, constrict, and fragment the unifying ideas that called it into being. These factors, however, create rather than obviate the need to lay bare the inadequacies of the structures we have. Precisely because all knowledge and organizational structures that house knowledge have this tragic, self-undoing quality combined with great staying power, criticism of the structures of knowledge is essential. Without such criticism, they retain a power to shape theological education's patterns of thought and activity that they do not deserve.

One reason, then, that the new literature on theological education has had limited impact is that some of its sharpest points have been blunted by misreading. Because of the technical density of some of the writing, because familiar meanings cling to terms long after new meanings have been proposed, and because the concrete referents of terms often supplant the abstract ones, many readers have drawn from these works messages nearly the opposite of those the authors appear to be sending. Often, in fact, readers take away from the literature messages that sound greatly like the conventional wisdom that the literature aims to undercut.

The new literature on theological education needs to be supplemented by another kind of scholarship. A second means of bridging the gap between the new literature and conventional thinking about theological education may be another kind of writing. In *Saving Work,* a text on theological education written from a feminist perspective, Rebecca Chopp calls for a "second generation" literature to supplement the work of Farley, Kelsey, and other writers.[30] Chopp characterizes the publications to date as "ideational": they strive to "get the idea of theological education correct, to understand appropriately and adequately the idea of theological education before [turning] to the subjects, to the reality of church, and to patterns of Christian symbolic practice."[31] Such "formal" quests for "a unity above or beyond the fragmentation and pluralism" are, in Chopp's view, valuable for feminists as well as others, but they are not enough.[32] Something further is needed: a literature that "return[s] to the controversial issue of concreteness and attempts to discern the historical, cultural and symbolic factors at work in present theological education."[33]

This literature should be, Chopp argues, Utopian, but in a different sense than Kelsey and Farley use when they apply this label to their work. The works to date are "ironic" critiques and constructions, deliberately unrealistic and distant from the way things actually are.[34] Chopp proposes a disciplined search for "the utopian" that is already present, at least in anticipation, in today's educational patterns and practices.

She suggests that Utopian visions are not made out of nothing: their shape and direction are prefigured, or at least intimated, in "emergent" new practices, changes now underway though not widely recognized. She illustrates the point by describing some new feminist "practices" of theological education that, she argues, not only represent a response to the crisis of fragmentation that Kelsey and Farley have described but may, in fact, have helped to identify the crisis, to make it visible and sensible, and may also have stimulated the search for some unifying alternatives.[35]

If Chopp is correct — if diagnosis of current problems and imagination of new possibilities are catalyzed by exposure to practices that have already begun to change — then an additional kind of research on theological education is required: studies that describe the practices of schools in thick detail. The new literature to date of course includes some descriptions of the current state of theological education, but they are highly general accounts of transinstitutional phenomena. To fill out and specify these phenomenological descriptions, there should also be full-scale ethnographies that portray processes of teaching and learning and the institutional cultures in which they are embedded in actual schools.[36] Some of the distance between the theological visions of the new literature and the efforts of actual faculties to make educational decisions may be covered by richly descriptive studies that show that more powerful patterns of theology and education are already partly present in the work that theological educators do every day.

Such studies may have an impact on attitudes toward educational change as well as ideas for it. Radical revisions of educational programs are rarely attempted because even the prospect of doing so many things differently is exhausting and because the benefits of investing so much new effort cannot be guaranteed. If it can be shown, however, that new goals and means of reaching them are to some extent already grounded in the ways things are being done now, the path to change may seem more sure and the will to attempt change may be easier to summon.

There are conceptual gaps in the current literature on theological education. A third reason that the new literature on theological education has had minimal impact on most people's thinking about theological education is, we think, that it has failed to address some topics that might connect its critical and constructive arguments to the kinds of questions that theological schools regularly have to address. The most important unattended topic is anthropology. Everyone agrees that theological education aims to shape *persons*, often for the purpose of leadership for the churches. But rarely is there awareness, much less critical analysis, of the views of human personhood that undergird pictures of church leadership and how to educate for it. On this count, the new literature, conscientious as it is at other points about defining terms and stating premises, is not much more explicit than everyday discussions have been.

Our goal in the remainder of this essay is to tease out the anthropological assumptions of the new literature and the usual ways of talking about theological education. This will be a very general attempt. Our intent is to begin rather than complete a discussion of the difference that careful attention to these matters might make to thinking about and doing theological education.

The anthropology implicit in the conventional wisdom about theological education as intellectually serious professional education seems to be that of the *affectively moved rational performer*. This is an "objective" view of persons that, on inspection, proves to be thoroughly individualistic, largely utilitarian, and basically ahistorical.

The anthropology is constructed like this. As professional education, theological education's aim is to prepare people to fill competently the functions of Christian ministry. These functions are pieces of behavior that can be described in an objective way from an observer's standpoint. Their goal, by and large, is a change in the state of feelings, beliefs, or will of another person (crude examples: feeling forgiven, believing that God is just, willing to keep the sixth commandment). These goals or ends of ministerial functions may be thought of as objective values to which ministers are committed as part of their faith framework. Any actual performance of any of these behaviors can then be evaluated as to its competence or effectiveness. Indeed, at least in principle, it ought to be possible to devise instruments by which to test people's capacities to perform these behaviors effectively. Professional education aims to help future church leaders acquire the skills they need in order to perform these behaviors effectively in ways that meet standards of professional excellence.

At the same time, as "intellectually serious," theological education's aim is to prepare future church leaders to know how to maximize their effectiveness rationally. To maximize effectiveness, a church leader needs to be able to assess the historical and cultural context in which she seeks to perform ministerial functions and to grasp historical and cultural theory that will help her function more rationally. She also needs to be able to assess the psychological and social dynamics of the people on whom she seeks to have an effect; a grasp of psychological and sociological theory will help her function more rationally in that respect. She has other "theoretical" needs to undergird her ministerial performance: for historical theory that will help her to understand the dynamics of the community of faith she is to lead; for theological and biblical insights that illuminate the goals of ministry. In every respect, "reason," the acquisition and use of bodies of theory, is instrumental to achieving the goals sought by performing ministerial functions. Intellectual seriousness consists in knowing bodies of theory and how to apply them to the practice of ministerial functions.

This is not to say that the conventional view of theological education is "intellectualistic," an anthropology that privileges mind over heart. Far from it. Understood instrumentally, "reason" may be a means to greater effectiveness, but it does not explain sustained engagement in the performance of ministerial functions. It is the intensity of her Christian experience, the depth of her religious feelings, the passion of her commitment to Christian beliefs that explain that. The assumption here is that the affective and volitional states of persons are related to their behavior as a cause is related to its effect. "Mind" may guide a church leader in her performance of ministerial functions, but it is "heart" that moves her, causes her to engage in those performances in the first place. Hence it is of utmost importance that an intellectually serious professional education of church leaders also persistently test and nurture the hearts of future leaders.

This is an anthropology, then, that sees persons in social groupings but does not see interpersonal relations as constitutive in any way of personhood. It sees persons set into historical and cultural context but does not see historical or cultural dynamics as constitutive in any way of personhood. It sees persons as embodied but does not see bodiliness as making any difference to personhood other than imposing limitations on the range of possible behavior. It sees persons as rational beings but rationality as wholly instrumental. It sees persons as emotional and volitional beings whose affects and wills cause their behavior. At its deepest level, it sees persons as objective units of reality set in networks of relationships that consist mostly of causing effects upon one another.

This is a stark sketch of the anthropology implicit in commonly used rhetoric about theological education, one that would, no doubt, be nuanced considerably if someone were to outline a defense of the conventional view (an attempt that has never, as far as we know, been made). We are convinced, however, that the basic themes would remain those we have identified. These themes provide a sharp contrast with the anthropologies that seem to lurk in the new literature that Farley pioneered.

We find two anthropologies in the new literature. Most of the texts presuppose one or the other or, like Farley's work, contain elements of both, though we shall outline the anthropologies, again starkly, without exegetical illustrations from anyone's work on theological education. One of these anthropologies sees human persons basically as *agents;* the other presents them as *expressive subjects.*

The view of persons as agents, which has deep philosophical roots in an intellectual tradition that moves from Aristotle though the medieval "Thomist synthesis" to certain strands in Anglo-American analytical

philosophy, takes the capacity for intentional action to be the distinguishing mark of human personhood. As living bodies, persons are
capable of a large variety of types of behavior. Much of it is bodily
movement, that is, behavior that can be adequately described from a
spectator's standpoint and explained by reference to causes other than
the person himself (just as the person is described in the rational performer view). Thus far, however, the behavior is not yet properly human
or personal. Properly personal behavior is bodily intentional action, action that can be adequately described only by reference to an intention
about which the agent himself is the final authority. Description of such
behavior is adequate only when it includes a first-person account from
the agent's own perspective.

Such behavior is not explained by reference to causes other than
the agent. It is explained by reference to the agent herself: "I, Mary,
did it" is the ground for saying "Mary caused it." Intentions are not
mental causes of which actions are the physical effects. Conceptually
speaking, causes and effects must be capable of being described and
identified in complete independence of each other. But an action can be
described and identified only by reference to its intention, and an intention is by definition an intention to "this" action. Here the body need
not be played off against some other causally effective (and perhaps
non-material, "spiritual") reality. It is the agent herself as a psycho-
somatically complex but integral unity that is terminal in the order of
explanation of, and in the order of accountability for, the action.

Two thematic features of this view are especially prominent in the
new literature. They infect a wide range of proposals, both those that
take their theological cues from ideas about the structure of faith and
those that view the practices of religious communities as central in the
restoration of *theologia*. One of these themes is culture. Agent's capacities for intentional action, in this view, is but one type of capacity among
many types of capacity for response to their physical and social settings:
responses in feelings, in imaginings and fantasies, in thought and in the
formation of beliefs, and in talk as well as action, and all of them are
conceptually formed, in a broad sense of "conceptual." That is, each
of them is made determinately the feeling, thought, image, belief, intentional action that it is in a way that can be communicated by some
culture's ordinary "language," whether of words or of significant ges-
tures and practices. Thus location in a culture and in the society whose
culture it is is the logically prior condition of being an agent. Cultural
location and social relationships are constitutive of being a person, in
this view, and not extrinsic or accidental.

Accordingly, when a person acquires radically new conceptual capacities, the person's reality is radically changed. Such changes cannot be
effected in another directly. Each must acquire it for herself or himself.

What one can do is to encourage it indirectly. It is against this background that it makes sense to see ministerial leadership, not as a set of functions, but as a set of practices comprised of intentional actions given form by the conceptual structure of Christianity and aiming at creating conditions in which others might undergo such deep changes in the conceptual capacities that form their own personhood that they are religiously transformed, liberated, redeemed.

The other important thematic feature of this view has to do with dispositions. An especially significant way in which persons come to be formed is by the acquisition of dispositions to respond, in appropriate circumstances, in consistent and characteristic ways. Admirable dispositions are traditionally called virtues. Persons may acquire dispositions to act under suitable circumstances in courageous or prudent ways (moral virtues), to think in clear or self-critical ways (intellectual virtues), to feel in grateful or in sorrowful ways (affective virtues).

The technical term for such dispositions is *habitus*. It is against the background of this anthropological view that it makes sense to see theological education as *paideia*, the shaping of agents by nurturing in them dispositions to act, think, and experience in ways formed by Christian understanding of God — in short, to see *paideia* as the formation in agents of a *habitus* called *theologia*.

A second anthropological model is in play in the new literature, most prominently the feminist proposals of the Mud Flower Collective and Chopp,[37] though aspects of it also inform Farley's and other work. This model of persons as expressive subjects is associated with otherwise quite diverse philosophical traditions ranging from absolute idealisms through many existentialisms to transcendental ontologies. In it, two closely interconnected features are definitive of human personhood. On the one hand, persons are subjects, not objects. Although persons may *have* objective bodies, which are items in the spatio-temporal continuum that may be perceived, thoroughly known and (at least in principle!) controlled, persons are, more deeply, systematically elusive centers of consciousness marked by an inexhaustible inwardness and an irrepressible spontaneity that can be known only as it manifests itself. On the other hand, persons do not just accidentally have bodies; it is necessarily by means of their bodies that they are conscious and expressively self-manifesting. So a human person simply *is* the dialectical relationship in which subjectivity manifests itself in an alien, objective medium. A person's identity is an identity-in-difference. Furthermore, since consciousness is always consciousness-of something else, persons are inherently relational. And since self-manifestation is manifestation-to another center of consciousness, subjectivity is inherently inter-subjectivity and subjects are inherently social.

Against this background, it makes sense to understand faith in God as a distinctive mode of subjectivity or inwardness, to see a religious mythos as the objectifying expression of that subjectivity that manifests it, and to see a community of faith as the social matrix in which such subjectivity is evoked and nurtured. Further, this model highlights the danger that, in their objectification of faith's mode of subjectivity, the symbols, narratives, beliefs, practices, and institutions of faith's mythos may more distort than manifest faith's inwardness. It makes sense against this background to say that the central task of church leadership is to guide communities in which faith is nurtured by providing interpretation of the various elements of faith's mythos as well as interpretation of larger social, cultural, and physical contexts in light of that mythos. Accordingly, theological education will be most aptly described as the process of preparing church leaders by equipping them not only to interpret faith's mythos and the world, but also to interpret *critically* in order quickly to identify efforts expressively to manifest faith that in fact simply distort it.

Human person as affectively moved rational performer, as bodied agent, as subject self-manifested in objective media: the first of these anthropological models dominates most everyday discourse about theological education; the other two suffuse the literature that has appeared during the last decade. Perhaps still other models are assumed in the various strands of the current discussion of theological education. The failure on all sides to surface anthropological assumptions is, we think, complicating much of the exchange. At their deepest levels, both theology and education depend on pictures of and theories about human being. Therefore, anthropological clarity, along with more careful reading of the impressive proposals that have already been produced and the development of a contrapuntal literature that describes theological education as it is practiced in actual schools, is essential if the remarkable theological education debate of recent years is to bear fruit in the future.

NOTES

1. Edward Farley, *Theologia: The Fragmentation and Unity of Theological Education* (Philadelphia: Fortress Press, 1983).

2. For bibliographies of this literature, see W. Clark Gilpin, "Basic Issues in Theological Education: A Selected Bibliography," *Theological Education* 25 (Spring 1989): 115–21; and Mark N. Wilhelm, "A Bibliography of Theological Education," *Auburn Studies* (Summer 1993): 15–20.

3. We have published other descriptions of the characteristics of the recent writing on theological education that amplify the brief account that follows. See David H. Kelsey and Barbara G. Wheeler, "Thinking about Theological Education: The Implications of 'Issues Research' for Criteria of Faculty Excellence," *Theological Education* 28 (Autumn 1991): 11–26; and Barbara G.

Wheeler, "Introduction," in Barbara G. Wheeler and Edward Farley, eds., *Shifting Boundaries: Contextual Approaches to the Structure of Theological Education* (Louisville: Westminster John Knox Press, 1991), 7–33. An extensive critical account of the work of Farley and others on theological education appears in David H. Kelsey, *Between Athens and Berlin: The Theological Education Debate* (Grand Rapids, Mich.: William B. Eerdmans Co., 1993), 95–229.

4. Many citations of such items, spanning a period of two centuries, are found among the several thousand entries in Heather F. Day, *Protestant Theological Education in America: A Bibliography* (Metuchen, N.J., and London: American Theological Library Association and Scarecrow Press, 1985).

5. A list of sponsored studies of theological education is provided in Mark N. Wilhelm, "Bibliography," 14.

6. H. Richard Niebuhr, *The Nature of the Church and Its Ministry: Reflections on the Aims of Theological Education* (New York: Harper and Brothers, 1957).

7. Edward Farley, *The Fragility of Knowledge: Theological Education in the Church and the University* (Philadelphia: Fortress Press, 1988). Farley has published other important essays on theological education: "The Reform of Theological Education as Theological Task," *Theological Education* 17 (Spring 1981): 93–117; "Theology and Practice outside the Clerical Paradigm," in Don S. Browning, ed., *Practical Theology: The Emerging Field in Theology, Church, and World* (San Francisco: Harper & Row, 1983), 21–41; "The Passion of Knowledge and the Sphere of Faith: A Study in Objectivity," *Theological Education* 25 (Spring 1989): 9–29; "The Tragic Dilemma of Church Education," in Parker J. Palmer, Barbara G. Wheeler, and James W. Fowler, eds., *Caring for the Commonweal: Education for Religious and Public Life* (Macon, Ga.: Mercer University Press, 1990), 131–45. See also Farley's "The Place of Poetics in Theological Education: A Heuristic Inquiry," and "Music and Human Existence, a Response," both in *Theological Education*, special issue on Sacred Imagination, the Arts and Theological Education, 31, no. 1 (Autumn 1994): 133–48, 175–81.

8. *Fragility of Knowledge*, 103–91.

9. An example is the "Standards for Accrediting" of the Association of Theological Schools, which were drafted in the early 1970s, when theological educators' attention was focused especially on "experiential" education and the new Doctor of Ministry degree. The current version of the "Standards," which reflects relatively minor changes made since that time, is "Standards for Accrediting," *Bulletin of the Association of Theological Schools* 40, no. 3 (June 1992): 23–79. See also "Theological Education in the 1970s: Redeployment of Resources," *Theological Education* 4 (Summer 1968): 757–845; and Celia Alison Hahn, ed., *INTERMET: Bold Experiment in Theological Education* (Washington, D.C.: Alban Institute, 1977), 1–66, 192–214.

10. The placement of social-scientific theoretical studies in this scheme has been a matter of great confusion. Psychology, for instance, which is present in most theological curricula in some form, is acknowledged to have a wide theoretical base, but it is usually taught in courses labelled "practical."

11. Michel Foucault, *The Archeology of Knowledge* (New York: Harper & Row, 1980).

12. *Fragility of Knowledge*, 104.

13. *Theologia*, 138. "Most of these schools have abandoned the deposit-of-revelation approach." This and similar statements have generated a controversy about Farley's work among evangelical readers, some of whom argue that a structure that gives priority to the study of the Bible is not necessarily "pre-critical." See Richard J. Mouw, "Evangelical Reflections on the 'Aims and Purposes' Literature," unpublished paper (New York: Auburn Theological Seminary, 1990); and Robert K. Johnston, "Being Theologically Capacitated," unpublished paper (Pasadena, Calif.: Fuller Theological Seminary, 1992).

14. *Theologia*, 137; *Fragility of Knowledge*, 104–5.

15. Historical perspectives and methods have also, Farley notes, heavily infiltrated biblical and theological studies, though often in ways that the arrangement of studies in the fourfold structure obscures (*Theologia*, 140).

16. *Fragility of Knowledge*, 105.

17. *Theologia*, 139–41.

18. Ibid., 127–31.

19. Ibid., 139–41.

20. *Fragility of Knowledge*, 3–55.

21. *Theologia*, 156.

22. Ibid., 166–68. A five-part scheme of the "interpretive modes" of *theologia* is set forth in *Fragility of Knowledge*, 133–70.

23. *Theologia*, 168.

24. Ibid., 175–77; *Fragility of Knowledge*, 159–62.

25. *Theologia*, 127–28.

26. Between 1982 and 1991, we had the opportunity to observe most of the public discussions of the aims and purposes of theological education that were organized in response to the work of Farley and others. We were working as program evaluators under commission from the Association of Theological Schools and Lilly Endowment, Inc. These two institutions had sponsored many of the writing projects whose results are cited in this essay, as well as the discussions we attended; their leaders, Leon Pacala and Robert W. Lynn respectively, are usually credited along with Farley and the other writers as creators of the new literature. In addition, we were invited to attend a number of faculty discussions of the literature in particular seminaries and divinity schools. Our generalizations about current discussions of theological education are based on these experiences, which are extensively analyzed in Barbara G. Wheeler and David H. Kelsey, "Final Evaluation Report: Lilly Endowment Grants for Theological Education Research," unpublished paper (New York: Auburn Theological Seminary, 1990). We also published our observations in a series of articles in *Theological Education* between 1984 and 1991.

27. There are several constructive proposals that make practice or practices central: Joseph C. Hough, Jr., and John B. Cobb, Jr., *Christian Identity and Theological Education* (Chico, Calif.: Scholars Press, 1985); Craig Dykstra, "Reconceiving Practice," in Barbara G. Wheeler and Edward Farley, *Shifting Boundaries: Contextual Approaches to the Structure of Theological Education*

(Louisville: Westminster John Knox Press, 1991), 35–66; Don S. Browning, *A Fundamental Practical Theology: Descriptive and Strategic Proposals* (Minneapolis: Fortress Press, 1991); Rebecca S. Chopp, *Saving Work: Feminist Practices of Theological Education* (Louisville: Westminster John Knox Press, 1995). Features of the proposals of Charles Wood and David Kelsey also align with the emphasis on practices: Charles M. Wood, *Vision and Discernment: An Orientation in Theological Study* (Atlanta: Scholars Press, 1985); David H. Kelsey, *To Understand God Truly: What's Theological about a Theological School* (Louisville: Westminster John Knox Press, 1992).

28. Dykstra, "Reconceiving Practice," in Wheeler and Farley, eds., *Shifting Boundaries*, 35–66.

29. Dykstra, "Reconceiving Practice," 57.

30. *Saving Work*, 11.

31. Ibid., 9.

32. Ibid., 10.

33. Ibid., 11.

34. Kelsey, *To Understand God Truly*, 16.

35. *Saving Work*, 19–20.

36. The only professional ethnographic study of a theological school is Sherryl Kleinman, *Equals before God: Seminarians as Humanistic Professionals* (Chicago: University of Chicago Press, 1984). There are a few journalistic accounts of seminary life, for instance, Ari L. Goldman, *The Search for God at Harvard* (New York: Ballantine Books, 1992).

37. The Mud Flower Collective, *God's Fierce Whimsy: Christian Feminism and Theological Education* (New York: Pilgrim Press, 1985); Chopp, *Saving Work*.

⇒ 12 ⇐

A Story of Freedom's Corruption

Sin as a Response to the Human Condition

NANCY J. RAMSAY

Pastoral care specialists and pastors daily respond to the suffering that arises from what Edward Farley describes as a tragically structured human condition. In *Good and Evil* Farley carefully delineates the tragic vulnerability of human reality in its personal, relational, and social spheres. He then addresses how sin emerges in response to this vulnerability as well as the possibilities for experiencing redemption. He provides a way of interpreting what is a painful blur at the concrete level of human experience. Farley's careful description of a tragically structured human condition is especially helpful for pastoral theological reflection on human experiences of suffering. His research provides a way to distinguish between the consequences of psychopathology and sin. Such distinctions are vital because each limits and distorts human freedom or agency differently and interactively. Moreover, the language worlds of psychopathology and sin include quite different normative visions for human life and community, though in popular culture they are often conflated.

In this essay we will use Farley's schema for the tragic structure of human reality to interpret a situation in pastoral care. Pastoral theology is a praxis-centered process of theological reflection. It moves from experiences of care to revised critical correlation of theological and behavioral resources in order to enhance both the practice of ministry and theological understanding. As an exercise in pastoral theological method, this essay begins with and revolves around a painful human experience.

Dick is a sixty-year-old Caucasian. He is divorced from his wife because of his admitted molestation of their daughter over a period of several years (age ten–thirteen), which she reported to her mother when a young adult. He had lost his job earlier when charged with indecent public exposure. Dick was reared by his mother after his parents di-

202

vorced. Prior to his marriage to Pat, Dick had a son with Joan, when she was thirteen and he was sixteen, but they did not marry. Dick, himself, is a survivor of sexual abuse. Dick is voluntarily participating in an intensive therapeutic program of recovery related to his sexually abusive behavior. He is also in individual therapy with a licensed clinical social worker. He accepts responsibility for his actions and is learning to identify the feelings and experiences that precipitated his acts of molestation and exposure. He is not currently in contact with his daughter or son, but he hopes for that. He is employed again.

Dick is now worshipping in a Presbyterian church in his new community. Members of the congregation know he is divorced and not in touch with his family. Dick has sought the supportive counsel of his pastor, Steve, as Dick comes to terms with the devastating effects of his behavior for his victims, his guilt and shame, and his efforts to find hope for the future. More details of Dick's experience will unfold in this essay as they would in a pastoral relationship.

Dick's situation presents Steve with a problem. It is clear that psychopathology is present. We have several different therapeutic resources for assessing Dick's situation, which may explore his own history of trauma, the family's dynamics — including his wife's — his lack of impulse control, and the convergence of such dysfunctional preconditions that together may account for Dick's deviant behavior.[1] No theory has won universal acceptance. These theories at best describe for us relevant psychological and relational factors to guide assessment and intervention. They help disclose the tragic vulnerability of human existence and the factors that may combine to yield extraordinarily destructive behavior.

These theories of psychopathology are less helpful in allowing us to explore the moral and ethical dimensions of Dick's behavior. In fact, the language of psychopathology avoids moral or ethical references. This is an important fact, for it signals a danger in conflating the language worlds of psychopathology and sin as is sometimes done in contemporary culture. If they are not the same, how do they differ?

Psychopathology, in varying degrees, diminishes at pre-conscious levels the relative autonomy of the person it affects. That is, it alters those intrapsychic structures by which we perceive and respond to the world so that persons may be less able to respond unselfconsciously and constructively to various situations in their environment. Sin describes the abuse or corruption of freedom. Traditionally sin assumes the formal capacities of freedom as ordinary autonomy. Its concern is rather with freedom as a symbol of life's goal to make life-enhancing, faithful choices — to be the self one is created by God to be. The concept of sin presumes freedom is God's gift, and it projects the ethical language of responsibility and accountability.

We must assess the extent to which victimization has reduced Dick's ability to act freely as well as his agency in corrupting his freedom to "choose life" in the abundance God intends. At stake in pastoral diagnosis is more clarity about how psychopathology and sin limit our freedom differently and how these two phenomena coinhere. This is especially true in a culture whose language often suggests psychopathology is sufficient to explain problematic behavior. Sin rarely appears as a useful or relevant category. Two concerns guide this essay. First, if the bondage that sin and psychopathology impose on our freedom is not the same, it is important to discern how that bondage differs. Second, is the language of sin truthful and helpful for responding to Dick?

Our classical Augustinian paradigm for the doctrine of sin affords Dick's pastor, Steve, crucial guidance in three important ways. First, it asserts that our true fulfillment lies in relationship to our Creator in whose love and justice our freedom finds its compass. Sin is not simply about the violence we do to others and ourselves. It is first a turning away from faithfulness to the One who calls us into life and whose love is the horizon defining our vision for life in communities of mutual respect and care. Awareness of sin casts life in a theocentric light. This theocentric vision is the normative context in which pastoral assessment takes place. Second, awareness of sin reminds us that what is at stake for Dick and for us is ethical accountability in the exercise of freedom. Classical Christian tradition has asserted that human evil arises as rebellion. It is a refusal to entrust our lives to God's care. As such, sin is an absolutization of our own desire for a sense of control or power achieved through idolatrous trust in some mundane good. Once our freedom is so alienated, the self is no longer able to "right its own course." The bondage of sin is thus self-imposed, radical, and progressive. That is, once our trust is shifted away from God, the fear that led to sin can only deepen because no mundane good can secure us. Third, human evil is not the same as our finitude. Evil is not a necessary response to our creatureliness but rather a corruption of the ideal of faithfulness to God and to love that is just, for ourselves and others.

These three claims have immediate implications for Steve's assessment of Dick's predicament. First, to say that awareness of sin casts life in a theocentric light points to the distinctively theological affirmation that sin bespeaks of a vision of faithfulness, prophetic transformation, and love that functions normatively in pastoral practice. The violence and violation woven throughout Dick's story are a tragic distortion of who Dick is called to be and how he is called to live. However, these distortions do not exhaust God's love for Dick or the possibilities for Dick to experience a renewed freedom.

Second, sin implies the possibility of redemption. Moreover, this redemption is not simply restorative. Just as sin underscores accountability

for the abuse of freedom, it also points to the transformative goal implicit in Steve's care for Dick. Steve intends not simply to ease sin's
bondage in Dick's life but to nurture freedom properly directed. The
freedom for love is a correlate of Dick's abuse of freedom and subsequent bondage to sin. But the term "bondage" signifies the radical,
progressive character of sin's effect so that Steve anticipates the way
sin's distortions have metastasized throughout the web of relationships
and experiences that shape Dick's identity. To lose sight of sin's radical and progressive bondage would have Steve vulnerable to Pelagius's
error, which presumes our undiminished freedom to choose rightly.

Third, in separating finitude and human evil, this doctrine helps Steve
avoid confusing the vulnerabilities of Dick's experience of familial and
psychological dysfunction with sin's bondage. Many are those who hear
stories like Dick's and find sociological and psychological explanations
sufficient. Theirs is the contemporary version of the Gnostics who presumed sin was the consequence of finitude.[2] But Steve realizes that while
the vulnerability that these behavioral sciences disclose no doubt interacts with sin's fearful self-securing, Dick's freedom as a human being is
not exhausted by dysfunctional family structures and psychopathology.
Nor does the freedom for love he envisions for Dick exist somehow
apart from or above the contingencies of historical existence. Rather,
it has to do with living ethically in the midst of such vulnerability.
Psychopathology and sin coexist interactively. Even these brief reflections on the guidance available in traditional concepts of sin suggest
that Christian pastors like Steve have important, distinctive, and truthful contributions to offer to persons like Dick and to broader societal
conversations about the roots of our violence against ourselves and
others.

However, there are difficulties in this classical understanding of sin
that require careful, constructive response if it is to prove adequate for
guiding Steve's efforts in Dick's behalf. Our problem begins with Augustine's reliance on a literal interpretation of Genesis and thus on a
historical schema for understanding the emergence of human evil. This
schema obscures the reciprocal influence of various forms of vulnerability and the emergence of sin. Making his way between the Scylla of the
Manicheans and the Charybdis of the Pelagians, Augustine asserted the
origin of human evil as the self-imposed, radical bondage of the will. It
arose as a refusal of finitude, which meant turning away from a fulfilling
experience of God's presence in Eden's paradisiacal setting.

In asserting a period of original righteousness for Adam and Eve in
an idyllic setting, Augustine differentiates creation and human evil, but
he clouds the reality of suffering and temptation as a context for sin's rebellion. In fact he writes: "All evil is the result of sin and punishment."[3]
This focus on voluntarism that helped rebut the fated perspective of his

day with its conflation of finitude and sin meant that his more nuanced passages received less attention. In the *City of God,* for example, he imagines that the first couple, like the angels, were vulnerable to sin in that they could not be certain of the "eternity of their happiness."[4] Later, perhaps in reference to the snake's role, he suggests that all sin began with the lies of the Devil.[5] Calvin also references the "serpent's deceit" of Eve.[6] But, with Augustine, he put the stress on a corruption of the will. A consequence for the Augustinian/Calvinist tradition has been inadequate attention to the tragic context in which sin's corruption of freedom arises.

Related to the problems posed by the concept of original righteousness are the difficulties posed by Augustine's doctrines of original sin and guilt. Augustine's historicism and assertion of a biological transmission of the propensity to sin[7] have made many fail to appreciate this doctrine's continuing relevance. The doctrine of original sin helps us deal with the tensive relation between the self-imposed character of sin's bondage and the weight of the tragic context for the experience of sin. A story like Dick's helps to illustrate what is at stake in rescuing this doctrine from Augustine's bio-historical schema, for surely Dick's experiences of early, severe trauma and violence suggest the influence of tragic vulnerability in shaping sin's corruption of freedom and the progressive radicality of that sin as bondage that is not merely occasional. But his experience also discloses the existence of at least a wedge of freedom[8] rather than fate; Augustine's references to "the law of sin as the strong force of habit"[9] echo in Dick's description of his molestation of his daughter.

Contemporary insights from the social sciences and developmental psychology render thoughts of biological transmission of sin and guilt very problematic. We need to adapt Augustine's insights about the radicality of sin's self-imposed bondage so as to include the complexities that external forces and developmental and intrapsychic vulnerability introduce. The need for such a constructive response is illustrated well in Steve's Presbyterian tradition. Having recently reunited two branches of the denomination, Presbyterians prepared and adopted a contemporary Brief Statement of Reformed faith in 1992 as a way of restating their identity. Its lines regarding sin are as follows:

> But we rebel against God; we hide from our Creator.
>   Ignoring God's commandments,
>   we violate the image of God in others and ourselves,
>   accept lies as truth,
>   exploit neighbor and nature,
>   and threaten death to the planet entrusted to our care.
> We deserve God's condemnation.[10]

As expected, these lines are deeply rooted in Augustine's classical emphasis on sin as the self-imposed corruption of freedom — a disobedient turn from God. Previous lines stress the radicality of such sin by noting the necessity of redemption. These sentences avoid Augustine's historical schema, but they do not reflect contemporary insights and resources regarding the tragically structured context in which sin arises. Rebellion here suggests a sheer, inexplicable turn away from God's good creation. This statement is a helpful description of the destructive consequences of sin, spiritually and relationally. Such a brief confession is necessarily limited in the development of any theological theme. However, Steve's pastoral care with Dick requires a better accounting of the dynamic interaction between the tragic vulnerability of the human condition and sin's anxious response. Certainly Dick's experience of sin is accurately characterized by rebellion, hiding, violation, deceit, and exploitation. But the corruption of freedom such actions disclose is more complex than the sheer voluntarism these lines suggest.

To summarize, we need to develop a constructive, contemporary response to Augustine's earlier profound insights into the origin and enduring bondage of sin. We must find a way to hold on to the central reality of sin as a self-imposed, radical, progressive corruption of freedom while also recovering and developing further Augustine's recognition that sin's unfaithful turn from God arises in the context of a tragically structured human condition. That is, we must explore sin not only as a cause of suffering but as a response to the tragic structures of the human condition and psychopathology in particular. We do so realizing that the influence of context and historical experience does not exhaust responsibility for the exercise of freedom but does affect the degree of freedom available to us. As Whitehead observed, our historical and relational particularity includes both constraints and possibilities for our freedom. Steve's hopes for Dick lie not simply in healing sin's distortions, i.e., freedom from sin, but in a larger freedom for love that arises through Dick's response to God's grace in his life. Clearly, a more adequate construct for analyzing the dynamics of sin in human experience requires our appreciation for the tragic structures of the human condition itself.

Human Reality and Its Condition

To the extent that we understand sin as a response to a tragically structured human condition, it is important to address three questions: (1) What is it about human reality that makes it violable? (2) What leads us to violate ourselves and others? (3) How is it that we may receive redemption? When we describe human reality as tragically structured, we are referring to the inescapable ambiguities of our context. Such ambiguities are especially apparent when we focus on our inherent relationality. From birth we know ourselves relationally. When young we are utterly dependent on such relationships and especially vulnerable to their fragility even as we require the strengths and meaning they may also afford us. At best our needs are met well enough rather than fully satisfied. Experiences of redemption and evil alike are mediated by the structures of relationality.[11] Certainly overcoming evil in such a context can be only partial.

The Violability of the Human Condition

Edward Farley suggests that one way to characterize human reality that helps disclose its structural vulnerability lies in attending to its three constitutive, interrelated, interdependent spheres: the interhuman, the social, and individual agency.[12] Primacy lies with the interhuman sphere because it is in relationships that we recognize a deep summons to transcend self-preoccupation and move toward a sense of compassionate obligation for one another in our fragility.[13] Very briefly we will sketch the outlines of these three spheres and the vulnerability they disclose in order then to focus on Dick's experience as illustrative of sin as a response to these tragic structures.

Interhuman Sphere. The interhuman sphere refers to the intrinsic relationality of human experience. We use relationality here both in the descriptive sense of lived experience and normatively to refer to the intentionality required to sustain relationships. In his explorations of this sphere, Farley suggests it has three formal dimensions: the radical otherness of our particularity, the relational fabric we presume even to know ourselves at all, and the sometimes profound experiences of emotional intimacy.[14] This sphere discloses distinctive elements of the tragic and the ethical in the human condition related to the primary experiential fruit that may arise from it: compassion and a sense of obligation.

Philosophers such as Emmanuel Levinas suggest that the interhuman is constituted by recognition of "the face" of the other. The face summons us beyond self-preoccupation into responsibility — having seen in the other their physical and emotional fragility mirroring our own vulnerability. Theologically, the face symbolizes an incarnational God disclosing the sanctity of life. In response to the face we realize compassion and obligation are required of us. As Levinas put it, "The face orders and ordains me."[15] Farley notes, along with philosopher Nel Noddings, that the interpersonal claim of care is a "primordial summons" foundational for life together.[16]

Two types of vulnerability characterize the tragic structure of the interhuman: interpersonal suffering and benign alienation, which arise in connection to the summons of the face.[17] By vulnerability we are referring to the frustration of needs and suffering that arise simply through living in community, i.e., the tragically structured human condition.

Interpersonal suffering is intrinsic to our deepest relationships, such as family, marriage, and friendship. These relationships shape us in significant ways — they are the context of joy as well as suffering. However significant, no relationship is secure from the contingencies of historical existence. Dick's parents, for example, found their love undermined and replaced by antagonism. Even in less extreme examples, it is clear that suffering inevitably occurs within the dailiness of relationships. Often interpersonal suffering is sharpened by the empathic connection with another's pain.

Benign alienation may be closely related to interpersonal suffering but describes more indirect suffering. It refers to the inevitability of suffering in light of the competing needs even of those who love each other. Divorcing parents feel this acutely as they seek to buffer their children's experiences of loss. While benign alienation refers to pain arising indirectly, rarely do we experience such pain dispassionately. Certainly Dick didn't as his parents divorced and his father remarried so that a half-brother received the attention Dick ached to have. These two types of suffering disclose well the tragic ambiguity of our relationality in which the very structures that provide opportunities for love, care, and joy also include possibilities for deep suffering.

Social Sphere. The "social sphere" refers to the complex environment of language, customs, institutions, and norms that shape us individually and interpersonally.[18] It expands the dynamics of relationships in the interhuman by virtue of the scope and interplay of institutions. For example, through this sphere arise the norms for care and family life; the assumptions carried in language; and the ethos surrounding gender, race, and class that frame and are in turn modified by our relationships. Farley suggests this sphere includes two kinds of vulnerability: social incompatibility and social suffering, and they represent a societal version of the vulnerabilities of relationality.[19]

Social suffering, for example, refers to a variety of ways the structures and systems of society may expand the possibilities for suffering that individuals encounter. When Dick's parents divorced, his mother's income dropped precipitously. The sexism that formed the context of the financial gulf between his parents reflects a structural or systemic consequence of patriarchy. The absence of adequate structures to assure help for children and affordable shelter for Dick and his mother illustrate social incompatibility — the societal form of benign alienation. Given the competing demands for limited social funding, legitimate needs are met inadequately, if at all. Of course, political priorities illustrate the interaction of these two forms of social vulnerability.

Sphere of Individual Agency. The complexity of the sphere of individual agency requires our attention to three interrelated dimensions, each with its particular form of tragic vulnerability painfully present in Dick's experience. These dimensions are subjectivity, physical embodiment, and what Farley describes as our elemental passions.[20]

Subjectivity — the experience of personal being — includes the tensive interdependence of our particularity, necessarily limited or determinate, and of our creative possibilities, or transcendence borne in our capacity for imagination and interpretation. Dick, for example, is a white man from the U.S.A. with a particular family history. However, he is never reducible to these several categories because he experiences himself as able to imagine and create alternative possibilities. This capacity for transcending particularity is the foundation for our agency and moral accountability. The specificity of our social historical location joined with this capacity for transcendence yields our autonomy.[21] It also discloses the tragic structure of personal being, for, as Charles Gerkin observed, we have infinite aspirations and finite possibilities.[22] There are real limits to our autonomy, but such limits do not exhaust the possibilities available to our imaginations.

Physical embodiment foreshadows the tragic condition of human reality in the sense that all creatures, by virtue of bodily requirements, experience limitations. Moreover, striving for the necessities of life and opposing whatever thwarts these needs occurs in an environment that, while abundant, is also indifferent and sometimes dangerous. Just as we experience benign alienation in the interhuman sphere, benign aggression describes a genetically necessary capacity to resist and defend ourselves from harm.

Bodily requirements for human life include the developmental character of human reality. While these developmental structures provide rich possibilities for human striving and relationships, they also render human beings especially vulnerable since we are dependent on others' care for an extended period. This makes us susceptible to enduring distortions conveyed through each of the three spheres here described. Dick's experiences of sexual abuse between the ages of seven and ten illustrate the developmental vulnerability of sexuality — a core dimension of identity and relationality — and the enduring, often tragic, consequences.

In his explorations of individual agency, Farley proposes the primacy of three elemental passions that fuel our agency and found and direct moral and reasoned actions such as love and justice.[23] These passions, as passions, can never be fully satisfied and always look beyond the moment. Just as hope far exceeds a wish, these passions anticipate broader states of affairs than a single event. They seek to negate what might obstruct fulfillment and therefore reflect a natural egocentrism. Two of these passions especially inform Dick's experience. The first we might call a passion for the survival and well-being of one's self, which draws on the capacity for transcendence to resist any challenge to autonomy, diminished determinacy, and threat of death. Dick's response to his loss of place in his father's attentions to a half-brother suggests the strength of this first passion. The second is a passion for mutually sustaining relationships in which we are valued and able to give care, i.e., relationships in which "the face" of one another is viewed. This is a passion for relationships in which we experience compassion and obligation. Dick's hopes for his marriage and life with Pat illustrate this passion. Of course, his story also illustrates the vulnerability of these passions to distortion — an issue to which we will return.

In sum, it is apparent that the tragic vulnerability attending our personal, embodied, and impassioned experience of individual agency is well illustrated in poignant ways in Dick's early life, for sexual abuse violates every dimension of the sphere of individual agency. In this tensive relation between determinacy and transcendence, we are vulnerable to others' refusing or distorting our determinacy. Certainly the older boys and later the stranger who molested Dick denied the determinacy and boundary of his body. Similarly, we are vulnerable to actions that humiliate, reduce, control, or objectify our embodied transcendence that sexual abuse dramatically illustrates. Abuse also illustrates well the vulnerability of the passions for survival and the reciprocity of care. Dick's passion for the survival and validation of his selfhood were utterly denied by his experiences of molestation. His hopes for reciprocity of care — especially with the older boys — were cruelly exploited.

Exploring these three spheres of human reality has disclosed our tragically structured existence. It has helped us recognize the remarkable vulnerability to violation of our psychic center or that self-initiating center of our identity.[24] Human suffering may accumulate as the daily humiliations of political tyranny or the debilitating effects of physical illness. In Dick's case, reviewing the vulnerability of his spheres of reality reveals the archaeology of psychopathology's onset with its corresponding limitations. The interpersonal suffering of a six-year-old boy feeling the security of his familial world disintegrate suggests the "cracks in the foundation" of his sense of safety. The sexism and classism mediated through the social sphere are especially important as the former established the context of Dick's sexual abuse and the latter contributed to his sense of poor self-esteem. In the sphere of individual agency the ac-

tual experiences of abuse exploit Dick's heightened longing to be valued
and his normal developmental vulnerability as a sexual being. It is easy
to imagine how these several particular events and enduring losses set in
motion psychopathological patterns of response that progressively limited Dick's freedom to trust others and himself. Dick's vulnerability to
suffering is the result of the cumulative effects of the violations he has
experienced, for these violations have led him to develop habitual styles
of defense and other symptoms of dis-ease.

These defenses alter freedom in pre-critical ways. That is, they origi-
nate in particular events and processes of violation, but then they endure
through altering the very structures of being such as our experience of
safety or our ability to love ourselves and others. When these structures
are altered, our capacity for self-determination is diminished — often
with little if any conscious awareness, for we are simply responding to
the world as we are able to perceive it.

We have seen how human reality is violable and the insidious consequences of that violation for human freedom. Now we turn to sin
as violation, drawing once more on Dick's experience as a victim and
perpetrator of sexual violence.

The Emergence of Sin

Our careful review of the tragic structures of the human condition, and
Dick's reality in particular, helps to clarify that evil or sin and human
suffering may be distinguished. But it is also apparent from Dick's experience that at the concrete level of human behavior such suffering
and human evil are closely intertwined. In his care of Dick, Steve will
likely find it difficult to distinguish suffering and sin. Having explored
a schema that discloses the tragic structure of human reality and the
particular ways psychopathology arises and endures in that reality, we
need to identify the ways in which sin arises and endures as a response
to such suffering. We will also pursue our questions about how sin
and psychopathology limit human freedom differently and interactively.
Such analysis may help Steve discern the interplay of sin and suffering in
ways that support his care for Dick and his empowerment of Dick's freedom for love. There are a number of perspectives from which to observe
this relationship between sin and suffering.

Original sin reminds us of the impersonal dimension of sin. It is true
that sin's alienation has a cumulative force carried transculturally and
transgenerationally, as sexism, racism, and various forms of abuse attest.[25] Dick's story suggests the way in which what begins as an objective
reality insinuates itself into one's subjective experience. He was born
into a nuclear family in which his parents experienced such conflict that

they chose divorce. Dick was an innocent party in this situation though the stress of a third child likely was an issue. Nonetheless, Dick is not at fault here, nor is he responsible for the serious economic differences that meant his half-brother's stock of toys and access to his father's care were superior to his. Dick did have a choice, a wedge of freedom,[26] in developing intense envy and malice toward his half-brother. However, given this complicity we would still need to acknowledge the weight of those forces at work in his childhood and youth that together served to diminish his freedom to choose life-enhancing possibilities. Moreover, as Dick assented to postures of malice, envy, and self-doubt, he contributed to the cumulative historical force of sin for others as well. As Paul reminded us in Romans — ironically — Dick chose sin's bondage. Original sin helps us recognize that he did so in a context tragically structured.

In addition to the massive historical force original sin describes, fear of the future and the death(s) it brings is a critical factor in sin's origin and dynamics in our lives. As Suchocki notes, fear itself is death-dealing.[27] Sin lies not in our anxiety about real or symbolic limits to our lives but in the ways we then choose to narrow our possibilities for experiences and relationships. We choose to foreclose the risking of ourselves that being fully alive entails.

In Dick's life story one can easily imagine how very poor self-esteem functioned to limit his hopes and possibilities as well as his willingness to risk new relationships. But his story also indicates how these origins of sin interweave, for his decision to begin acts of sexual violence occurs in response to a marriage in which he describes the emotional withdrawal of both partners. Each seemed to hide more of themselves, closing off the future of their marriage.

Clearest in Dick's story is the reality of sin as violation — the absolutization of one's own satisfaction or the absolutization of others' needs in such a way that relationality and interdependence are negated.[28] On the one hand, we see Dick's response to Joan's pregnancy and her subsequent disregard for him as a good description of false dependency. He absolutized her and their son's needs at the expense of his own despite her refusal of mutuality and interdependency. Later, when Pat rejected possibilities for emotional and physical intimacy and relationality, Dick began a pattern of violation earlier perpetrated against him. This time he absolutized his own needs, violating those to whom he exposed himself and later his daughter. His victims are valued only according to the egotism of his own needs and thus are dehumanized through this process of objectification. In a rather paradoxical way his earlier response of false dependency was similarly controlling in that his construal of the situation provided some sense of control and also effectively cut off possibilities for genuine relationality as he sought to live through others by providing for their needs.

The common denominator in these various perspectives on sin's emergence is pretense — the distortion of the tragic structure of reality into some more tolerable version. Sin as "the lie" is Suchocki's way of describing the assent to sin in its various forms.[29] We lie to ourselves that we were/are not free to act differently.

Farley describes this lie as the refusal to accept the tragic structures of our human condition and the insistence on interpreting such vulnerability as contingent on others' or our own control.[30] In the Christian paradigm these postures of refusal and resistance are the idolatrous turn, for our anxiety requires some relief from our fearful recognition of these tragic structures. We attempt to make some mundane good fulfill our passion for being and our longing for reciprocity in intimate, caring relationships.

Once we make this anxious turn the lie requires, then, the destabilizing dynamics of sin compound our dis-ease because no penultimate good can satisfy our needs. Resentment, greed, fear, malice, etc. arise in place of a more secure and authentic posture of openness and reciprocity. Sin's bondage, which begins as fearful self-securing (pretense), diminishes our freedom to actualize capacities for love of God, self, and neighbor.

Sin is not the only way human beings deal with our tragic vulnerability and our discontent. Sometimes — perhaps because of biochemical reasons or other developmental disabilities — persons may find themselves relatively incapable of discriminating between actions that are life-enhancing and destructive or relatively unable to control such choices. Alzheimer's disease and forms of schizophrenia are illustrative here.

However, psychopathology that is more experiential in origin — such as Dick's history of trauma suggests — illustrates the way evil's corruption of human experience alters another's possibility for historical freedom. Sin involves a corruption of freedom's normative vision for life-enhancing behavior for one's self, others, and creation. It presumes sufficient autonomy for accountability. Psychopathology describes the pre-critical erosion of one's relative autonomy. It diminishes those intrapsychic structures by which one perceives and responds to the world rendering one less free or able to be unselfconscious and constructive.

The destructive consequences of shame that arise as psychopathology from experiences of victimization particularly illustrate the ways in which sin and tragic vulnerability intertwine. Shame diminishes our freedom to be unselfconsciously present and at ease with ourselves, others, and our environment. It does so by coloring our perceptual capacities with fear. Shame organizes the psychological reality of adults molested as children through its effects on the individual's sense of self and consequent diminished capacities for relationality that are shaped by love and trust.

Identity is that sense of individuality that has continuity over time. It is that "vital sense of who we are as individuals, embracing our worth, our adequacy, and our very dignity as human beings."[31] Ordinarily, identity emerges as a child's natural needs are met in mutually significant caring relationships. An inner sense of wholeness, belonging, and connection develops through a reciprocal process of identification and differentiation. Shame ensues when a devastating experience of rupture breaks that interpersonal bridge...[with trusted or valued persons] and brings a consequent sense of betrayal and the unexpected exposure of unmet internal need.... When such experiences in relationships are not repaired or are chronic, they leave the individual's sense of [self] diminished, painfully small or belittled, filled with self-doubt, and overwhelmed by self-consciousness.[32]

Dick's experience of shame, not met by any repair, does reflect this internalized experience of shame, i.e., he now feels toward himself the contempt he experienced from others whose acceptance he valued. As we noted earlier, the interdependence of our spheres of reality means that, once internalized, such self-contempt renders Dick vulnerable to diminishment in every aspect of his experience. Thus, unrepaired, shame has progressively destructive consequences for Dick's experience of agency, relationships, and the social sphere as well. Moreover, sexual abuse arises around the violent experience of bodily invasion that includes the experience of powerlessness to protect one's self. Thus one's sense of safety in the world is reduced. Dick's sexual abuse experiences, especially unmet by efforts to repair broken trust, mean that his freedom to be at ease with himself and others or to feel secure in his environment is significantly diminished. The primacy of relationality is apparent in the fragile, developmental processes of our emerging personality structures as children, so that the familial deprivation and sexual abuse Dick experienced did constrict his possibilities for life-enhancing freedom. Remembering that sin arises from fearful insecurity, it is obvious that Dick's experiences of victimization reflect the significance of the context to which sin is a response.

Yet, not all victims of sexual abuse become perpetrators. As Dick acknowledges, he chose to violate his victims — though he describes such occasions in the language of compulsive behavior illustrative of sin as "the lie" even as it also bespeaks the constricting legacy of his victimization.

Sin is a refusal — an active resistance — to our tragically structured finitude. Its origin is distinct from the victimization of psychopathology. But, precisely because the structures of existence are so closely intertwined, the corruptions of sin and the constrictions of psychopathology, while limiting our freedom differently, do inform one another as Dick's experience of victimization and perpetration illustrate. The shape and effects of sin vary in the several spheres of human reality as does its interrelation with psychopathology. We turn now to explore how it is that sin arises and corrupts Dick's experience of human reality in its several spheres: individual agency, the interhuman, and the social.

Sin and the Spheres of Human Reality

Individual Agency

Our earlier exploration disclosed several dimensions operative in this sphere: personal being, the passions, and embodiment. Again, drawing on Dick's experience, it is striking to see how sin corrupts these dimensions of his agency.

Personal Being. In the realm of personal being distortions of the tensive relationship between transcendence and determinacy lead to several patterns of sinful behavior. For example, when Dick locks in the present for the immediate gratification of his need for control, he also absolutizes his particularity or determinacy and those needs begin to define him. He cannot bear the self-transcending functions of criticism or vulnerability in relationships so they are reduced. This reduction of transcendence is a corruption of Dick's autonomy because now he has absolutized his needs and objectified other persons so he no longer is drawn past himself toward authentic relationality but is motivated by a narrow priority for himself.[33]

The Elemental Passions. The corruption of our elemental passions for subjectivity and the reciprocity of caring relationships takes the form of either a false optimism or despair. It is also the case that the corruptions of these passions are interactive and at the same time serve to isolate them, subverting their interdependence.[34]

Let us look more closely at the corruption of Dick's desire to be valued and affirmed relationally and to reciprocate that caring. This passion for the reciprocity of care refers not to the sphere of the interhuman and its actual relationality but rather to our deep desire for the experience of giving and receiving care.[35] Dick's longing to receive and give such acknowledgment is intense and likely reflects the losses of early shaming experiences he had surrounding his parents' divorce and his two experiences of sexual abuse. This passion for the reciprocity of care corresponds with developmental needs for trustworthy relationality especially in the early years of life.

Dick's early shaming experiences, especially with his father, the abusive older boys, and the stranger, significantly distorted his sense of
self-esteem and confidence in his value to others. These experiences of
victimization then coinhere with the vulnerability of his normal developmental needs for experiences of acknowledgment and the possibility
that his care would be valued. Not surprisingly, several years later, we
find Dick seeking to secure himself through relational dependence with
Joan, the young adolescent with whom he fathered a child when himself
a teen. Dick's false optimism regarding this relationship and later his relationship with Pat, his wife, bespeaks the corruption of pretending he
could secure himself through absolutizing the good of their love. It may
be that his sexual misconduct was precipitated by the recognition that
Pat had rejected his care. It does seem clear that shame and the corruption of Dick's passion for an intimate, caring relationship destructively
coincide to lend a primacy to this dimension of his experience in our
assessment.

Embodiment. Closely related to the distortions of our passions and
subjectivity is the category of bodily life that Farley includes in his treatment of this sphere of individual agency. The natural egocentrism of
our needs for satisfaction and competition begin as biological urges and
are soon extended by the values and symbols of culture.[36] Because our
agency is embodied, there is an immediate reciprocity among our several
spheres of reality: individual agency, relationality (the interhuman), and
the social. Corruptions of human reality or contrasting experiences of
being-founded (secure in God's love) in any sphere will affect us biologically. Because our agency is embodied, our benign, biologically rooted
capacity to resist what frustrates our striving may be corrupted into a
posture of enmity when the dynamics of idolatry lead us to absolutize
whatever resists us.[37]

Because we remember the past, resentments and old assaults —
both personal and cultural — accumulate and structure our personality. Malice and control are two resulting forms of enmity.[38] Malice is
a personalized form of resistance to those identified as enemies because
they have in some way threatened what we have absolutized for a sense
of security. Control represents a less personalized response to persons
or institutions that seem to threaten the conditions deemed necessary
to assure the continuation of our absolutized satisfaction.[39] Of course,
malice and control may also be combined.

Dick describes the cumulative resentments that yielded a posture of
malice toward his half-brother because of his apparent favored status
and privileges due in fact to the divorce of Dick's parents rather than
any action by this child. But how does Farley's schema offer us insight into Dick's sexual violence, first through his exposure of himself

to young girls he did not know and then through the molestation of his daughter?

To answer this fully we will need to include how idolatry or "the lie" corrupts the sphere of the interhuman or relationality. But it is important to discern the possible significance of the ways Dick's experience of sexual abuse may have altered the freedom of his bodily life. Remember that corruptions in any of the several spheres of human reality have access to our biologically rooted striving for satisfaction or resistance and may corrupt those benign forms of our resistance.[40] When eight years old, Dick's passion for the interhuman — the longing to have his being and need for belonging confirmed — was exploited and cruelly violated by much older adolescent boys who required he submit to oral sex as an initiation into their group and rejected him even after such humiliation.

Vast are the destructive consequences of such an experience of violation. This abuse was an utterly dehumanizing, insulting disregard for the irreducible uniqueness and value characterizing the way Dick or any of us experience the unity of our embodied selves. As Farley noted, we give meaning and value to our biological and physical givenness. Though not yet sexually aware, Dick realized he had experienced evil/violation and the humiliation otherwise described as shame from those whose affirmation he had absolutized. Shame's destruction is now intertwined with the vulnerability of physical sexuality. What Levinas describes as face — that fragility of being that ideally elicits reciprocities of compassion and obligation — was utterly violated. Later at the age of eleven a stranger also sexually violated Dick, which he describes as a source of great shame. To some extent the consequences of such violations are subject to a victim's idiosyncratic psychical structures and history, but we can discern that these violations set in motion severe deprivations that would metastasize from this sphere of individual agency to the spheres of the interhuman (relationality) and the social.

The medium of sexuality is highly symbolic for gender identity and communication. If one's sexuality is the locus of extremely shameful and violent experiences of evil and powerlessness, it is not difficult to imagine how one's freedom to be at ease with one's self or others of the same or different gender would be significantly diminished. That Dick's perpetrators were male is also complicating because of this culture's pervasive homophobia. His sense of self-contempt originates in his sexuality. Moreover, such violations no doubt accumulate resentment that may contribute to subsequent postures of malice and control. It is no accident that Dick began to perpetrate sexual violence when his wife abruptly ended all physical and emotional intimacy. He experienced this rejection through the frame of one whose security in the world lay in this relationship and whose sense of self-esteem and powerlessness made direct confrontation seem impossible. The psychopathology of shame and the lies sin requires weave tightly together in this story.

The Sphere of the Interhuman

In describing this sphere of relation, Farley draws our attention to a phenomenon easily missed because we focus on individuals or social structures rather than on the more elusive relation between persons. Violation in this sphere effects two reciprocally related sinful postures: resentment and guilt.[41] The posture of resentment is an "enduring wound" created by another's violation of the wounded one's personhood. That is, the vulnerability we bring to relation (the summons of the face) is disregarded or abused. When relationships experience violation, the summons of this fragility or vulnerability changes to accusation. Recognition that one has violated the implicit relational obligation to care for the other elicits a corresponding guilt. These two responses affect the relation itself and are not simply internalizations of individual participants. However, these wounds also are internalized and thus have widespread effects.

We find in Dick's story several significantly alienated intimate relationships characterized by these dimensions of resentment and guilt as well as his personal history of victimization and his reported postures of resentment. Imagine in Dick's relationship to his daughter the toxic effect of the feelings each experience. We do not know her feelings directly, but judging by her decision not to see him, it is fair to presume resentment. We do know Dick describes enormous guilt. The gulf between them is currently unbridgeable. His guilt has sometimes created suicidal feelings. His sense of value and worth have been minimal. His guilt and her resentment are enduring factors in any future relation between the two. In Dick's marriage certainly his perception of Pat's rejection left him feeling deep resentment. If his assessment be accurate, she too acted out of resentment not only with him but with earlier husbands who violated her. Those old wounds — internalized earlier — festered and poisoned this later relationship.

His relationship with Joan, the thirteen-year-old with whom he fathered a child, was certainly colored by his sense of violation and eventual resentment. At the time he reports his first acts of public sexual exposure, Dick describes a seriously alienated marriage in which he felt utterly and unfairly rejected by his wife, Pat. At the time he only knew that she had emotionally and sexually withdrawn from their relationship. Now he believes she was reacting to her own history of sexual and physical abuse. What he felt was that once again what had been promised (as with his father and the abusive boys) was withheld.

It is not difficult to imagine how responses of malice, control, resentment, and guilt could arise from Dick's personal and relational history. He brought to this marriage deep relational needs hoping they would be honored and his need to offer care would be welcomed. The respective relational and sexual humiliation he felt with his half-brother and with the older abusive boys created a significantly heightened vulnerability to further emotional losses with a far less resilient sense of self. The relationship he describes with Joan is characterized by what Farley terms "false dependence" and current therapeutic language names as co-dependency — an emotional dependence in which one's own needs are met derivatively. This emotional vulnerability is certainly predictable given Dick's history. It is tragically predictable that having known first-hand the humiliating objectification and dehumanization of sexual abuse, Dick would choose this same medium in which to reclaim his sense of power and agency though finding he needed to increase the frequency of his exposures to satisfy his need for a sense of control.

Once again we find the inextricable relation of shame-based postures of release and control and the idolatrous corruption of the spheres of individual agency and relationality or the interhuman.[42] The shame seems to add a paradoxical counterpoint of self-loathing that exacerbates the fearful threat feeding Dick's cycle of sexual violence. Indeed, he describes that self-loathing as deepening with each act of exposure, increasing his need for the power and confidence such acts brought, albeit briefly.

Placing a theological analysis alongside the therapeutic lens of shame-based compulsive behavior illumines further the tragedy of Dick's sexual violence. Now we can see more clearly the consequences of freedom diminished by victimization and corrupted by fear. Our analysis is incomplete, however, without attention to the larger social sphere also formative and interactive with Dick's behavior.

The Social Sphere

Farley refers to the way sin arises in social structures as processes of social infection and the maintenance and extension of such infection as collusion in which sin takes the form of subjugation. For example, the idolatry of racial purity pervades a school system and maintains itself in the angry defense of segregation.[43] Sin as subjugation presupposes the infection of social structures. It represents the way self-absolutization in the sphere of individual agency here expands to corrupt the particularity of an institution, ethnic group, or nation. Such entities then fearfully abuse their power to deny to other groups all elements of compassion that would summon obligation to them.[44] Now these other groups and individuals may be used or violently opposed as racism illustrates painfully well.

Suchocki describes corruption in the social sphere in the tradition's language of original sin and the demonic. She describes the tragic structure of the social sphere as demonic — the cumulative result of sin in the personal and relational spheres. This demonic element surrounds individuals with overwhelming powers of destruction and inevitably involves all in the alienation of sin.[45] Unfortunately those who experience subjugation likely internalize the alienation and violence projected toward them, further diminishing their freedom and well-being. Those who subjugate others assent to evil, thus deepening their own bondage and increasing the force of the demonic.[46] She stresses that however forceful this power of the demonic may be, one engages in "the lie" if one denies the possibilities present for life-giving choices also available when "choosing" the demonic.[47]

In Dick's story we see evidence of the tremendous force of patriarchy in which the interests and goals of white men are granted priority with the corresponding right to use power unilaterally to subjugate women, people of color, and others whose status is deemed inferior. The predominance of sexual abuse by older boys and men against children suggests the interpenetration of corruption in the three spheres but certainly the emergence in the social sphere of the tolerance of violence and the objectification of those "of no use" or "in the way." The abusive older boys assented to the demonic character of patriarchy in trivializing the no doubt irritating pleas of a lonely little boy whose mama had just brought him along when she moved in with a man whose trailer was in their rural area. They had learned power was joined with their sexuality, and they abused Dick's vulnerability. Even as a young boy Dick had learned the constraints of sexism, which inhibited his freedom to seek comfort or help after his experiences of abuse. He bore it "like a man" and certainly didn't want to encourage homophobic suspicions.[48] As a man, Dick carried his history of such humiliation alongside the second rejection by a woman in whom he had absolutized his worth and hopes. He, too, had learned that in this culture he could objectify and control young girls. Even with his diminished self-esteem, these girls could be objectified for his use, and they were — the anonymous girls to whom he exposed himself and his daughter. He assented to the demonic force of this ideology as it interacted destructively with the corresponding vulnerabilities in his individual and relational life. And he assented to "the lie" that he was not free to act otherwise.

A Normative Vision of Historical Freedom

Having ventured into the destructive consequences of human evil, it is important to explore the normative, Christian vision of historical freedom and faithfulness against which the language of sin's bondage and idolatry are so starkly drawn. Suchocki's "lie" and Farley's refusal and resistance both depict persons unable to tolerate the precarious ambiguities of historical existence who give way to the pretense of some more immediate sense of security, meaning, and love. But evil originates in this active refusal or lie because it leads us away from God's power to found or secure us and initiates destructive distortions of mundane goods now forced to satisfy ultimate longings.[49]

Rather than a stoic bravado, the Christian paradigm asserts only God's sacred presence as Creator can found our longing for meaning and care. Such redemptive experience is mediated historically through the milieu of a community of faith, and faith is witnessed through acts of love. In historical communities, of course, we are not immune to the dynamics of evil, but these are mediated in conjunction with God's saving presence through disciplines of worship, service, and prayer.[50]

This experience of "being-founded" is the moment in which the bondage of sin yields to true freedom — a posture from which we can relativize the value of mundane goods and restore to them a penultimate status; consent to our historical existence with appreciation for what is beautiful and good; and, trusting God's care, risk venturing amid the ambiguities of historical existence with courage and hope.

In this Hebraic-Christian paradigm the evil we have described is a refusal or lie about God's power to found or save. Hence, this communally mediated experience of God's gracious presence is one of reconciliation. Acts of relativization, consent, and risk are dimensions of faithful obedience. In fact, Dick describes his process of recovery as including very different transformative experiences of God's presence. He describes the sense that as a perpetrator, "I was turning my back on God," but as he has acknowledged his violation of others and faced his accountability as well as his own history of abuse, Dick now says, "I am receiving unconditional love I couldn't get from anywhere else." Dick is describing the historical freedom made possible as he rejects the lies of his earlier perpetration of abuse and the distortions of the psychopathology that contributed to his diminished freedom. It is important to recognize that just as the corruptions and constrictions of evil and psychopathology destructively intertwine, the liberation of faithfulness and healing are similarly expansive. Of course, this normative vision of historical freedom or redemption is not simply the absence of idolatrous distortion. Rather it arises through the experience of being-founded by God's reconciling presence. It is not simply a freedom from sin. It is a freedom for love.

One description of this normative vision for love guiding Dick and his pastor is briefly articulated in "A Brief Statement of Faith" mentioned earlier. Here Steve has a communally shared resource for encouraging

Dick to deepen his experience of being-founded by God's reconciling love. The themes of reconciliation, the relativization of mundane goods, consent to the limits and possibilities of historical existence, trust of God's care, and the risks of discipleship are accessible for their reflection together and their shared experience of worship.

> We trust in God the Holy Spirit,
>   everywhere the giver and renewer of life.
> The Spirit justifies us by grace through faith,
>   sets us free to accept ourselves and to love God and neighbor,
>   and binds us together with all believers
>   in the one body of Christ, the Church....
>
> In a broken and fearful world
> the Spirit gives us courage
>   to pray without ceasing,
>   to witness among all peoples to Christ as Lord and Savior,
>   to unmask idolatries in Church and culture,
>   to hear the voices of peoples long silenced,
>   and to work with others for justice, freedom, and peace.
>
> In gratitude to God, empowered by the Spirit,
>   we strive to serve Christ in our daily tasks
>   and to live holy and joyful lives....[51]

This description of life in the Spirit, or being-founded, suggests a life of faith that relies on the possibilities inherent in the several spheres of reality. But these lines also disclose an awareness of a constant tension with the possible corruptions of these same spheres of agency, relationships, and social structures. The bondage of evil and suffering are the backdrop of this vision as it describes in previous lines sin's corruption in the human community and among people of faith. The struggle is contemporary, for this world is described as broken and fearful. Who could repeat these lines thinking faith's trust or the life of faith is easy? Such vulnerability requires courage. The life of faith is a commitment to justice shaped by reverence and joy. Gratitude to God is the "habit of being" for those who experience God's founding love.

Conclusion

We began this exploration with the troubling realization that our classical theology of sin was not adequate for helping us discern how Dick could choose to perpetrate sexual violence. We have carefully explored the proposal that sin arises as a response to the tragic structures of our human condition rather than as sheer, inexplicable volition in rebellion against God and a violation of neighbor and self. On the other hand, we have been able to confirm with the tradition that sin is not equated with the suffering of the human condition however oppressive its destructive force may be. In taking this context of tragic vulnerability seriously, we have recognized the centrality of the theme of freedom in exploring the different ways sin and psychopathology arise and endure in human experience.

Through the tragedy of Dick's experience, we have also observed how closely sin and the victimization of psychopathology interpenetrate, shaping each other interactively. The victimization of shame metasticized like cancer throughout the three spheres of Dick's reality. Deepened by his alienating and fearful behavior, it created the particular vulnerabilities his controlling, angry resentment and his guilt would exploit in futile efforts to secure himself in a relational environment that was ambiguous at best and often hostile. Those structures of Dick's life most affected by victimization — self-esteem, sexuality, and relationality — were precisely the points of fearful vulnerability at which the corruption of sin occurred. Dick's angry control, resentment, and guilt erupted in the repeated subjugation of young girls through sexual molestation — both anonymous and incestuous. It is a tragic illustration of the way sin and psychopathology interact deepening their destructive consequences.

This exploration of the different ways sin and psychopathology impose bondage on our freedom reinforces the importance of refuting any conflation of these two categories in pastoral diagnosis. Sin is a distinctive, truthful, and important lens for interpreting the roots and dynamics of the violence and suffering tearing the fabric of the human community. There is much room for fruitful dialogue between therapeutic approaches and theological analysis around such themes as freedom, shame, power, and fear. While our focus has been sin, the lens of shame offers promise of further insight as a common psychological and theological resource for understanding the bondage of sin and psychopathology as they interact.[52]

Beyond assessment, the experience of being-founded and the freedom emerging in faithfulness are also suggestive for the helpfulness our theological resources offer toward healing and the profound freedom for love. What is encouraging about this attention to the significance of sin as a response to our tragic context is that the interpenetration of these spheres of human reality that contributed to sin's power to corrupt also extends the life-giving experience of being-founded by God's grace. Moreover, the interdependence of sin and psychopathology suggests how healing the wounds of victimization and reconciling the alienating corruption of sin inform one another. Attention to sin's reality and power will enhance our resources for mediating the enlivening power of God's gift — the freedom for love.

NOTES

1. For particularly helpful discussions of current therapeutic theories, see David Finkelhor, *Child Sexual Abuse* (New York: Free Press, 1984), and Terry S. Trepper and Mary Jo Barrett, *Systemic Treatment of Incest* (New York: Brunner/Mazel, 1989).

2. For a further exploration of the correspondence of the ancient debate about sin and freedom and our contemporary context see Robert R. Williams, "Sin and Evil," in Peter C. Hodgson and Robert H. King, eds., *Christian Theology* (Minneapolis: Fortress Press, 1982), 168–95.

3. Augustine, *On Free Choice of Will*, trans. Anna S. Benjamin and L. H. Hackstoff (Indianapolis: Bobbs-Merrill Company, Inc., 1964), III.xvii.

4. Augustine, *City of God*, trans. Gerald Walsh, Demetrius Zema, Grace Monahan, and David Honan (New York: Image Books, 1958), XI.12, p. 221.

5. Ibid., Book XIV.3., p. 330.

6. John Calvin, *The Institutes of the Christian Religion*, trans. Ford Lewis Battles, vol. 1 (Philadelphia: Westminster Press, 1960), Book 2.1.4, p. 245.

7. Augustine, *City of God*, XIV.1, p. 295.

8. Marjorie Hewitt Suchocki, *God, Christ, Church*, new rev. ed. (New York: Crossroad, 1993), 17.

9. Augustine, *Confessions*, trans., Rex Warner (New York: New American Library, 1963), 8.6., p. 169.

10. Presbyterian Church (U.S.A.), "A Brief Statement of Faith" in *The Book of Confessions* (Louisville: Office of the General Assembly, 1991), 10:3.

11. Cf. Marjorie Hewitt Suchocki, *The End of Evil* (Albany: State University of New York Press, 1988), 81, for a fuller discussion of this ambiguity.

12. I am indebted to Edward Farley's careful philosophical reflections on the nature of human reality and the tragic structures of the human condition that are a significant context for the origins and dynamic process of human evil. Farley's discussion of three spheres of human reality provides the structure for the following reflections on the human condition. See Edward Farley, *Good and Evil* (Minneapolis: Fortress Press, 1990), 124–30.

13. Farley makes an essential move here to establish the interhuman as a key to understanding tragic and ethical elements of human reality. Noting the short-comings of cognitive and utilitarian foci on relationality, he relies especially on Martin Buber and Emmanuel Levinas, philosophers of dialogue. They attend to the irreducible mystery of face, co-discerned fragility, and summons to compassionate obligation that may be honored in the sphere of relationality. Cf. ibid., 37–44.

14. Ibid., 33–40.

15. Emmanuel Levinas, *Ethics and Infinity*, trans. R. A. Cohen (Pittsburgh: Duquesne University Press, 1985), 97.

16. Edward Farley, *Good and Evil*, 41, and Nel Noddings, *Caring* (Berkeley: University of California Press, 1984).

17. Farley, *Good and Evil*, 43.

18. Ibid., 47.

19. Ibid., 57 ff.

20. Ibid., 63–113.

21. Ibid., 72.

22. Charles Gerkin, *Crisis Experience in Modern Life* (Nashville: Abingdon, 1979).

23. Farley, *Good and Evil,* 98.

24. See Edward Farley, "Psychopathology and Human Evil: Toward a Theory of Differentiation," in Ronald Bruzina and Bruce Wilshire, eds., *Crosscurrents in Phenomenology* (Boston: Martinus Nijhoff, 1978) for an extended discussion of the different ways psychopathology and sin arise and endure in human experience and the ways they limit freedom differently.

25. Cf. Suchocki, *God, Christ, Church,* 14–17.

26. Ibid., 17.

27. Ibid., 22.

28. Ibid., 24.

29. Ibid., 18, 26–27.

30. Farley, *Good and Evil,* 132–33.

31. Gershen Kaufman, *Shame: The Power of Caring,* 2d ed. rev. (Cambridge, Mass.: Schenkman Books, 1985), 7.

32. Kaufman, *Shame,* 11, 29–30, cited by Nancy J. Ramsay, "Sexual Abuse and Shame: The Travail of Recovery," in Maxine Glaz and Jeanne Stevenson-Moessner, eds., *Women in Travail and Transition* (Minneapolis: Fortress Press, 1991), 112–23.

33. Farley, *Good and Evil,* 160–64.

34. Ibid., 209.

35. Ibid., 185–90.

36. Ibid., 214.

37. Ibid., 222–25.

38. Ibid., 224.

39. Ibid., 225.

40. Ibid., 222.

41. Ibid., 238–42.

42. For a helpful discussion of shame-based patterns of compulsive cycles of behavior, see Merle A. Fossum and Marilyn Mason, *Facing Shame* (New York: W. W. Norton and Co., 1986).

43. Ibid., 256–60.

44. Ibid., 260.

45. Suchocki, *God, Christ, Church,* 15.

46. Ibid., 17–18.

47. Ibid., 18.

48. For an insightful exploration of the consequences of patriarchy on men's sexuality and spirituality, see James B. Nelson, *The Intimate Connection.* (Louisville: Westminster John Knox Press, 1988).

49. Farley, *Good and Evil,* 144–50.

50. Cf. Craig Dykstra, "The Formative Power of Congregations," *Religious Education* 82, no. 4 (Fall 1987): 530–46.

51. Presbyterian Church, "Brief Statement of Faith," 10.4.

52. For additional reflection on the relation of shame and experiences of freedom and sin, see Don Capps, *The Depleted Self* (Minneapolis: Fortress, 1993), and Nancy Ramsay, "Sexual Abuse and Shame: The Travail of Recovery," in *Women in Travail and Transition.* See also Susan L. Nelson, "Soul-Loss and Sin," in Richard Fenn and John McDargh, eds., *Losing the Soul: Essays in the Social Psychology of Religion* (Buffalo, N.Y.: SUNY Press, forthcoming).

❯❯ 13 ❮❮

Dismantling Racism
Strategies for Cultural, Political, and Spiritual Transformation

SHARON D. WELCH

In her presentation at the 1993 meetings of the American Academy of Religion, Dr. Barbara Andolsen challenged ethicists to once again turn our attention to the problem of racism.[1] She acknowledged that ethicists have developed clear and persuasive condemnations of racism, yet she reminded us that more needs to be done. Racism continues to pervade and distort the structures of our common life, our workplaces, and our religious traditions. Derek Bell, for example, identifies six features of contemporary racism in the United States: despite integration, educational inequity; civil rights laws passed, but not enforced; growing disparity between incomes and assets of black and white Americans; tensions between marginalized racial groups; resistance to affirmative action; appeals by white politicians to white voters to maintain white privilege.[2]

For the past three years at the University of Missouri I have worked with people and programs focused on dismantling racism and integrating work against racism with work against sexism, homophobia, and other forms of oppression. This work has taken many forms: attempts to strengthen degree programs in Black Studies and Women Studies, efforts to establish and maintain coalitions between Black Studies and Women Studies, training for faculty and graduate assistants in educational strategies that enhance diversity, and building coalitions to support multicultural education throughout the university. These efforts have been directed primarily toward faculty hires, curricular development, and faculty promotion and tenure. In addition to this work on the curriculum, we have developed teams of faculty, students, and staff trained to lead diversity workshops addressing barriers to full inclusion in all aspects of university life. In the area of student affairs, there has been a consistent attempt by the staff of the Black Culture Center to address the strengths and challenges of black women as well as those of black men, and, correspondingly, the Women's Center has made deliberate efforts to address the needs of women of all races. These efforts at curriculum development and student programming have been accompanied by systematic efforts to recruit and retain African-American students.[3] These efforts have included sustained outreach to high schools with large numbers of minority students, summer institutes for prospective students, and mentoring programs for minority students. As a result of these efforts, the number of African-American students enrolled at the university increased from 642 undergraduates in 1993 to 801 in 1994.

While there are tangible results of our work, other aims are not as easy to measure. The challenge facing us is immense. How can we regenerate culture on the basis of equality and justice? How do we sustain and evoke forms of white identity that are not predicated on racial domination? Individual change, although essential to the process, is not enough. To paraphrase Theophus Smith, How do we give institutional, communal, and cultural expression to our visions of whiteness without racial domination and of blackness without racial victimization?[4]

There have been many successes in our work at the University of Missouri, and there have been as many, possibly more, failures. In this essay I want to address the failures, and most specifically, the failures that come, not primarily from opposition from external forces, not primarily from people opposed to racial justice or opposed to full attention to race, gender, class, and sexual orientation. My focus is on the conflicts that occur within groups that share a commitment to social justice and yet find ourselves in debilitating and destructive power struggles. Why is it so hard for us to maintain coalitions? And once we gain some measure of power (there is a grain of truth, after all, to the conservative fear of tenured radicals — some of us do have tenure, and we sometimes find ourselves as directors of programs, deans, provosts, and university or college presidents) why, then, is it so hard to utilize our power within institutions to implement basic institutional change? Why do we find ourselves so often locked in conflict with each other just as we have the opportunity to transform the structures of our workplaces? Michael Lerner has written of the strange proclivity of the left to snatch defeat from the jaws of victory — a peculiar talent that, among some circles, has been honed to a fine art. Why do we defeat ourselves?

What are the structural barriers to living out our ideals? And, correspondingly, what are the cultural, political, and spiritual practices that can evoke and sustain work for social justice? The barriers to sustained work for social change vary depending on the level of social change achieved. Rosabeth Moss Kanter describes what happens to women when we first enter a predominantly male workplace.[5] Her model of social change and resistance has been utilized by Leola Johnson to examine

the power dynamics that accompany the formation of coalitions between black caucuses and women's caucuses in the newsroom.[6] Kanter
describes what happens to women when we first enter a previously predominantly male workplace as managers, leaders, and decision-makers.
She speaks of two types of organizations, "skewed" and "tilted." In
a skewed workplace, women are less than 15 percent of the decision-
makers. In a tilted workplace, women make up 15 percent to 35 percent
of those who are managers. Kanter found that in the skewed environment, women were perceived by themselves and others stereotypically,
and they tended to either overachieve or underachieve. In a tilted environment, women began to exercise the power of self-definition. Women
viewed themselves and were viewed by others less stereotypically. Also
the achievement of women was more balanced, reflecting a range and
proportions more like that of men in the organizations.[7] Johnson found
the same dynamics operative with the inclusion of other racial groups in
a formerly all-white environment.[8]

As formerly excluded groups gain influence and power, the dynamics of support and resistance shift. Within a skewed organization, some
members of the dominant group are likely to be strong and effective
allies, working with women or racial minorities to break barriers and
bring the first people from different groups into the organization.[9] When
power shifts and there are more than token representatives of different
groups, new forms of resistance emerge. Those who were allies, active
in bringing in the "token" representatives, may find themselves defensive and resistant to further inclusion and to the impact of the inclusion
achieved thus far. For, as the numbers increase, the power of naming
shifts, and the balance of power shifts as well. The new groups begin to
change not only how they name themselves and are defined and named
by others but challenge the normal codes of operation — what counts as
business as usual, what the mission and focus of the organization should
be. At this point, former allies may resist, feeling the loss of power,
feeling the challenge to their powers of naming.

Once we recognize that these tendencies are at work, what difference
does it make? Kanter's theory can serve as a cautionary tale for those of
us who are dominant — realizing that against our will, outside of our intent, we may very well become defensive and resistant when our powers
of naming are challenged. For those of us who are exercising the power
of naming, we should not be surprised that our success leads to new
forms of resistance, and that those who were allies at an earlier stage
may not be allies at a later one. Furthermore, those of us accustomed
to the political struggles of the skewed organization may find ourselves
thrown off balance by the challenges of working for change within an
organization that is now tilted toward equality.

Let me give an example of differential resistance. A friend described the tensions she encountered as chair of a department of ethnic studies. She described the phenomenon of people coming into power as tokens — always being challenged, constantly having to fight to have their point of view taken seriously, always aware of the misunderstandings and ubiquitous attempts to coopt the few in order to placate the many (i.e., giving a few people highly visible but essentially powerless positions). She claimed that many of us who have had to fight our way into positions of power then only feel radical when we are embattled, struggling with an enemy who clearly does not share our agenda of social justice. My friend described what happens when we then gain power and may even have a measure of support from a formerly hostile administration. We may even *be* the administrators. She described how hard it is to shift from radical opposition to coalition building and institutional change. When people feel radical and alive only when they are opposed, she found faculty turning on each other or turning on students as being insufficiently radical, thus keeping alive, although now in self-destructive internal power struggles, the drama and energy of "the good fight."

When we have the power to name, the power to shape our institutions, when we have allies, how do we grasp this opportunity and utilize it effectively? The challenge is most basically one of practices, not of ideas. In his recent book *Conjuring Culture*, Theophus Smith provides a framework for examining this dimension of religious and political life. He takes the notion of "conjure" and uses it to highlight the intrinsically religious and political dimensions of social transformation in African-American life. Conjure involves eliciting spiritual power, transforming internalized oppression, evoking and sustaining acts of political transformation through a complex interaction of religious symbol systems, ritual performances, and political actions. Conjure describes the healing of an entire people, a challenge to systems of domination. Smith analyzes "cultural performances that involve curative transformations of reality by means of mimetic operations and processes."[10] Conjure "encompasses social-historical transformations as well as folklore practices."[11]

> I refer to such transformations as instances of *conjuring culture*, specifically where I find (1) ritually patterned behaviors and performative uses of language and symbols (2) conveying a pharmacopeic or healing/harming intent and (3) employing biblical figures and issuing in biblical configurations of cultural experience.[12]

In his work Smith analyzes instances of conjure and explores the need for further conjurational practices by African Americans. His book also raises a sharp challenge to Euro-Americans. We, too, are certainly in need of healing, healing from the deadly constructions of whiteness as domination, healing from identity formations that mask complicity with

232   SHARON D. WELCH

oppression, while they simultaneously elicit such oppression. He does not apply conjure to the spiritual-political-cultural dimensions of Euro-American religion, for we lack the systematic integration of material work, political activism and spiritual practice. Smith states that he "reserves the term conjure" "for African American transformations because of their more clearly articulated pharmacopeic, ritual and magical orientations."[13] What we Euro-Americans need, however, are practices that are explicitly conjurations of freedom, freedom from domination, freedom for risk, freedom from constructions of virtue and responsibility as control.

How do we conjure our way out of domination? Smith offers a key ingredient in his very definition of "conjure." By definition, conjure escapes the simplistic oppositions of good and evil, sacred and profane. Working with the notion of the *pharmakos,* he reminds us that that which heals can also harm.

> Concisely stated, conjure is not only sorcery or witchcraft but also a tradition of healing and harming that transforms reality through performances and processes involving a mimetic use of medicinal and toxic substances.[14]

Citing Raboteau, Smith reminds us that "we should be careful not to collapse the defensive and offensive distinction into the moral dichotomy of good versus evil.[15] That is to say, offensive conjure as well as defensive conjure can be good, and either can be malign."[16] It is this denial of the coincidence of good and evil, of help and harm, that is an intrinsic aspect of the evocation of domination and enmity.[17] People who locate evil and harm primarily in someone else, either the benighted masses or the heretical enemy, miss their own complicity in systems of oppression, often fail to see the possibilities for transformation in the "enemy," and find a justification for the exclusion or domination of the "enemy."

Can our focus on conjure be interpreted in the context of Farley's focus on *habitus* and *theologia* in his critique of theological education? Farley traces the loss of theology as *habitus* and seeks to return theological education and theology to a dialectic that resolves the theory-practice split. Farley states that in the medieval period theology was viewed as a "sapiential knowledge," an "aptitude of the soul," or, in other words, "theology is a *practical,* not theoretical habit, having the primary character of wisdom."[18] For Farley, theological understanding, or *theologia,* is both a *habitus,* a way of living, and critical reflection on the relationship between faith and life.

There are formal similarities between "conjure" and *habitus:* each is an understanding of faith that focuses on wisdom, on the sapiential end of theological knowledge. Like *habitus,* conjure is explicitly and thoroughly collective: the wisdom that is sought is grounded in, expressed in, and finds its end in the life of a people working for salvation/ justice. Conjure and *habitus* differ, however, in at least three senses. Farley proposes that *habitus* is best served by a type of critical reflection, *theologia*, which focuses on *appraisal*, the appraisal of "constitutive (ontological) features or ciphers of the human being's being and situation in the world," "the discernment of its [ecclesial] existential truth, its disclosive character, its enduring illuminating power," appraisal of "how the 'truth' of ecclesial existence pertains to choices, styles, patterns, and obligations of individual human life," appraisal "of the enduring truth of ecclesial existence and the public world."[19]

The aim of conjure incorporates appraisal, but is focused most properly on a complex of political, individual, cultural, communal, and spiritual transformation. Conjure begins after the work of appraisal. Once we have an analysis of the political and spiritual challenges facing us, how then do we act? Given the depth of injustice, merely providing a rational critique of systems of oppression does nothing to transform those systems, does nothing to free people from the construction of group identity and individual identity by hierarchical structures and imbalances of power. Thus the analytical dimensions of conjure include developing practices of spiritual and political transformation and then evaluating the actual effects of specific religious practices.

Second, the work of conjure unifies not only the theory/practice split, but the material/spiritual split as well. The means of conjure are material (the use of herbs, dance, physical discipline) as well as practices more commonly understood by Euro-Americans as mediums of the spiritual (prayer, meditation, preaching, poetry, drama). For example, one of the essential dimensions of resistance to apartheid in South Africa was the use of dance in mass marches. Thousands of people would join arms, the rhythm of the dance, the support of other bodies, making it possible for people to march for hours. When freed from prison, Nelson Mandela danced these same steps onto the platform for his press conference. While the dance alone could have accomplished nothing, it was also crucial, a means by which people who had worked together to appraise a given situation, who were committed to political and social transformation, could act together in a way that embodied a sense of power, of community, of movement. The marches, with the jubilant rhythmic dance, helped constitute a sociality that could sustain the long work of dismantling apartheid.

Thirdly, conjure incorporates both the capacity for harm and for healing. The community that is shaped by conjure, the conjurors themselves, remain even in the transformative practice of conjure capable of error, illusion, and self-deception. The strengths of the conjurors carry with them limits and weaknesses. Furthermore, that which heals in one situation may be toxic in another. Conjure is a way of moving within the dialectic of good and evil, help and harm. It is not a way of freeing ourselves from the possibility of evil and harm. *Habitus,* on the other hand, seems to be shaped by the Christian hope of transcending or vanquishing evil.

What does a focus on conjure and on *habitus* provide for people involved in social and political change? With Farley, we can reclaim the medieval understanding of *habitus,* the recognition that the object of our concern is far more than correct ideas about politics, ethics, or even so-called spiritual truths. We are concerned with habits of living, ways of attending to the world, to nature, to other people, to conflict, and to political struggles. We are examining habits of attention and response and the impact that these have on other people and the natural world.

With Smith's notion of conjure, we can complicate our understanding of habits in several ways. First, the development of the habits that lead to justice and equity requires the fusion of the material and the spiritual. Ritual, worship, dance, and physical discipline are as much a part of the process as rigorous critical thinking. Second, the development of certain habits does not free us from error or illusion, even from self-interest and the ability to misuse power for our own ends. Rather, conjure is a way of moving within the messy, conflictual, yet often beautiful and joyous dimensions of life without denial of either our possibilities for help or for harm.

Once again, what does this mean for groups working for social justice? What are our habits, how do we attend to our "enemies," those on the outside, those on the "inside" who are getting in the way of "truly effective work" because of their commitment to the "wrong" strategy or persistence in the "wrong" analysis? How do we work with our own proclivities toward self-interest and the abuse of power? How do we move with the chaos and conflicts that accompany group decision-making and institutional change? I contend that looking at these habits provides clues to understanding how we defeat ourselves, how it is that internal political struggles become deadly rather than remaining part of the necessary process of working with other people.

I have found two sources especially helpful in describing typical and problematic habits of self- and other-regard, habits of viewing ambiguity and opposition that often occur in groups. Both writers focus on the concrete process of making effective decisions in certain limited situations. Rosabeth Moss Kanter's book is based on her study of decision-making and change within major U.S. corporations. Gary Oxenhandler's essay is based on his work as a practicing attorney, conferring with clients, participating in committees, working with people in situations in which decisions have to be made and negotiation with an actual or potential adversary is necessary. Oxenhandler, in his description of "the dynamics that drive groups and individuals in their decision-making," and Kanter, in her analysis of the "art and architecture" of institutional change, provide glimpses into the complex of ethical and theological assumptions, habits, and dispositions that I claim are intrinsic aspects of a culture of domination.[20]

Oxenhandler and Kanter are focused on practice: what attitudes, questions, assumptions can help individuals and groups make decisions more effectively? In their divergent accounts of effective decision-making, I claim that we can find the resonance of other habits, habits of self-definition, habits of viewing the other, habits of seeing, naming, and responding to the complex of "good and evil," better and worse, right and wrong, effective and ineffective.

Oxenhandler describes the "mental posturing" that "all of us *initially* take when decision-making involves opposition or an adversary":

I am invulnerable.
I am psychologically stronger than my adversary.
I am financially stronger than my adversary.
I am a better negotiator than my adversary.
I have the best advice and I am listening to it.
I am right and my adversary is wrong.
God is on my side.
I will win and my adversary will lose.[21]

Those of us whose identities are shaped by both privilege and exclusion may not be able to make all of these assumptions (few women would claim invulnerability or greater financial strength, for instance), but we can make enough of them to find ourselves manifesting the illusions of what Oxenhandler calls SelfConsensus. In his description of SelfConsensus, Oxenhandler builds on Janus's analysis of GroupThink. SelfConsensus is the process by which we "positively reinforce our own conclusions so as to convince ourselves that we are right," and this process shares with GroupThink a complex of illusions. Janus describes eight illusions of GroupThink, two of which are especially pertinent for our purposes: "An unquestioned belief in the group's inherent morality, inclining the members to ignore the ethical or moral consequences of their decision" and "direct pressure on any member who expresses strong arguments against any of the group's stereotypes, illusions or commitments, making clear that this type of dissent is contrary to what is expected of all loyal members."[22]

Kanter describes a similar process at work in the "art and architecture of change."[23] She notes that there is often a clear disjunction between the institutional memory of change and the process of change itself. While the memory of change focuses on clarity, certainty, rightness, and consensus, the process of change is characterized by conflict, risk, errors, and confusion.

Where groups or organizations appear to "act," there are often strong individuals persistently pushing.

Where recent events seem the most important in really bringing the change about, a number of less obvious early events were probably highly important.

Where there is apparent consensus, there was often controversy, dissent, and bargaining.

Where the ultimate choice seems the only logical one, unfolding naturally and inevitably from what precedes it, there were often a number of equally plausible alternatives that might have fitted too.

Where clear-sighted strategies are formulated, there was often a period of uncertainty and confusion, of experiment and reaching for anyone with an answer, and there may have been some unplanned events or "accidents" that helped the strategy to emerge.

Where single leaders or single occurrences appear to be the "Cause" of the change, there were usually many actors or many events.

Where an innovation appears to have taken hold, there may be contradictory tendencies in the organization that can destroy or replace it, unless other things have occurred to solidify — institutionalize — the change.

And where there appears to be only continuity, there was probably also change. Where there appears to be only change, there was probably also continuity.[24]

According to Kanter, those who master change must know and understand the conflictual and chaotic processes of change, but they must also utilize and create myths that deny that very process. She argues that change masters create myths in which "conflicts disappear into consensuses," "equally plausible alternatives disappear into obvious choices," and "accidents, uncertainties, and muddle-headed confusions disappear into clear-sighted strategies" and "the fragility of changes (that exist alongside the residues of the old system) disappear into images of solidity and full actuality."[25] She claims that

> To get commitment and support for a course of action may require that it appear essential — not as one of a number of possibilities. By the time a decision is announced, it may need to be presented as the only choice, even if there are many people aware of how much debate went into it or how many other options looked just as good. The...champions of the idea...have to look unwaveringly convinced of the rightness of their choice to get other people to accept the change.[26]

Kanter assumes as inevitable, and even productive, an intrinsically hierarchical situation — there are those who engineer change and those who are affected by it. Those who engineer change understand the complexity of the change process, but they use myths of clarity, consensus, and certainty to gain assent. As Kanter states, "Those who master change know that they can never tell the 'truth,' but they also know what the 'truth' is."[27]

Contrast Kanter's change master with Oxenhandler's deliberate challenge to illusions of certainty, morality, invulnerability, and success.

> Always, always, always bear in mind that you *are* vulnerable; that your adversary *may be* psychologically and financially stronger than you; that although you *may be* getting the best advice, you *may not be* listening to it; that you *may not be* right; that everyone has their own God (and that even though your God is on your side, your adversary's God may be on their side and may be more powerful than your God); and, that you *may not* win.[28]

Oxenhandler's model strikes at the heart of the illusions necessary for domination — certainty of both power and the right to use that power, secure in the wisdom of one's own analyses, motives, and plans. Kanter's model, however, has deep resonance with the founding myths of Western culture. Note the similarity between her change master, successfully evoking myths of inevitable choices and widespread consensus with Weber's description of the charismatic political leader — one who convinces his or her followers that they are at the very heart of things, certain of eventual triumph, part of a process that is larger than the human agents who participate in it. Geertz, in his discussion of charisma, goes so far as to posit a necessary and intrinsic sacrality of central authority, a human need for the right answer and submission to a powerful leader who implements that right answer in political and cultural life.[29]

It is easy for us to see the danger of charismatic authority, of certainties of victory and rightness when they are held by our adversaries: we see the exclusion of dissent, the legitimation of violence against scapegoats, against those who obstruct and oppose the grand vision of society. I must admit, for example, that Newt Gingrich's promise "to bury any remains of what he disdainfully called the Great Society counterculture McGovernick legacy and return American to a more black and white view of right and wrong" makes *my* blood run cold.[30]

But what about the operation of this mindset among us — those of us on the left, among feminists, progressives, those committed to work for racial justice? Do we not make the same mistakes, participate in the same error — so certain of our commitment to social justice that we assume that our strategies for attaining justice must also be right, pure, and untainted by error, illusion, and self-interest? Do we not also silence those who offer sharply divergent strategies for achieving equality and justice? I find that all too often our work for social change is marred by internal struggles over who is feminist enough or who is black enough, enforcing uniformity, being threatened by real differences all the while we sincerely and wholeheartedly want to celebrate and sustain difference in mutually challenging as well as supportive interactions.

This is the place where conjure is needed, where our habits of evoking and celebrating power, vitality and energy fail us. I contend that Kanter's model is too dangerous and, while no strategy is free of toxic elements, too infected with the poison of domination to be useful. Domination is intrinsic to the myth of the change master: it assumes an elite that understands the complexity of change, and yet masks it from those affected by and those who actually implement the change. It leads too easily to illusions of moral purity, and thus the sanctioning of violence against scapegoats endemic to Christian cultures. Smith describes this phenomenon well in his discussion of the Christian apocalyptic imagination:

> A troubling aspect of Christian apocalyptic traditions in general can also be found in black American apocalyptic. In each case one finds a theological irony: the irony of a religion that espouses forgiveness and reconciliation, on the one hand, and yet harbors a vigorous hope for divine wrath and retribution on the other.[31]

We find in the Christian apocalyptic imagination a conjunction of protestations of universal love — love for all human beings, a desire to share the fruits of the gospel with all the earth, and, simultaneously, a desire for vengeance, a celebration of the wrath of God that destroys those who fail to accept the proffered message of love and reconciliation. There is a logic here — the lie of certain truth maintained only by violence against those who remind us of the tenuousness of our claims to morality, truth, and victory.[32]

On the surface, Kanter's model of the change master and Geertz's model of sacred authority and certain purpose appear affirming of human dignity and strength. After all, they offer the myth of being right, of being on the winning side, of being wise and creative and engineering and implementing not merely a good idea but the best idea, the necessary way of organizing human society. They offer a chance to be unambiguously on the side of the angels. And yet these seeming glorifications of human capacities in service to a legitimate authority or purpose mask a deep contempt for other people — a contempt expressed in the division between those who know the truth and those who are manipulated by myths, a contempt manifest in the scapegoat phenomenon and its exclusions and violence.

At first reading, Oxenhandler's model seems pessimistic, almost misanthropic. Here we find not glorification of human intelligence or wisdom, but a reminder of our capacity for self-deception, error, and illusion. Yet paradoxically, this mindset, when grounded in connection, manifests both deep respect for other human beings, and, not coincidentally, the potential to counter the toxins of elitism and domination. Let me explain. To acknowledge one's limits includes acknowledging the limits of others, and it also includes acknowledging the potential wisdom and insights of others as well as oneself. The tenor of this respect is described most clearly by Buber in his account of what occurs in the relationship of I and Thou:

> Love is a cosmic force. For those who stand in it and behold in it, [people] emerge from their entanglement in busyness; and the good and the evil, the clever and the foolish, the beautiful and the ugly, one after another become actual and a You for them; that is, liberated, emerging into a unique confrontation. Exclusiveness comes into being miraculously again and again and now one can act, help, heal, educate, raise, redeem.[33]

Buber affirms humanity with our faults, with our illusions and self-deceptions. From this matrix of seeing ourselves as flawed, but without attributing to that flaw fall, shame, or guilt, there can emerge another vocabulary of strength and weakness, of insight and deception — one that emphasizes accountability, not guilt, a sensibility that encompasses a good-humored recognition of the accidents, the surprises, the muddles that characterize our attempts to implement the good.

Is there room for passion for justice, for outrage, for commitment in a sensibility that acknowledges our vulnerability and capacity for error? It is difficult to imagine this sensibility, for much of our religious and political symbol systems are so precisely the contrary. We don't have to resort to "onward Christian soldiers"; "once to every man and nation" is enough. In our familiar hymns as in our seemingly secular constructions of efficiency and success, we are shaped by the assumption that momentous choices, those that have both theological as well as ethical and political import, are crystal clear and that we can respond, with truth, power, and majesty to the call for justice.

Can we find glimpses of another sensibility? I think so. I think it is there, pulsing in the rhythms of the blues, singing in the evocative prose of Toni Morrison. Smith cites Ralph Ellison's description of the transformative nature of the blues:

> The blues is an impulse to keep the painful details and episodes of a brutal experience alive in one's aching consciousness, to finger its jagged edge, and to transcend it, not by the consolation

of philosophy, but by squeezing from it a near-tragic, near-comic lyricism.[34]

In contrast, Smith reminds us of James Baldwin's claim that for Euro-Americans, our music is either happy or sad — an emotional state that correlates deeply with illusions of victory and rightness: we're either right, successful, and happy, or wrong, defeated, and miserable. What the wisdom of the blues evokes is a very different awareness, one that cannot be described as either optimism or pessimism, and most certainly is not adequately described as a tragic sense of life. Again, citing Jahn-heinz Jahn, Smith highlights the homeopathic power of the blues, noting that "the melancholy is a camouflage."

> If we read the text of the blues songs without prejudice and no-tice the double meaning, which all authors emphasize, we find them mocking, sarcastic, tragi-comic, tragic, dramatic and ac-cusing, often crudely humorous ... [but] only exceptionally ... [is there] melancholy.[35]

What would it mean for those of us shaped by the identity of dom-inance to embrace the spirituality and sensibility of the blues? We can stop taking ourselves too seriously so that we can respond, with utmost seriousness, to actual threats to human life. And in that response, we may remain fully aware of the limitations of our insight, our imagina-tions, and our courage. To move out of our identities as the dominant race, we must learn to fail — because we will, often and embarrassingly and repeatedly. It is not easy to dismantle centuries-long structures of racial oppression, a self-definition predicated on racial divisions. And yet, as Myles Horton knew and celebrates in his work *The Long Haul,* it is often in our failures that we learn the most, often in our failures that we discover deep ties with other people, in our failures that we plant the seeds of later victories.[36]

What religious sensibility can be conjured? What practices can emerge from this sensibility and then in turn sustain it? Music that embodies the complexity, both the pain and the joy of work for justice, music that carries through tone and tenor and rhythm the simultaneous hope for justice and a memory of the costs of oppression, the weight of all that has been lost; spirituality that affirms our humanity as in-trinsically capable of wisdom and error, kindness and self-centeredness, insight and self-delusions — without assuming that we'll ever be able to rid ourselves of the proclivity for error and harm. Toni Morrison evokes this sensibility most clearly, both in *Sula* and in *Beloved.* Here we find a language of good and evil, struggle and hope, that maintains the passion for justice without an illusion of ultimate victory, that acknowledges the persistent challenge of evil without resignation, nihilism, or cynicism. In

Sula, the images are stark and compelling — evil is something to be endured, not defeated.[37] In *Beloved,* the community that was complicitous in Sethe's tragedy returns to reclaim her, and this reclamation, while profound and healing, is itself partial. Sethe is reclaimed, Beloved is expelled, and yet the healing, for all its partiality, is a healing nonetheless, the matrix of further change, of life, of hope.[38]

Another intimation of a spirituality that can counter the toxins of domination is expressed in the poetry of Muriel Ruykeyser:

> A miracle has even deeper roots,
> Something like failure, some profound defeat.
> Stumbled-over, the startle, the arousal,
> Something never perceived till now, the taproot.[39]

What is this taproot grasped only in failure, stumbled over in defeat and betrayal? It varies, yet emerges in human connection: the resilience of our love for each other; the resilience of respect for ourselves and others in our illusions and error; the fact that in spite of, and even through, our limitations, we are yet capable of kindness and compassion, and maybe at times even justice. And while those attempts are partial, as they will always be, the taproot is the courage and humor of a community that continues to learn, to love, to acknowledge our capacity for harm — and from that acknowledgement find together balm for the journey, presence and witness to the struggles and joys of life.

NOTES

1. For her detailed critique of racism, see Barbara Andolsen, *Daughters of Jefferson, Daughters of Bootblacks: Racism and American Feminism* (Macon, Ga.: Mercer University Press, 1986).

2. Derek Bell, *And We Are Not Saved: The Elusive Quest for Racial Justice* (New York: Basic Books, 1989).

3. Administrators at the Missouri University have focused on the recruitment of African-American students because there are substantial numbers of African Americans in Missouri yet few Hispanics, Asian Americans, or Native Americans.

4. Theophus H. Smith, *Conjuring Culture: Biblical Formations of Black America* (New York: Oxford University Press, 1994), 162, 174, 253.

5. Rosabeth Moss Kanter, *Men and Women of the Corporation* (New York: Basic Books, 1977).

6. Leola Johnson, "Black Caucuses and Women's Caucuses in the Newsroom," lecture delivered at the University of Missouri, Columbia, March 1993.

7. Kanter, *Men and Women of the Corporation,* chapter 8.

8. Johnson, "Black Caucuses and Women's Caucuses in the Newsroom."

9. Let me give a personal example of the experience of working with allies within a "tilted" organization. When I attended Vanderbilt Divinity School (1975–1981), there was a critical mass of students interested in theologies of liberation. During this period women were redefining the nature, method, and scope of the theological enterprise from our vantage point as people formerly marginalized by and excluded from theological education. The faculty embodied the best of liberal Protestantism, welcoming our questions, and while not necessarily arriving at the same answers, supporting us in the process of foundational critique. We were encouraged to assume the "power of naming," challenged to be rigorous in our critique and redefinition of our identities within the Western theological and philosophical tradition. Many of us experienced the faculty at VDS as allies in this process of construction and critical inquiry. As a student of theology, I was most supported by the work of Edward Farley, Sallie McFague, Peter Hodgson, Gene TeSelle, and Jack Forstman.

10. Smith, *Conjuring Culture,* 5.

11. Ibid., 6.

12. Ibid.

13. Ibid., 56.

14. Ibid., 31.

15. Ibid., 43.

16. Ibid.

17. Susan Thistlethwaite provides a cogent critique of the dualities of good and evil in her analysis of racism, feminism, and Christianity. Susan Thistlethwaite, *Sex, Race, and God: Christian Feminism in Black and White* (New York: Crossroad, 1989), chapter 4.

18. Edward Farley, *Theologia: The Fragmentation and Unity of Theological Education* (Minneapolis: Fortress Press, 1983), 35.

19. Ibid., 186–87.

20. Gary Oxenhandler, "GroupThink and SelfConsensus," unpublished essay, 1992. Rosabeth Moss Kanter, *The Change Masters: Innovation and Entrepreneurship in the American Corporation* (New York: Simon and Schuster, 1983).

21. Oxenhandler, "GroupThink and SelfConsensus," 3.

22. Irving L. Janus, *Victims of GroupThink,* cited by Oxenhandler, "GroupThink and SelfConsensus," 2.

23. Kanter, *The Change Masters,* 288.

24. Ibid., 288–89.

25. Ibid., 285–86.

26. Ibid., 285.

27. Ibid., 288.

28. Oxenhandler, "GroupThink and SelfConsensus," 5.

29. Clifford Geertz, *Local Knowledge: Further Essays in Interpretive Anthropology* (New York: Basic Books, 1983), 146.

30. *New York Times,* November 10, 1994.

31. Smith, *Conjuring Culture,* 223.

32. This argument is developed in detail by Rosemary Radford Ruether

in *Faith and Fratricide: The Theological Roots of Anti-Semitism* (New York: Seabury Press, 1974).

33. Martin Buber, *I and Thou*, trans. Walter Kaufmann (New York: Scribner's, 1970).

34. Ralph Ellison, *Shadow and Act* (New York: Random House, 1964), 78, cited by Smith, *Conjuring Culture*, 123.

35. Jahnheinz Jahn, *Muntu: The New African Culture* (New York: Grove Press, 1961), 223, cited by Smith, *Conjuring Culture*, 123.

36. Myles Horton, with Judith Kohl and Herbert Kohl, *The Long Haul: An Autobiography* (New York: Anchor Books, 1990).

37. Toni Morrison, *Sula* (New York: Bantam Books, 1973).

38. Toni Morrison, *Beloved* (New York: Knopf, 1987).

39. Muriel Ruykeyser, "Fable" in *Collected Poems* (New York: McGraw-Hill, 1978), 554.

PART FOUR

Reply by
Edward Farley

⟫ 14 ⟪

Response

EDWARD FARLEY

Responding to these essays has been an exercise in frustration. The essays have focused laser-like beams on themes and texts of my work, exposing thereby things (good and bad) I was not aware of and pressing me to think about matters that I knew I had problematically handled. In some cases I would have liked a whole chapter, perhaps a book, to really engage the issue. And I am fortunate to have certain writings looked at from such diverse angles as process, Hegelian, liberation, feminist, and deconstructive thinking. Thus some see what I have done as ontologically reified: others as insufficiently ontotheological. In Section I, I shall take up both major themes and also particular essays. In the sections on history and praxis, I shall reply to each essay.

I. Philosophy and Theology

Several of the essayists (Hodgson, Williams) have noted my proximity to Friedrich Schleiermacher, a dependence I fully acknowledge. I would, however, qualify their interpretation of that dependence. Hodgson wonders whether I reduce christology and pneumatology to anthropology. If this means deriving world and God from "states of self-consciousness," I think not. If it means that redemption is the primary instance and location of *theological* discourse about world and God, then I think so. In my view very little if anything can be *derived* from states of self-consciousness. Hodgson is quite right in calling for a christology and some account of God's role in redemption, themes that constitute the companion volume to *Good and Evil,* soon to be published. Williams rightly senses a similarity between the "utter dependence" of Schleiermacher and my "being-founded." I must add, however, that structurally, the counterpart to utter dependence in *Good and Evil* is not being-founded but the motif of eros, elemental passions before an eternal horizon. A very different (more Blondelian) fundamental ontology and

247

formal account of incipient piety is thus at work here than in Schleiermacher. It is perhaps true to say that I "refuse an ontological philosophy
of religion" by making being-founded an ontic matter. Again, I add that
this ontic element correlates with the ontology of desire before the eternal horizon. Like Schleiermacher I refrain from labeling the object of
desire "God," since the full symbolic content of the term "God" does
not attend desire itself but rather redemption. On the other hand, from
the perspective of redemption, one can properly say that the yearned-
for *desideratum* or eternal horizon was in fact God. I have in other
words attempted to mediate the face-off between an ontotheological and
anti-ontological approach to theology.

Four themes are voiced by a number of the essays: the face, the status
of the tragic (or chaos), universality and parochialism, and reification.
As to *face*, Hodgson is especially concerned to apply that theme to God,
the universal face, making it a term for the self-presented, divine presence, glory, or grace. I can only say that I have strongly qualified (in the
companion volume to *Good and Evil*) all discourse about divine presence, and therefore I can discuss the metaphor of a divine face only if
these cautions are in place. Williams, Lowe, and Scott all note my taming of Levinas's motif of face. The result of this taming is to suppress
radical, uncontrollable otherness, the absolute demand of non-human
strangeness (Lowe), and to opt for the more Buberian notion of relation and mutuality. I must acknowledge the force and rightness of these
criticisms. In *Good and Evil* I appropriated Levinas's term "face" and
reset it into the realm of the interhuman. Hence, my discussions of face
do not retain Levinas's radicality. There was a reason for this. I am
convinced that, as a sphere of human reality, the interhuman is not reducible to either agency or sociality. In the interhuman, very subtle and
complex dynamics of interaction, inter-intentionality, discerned alterity,
guilt, and resentment take place. As a sphere it is subject to distinct corruptions and, I think, redemptions. I could not, therefore, omit all this,
simply to be true to Levinas, who is up to something quite different.
While I do not think Levinas's criticisms of Buber successfully destroy
the interhuman or mutuality, I do think he has shown a non-mutual and
radical alterity that is not capturable by human reciprocal relations. And
I do think that this asymmetrical otherness is a necessary ground of the
critique of totality.

Lowe and Williams both advance penetrating questions on my han-
dling of the theme and status of the tragic (chaos). Lowe agrees with the
critique of the classical tradition but worries that my placing of sin and
human evil against the background of the tragic make lucid what must
remain mysterious. At the same time he acknowledges that the tragic element limits explanation. Perhaps I have not been clear on this matter.
I do think there is a connection between the tragic condition of human

beings and the dynamics of idolatry, simply because an attempted refusal of that condition is part of that dynamics. But with Kierkegaard (cf. the leap) I do not think this explains evil. It is just this juncture of tragic condition and human response that eludes efforts of explanation, and it is at this juncture I would locate the mystery of the origin of evil.

Williams senses (rightly) certain ambiguities in my treatment of the tragic. I do see the *experience* of the tragic as intrinsically ambiguous because (as Williams points out) the tragic has connotations both of the chaotic and unpredetermined element in finite being without which no entity could be self-determining or creative and of the inevitable disharmony that ensues when self-determining entities exist together. Chaos thus is both a *sine qua non* and the perilous environment of freedom. More seriously yet, Williams senses an ambiguity concerning the *status* of the tragic. Is it ultimate, at the center of things? And if it is, is not this a nihilistic view? His own position seems to be that it is at the center, but because it is in God Godself, it does not triumph. There is one sense in which I see the tragic as ultimate. It comes inevitably with created or finite being. Finite being in the sense of activity can never exist in the mode of pure realization and hence embodies a gap between realization and any projected ideality. And this relativizes all projected triumphalisms. But chaos or the tragic is not ultimate in the sense of a positive and competing being or entity. That which is positive and has being (however much it exists from and needs chaos) is thus open to the divine activity. Accordingly, this notion of tragic finitude does not amount to nihilism.

Both Williams and Cobb raise questions concerning the way in which I understand how what is determinate about the ecclesial paradigm of redemption relates to what is universal or to other faiths. Williams senses a lack of resolution on the issue of foundationalism. He sees my locating of redemption and being-founded in historical determinacy (thus as ontic) as anti-foundational. And he wonders if this is a parochialism that would withhold being-founded (redemption) from other faiths. To counter such parochialism would require a foundationalist element. Both alternatives seem unfortunate, the one parochial to the point of exclusivism, the other universalist to the point of imperialism. There is a foundationalist element in *Good and Evil* that finds expression neither in a metaphysics of being or world nor in a universal transcendental human condition. It is the picture (Part One) of tragically structured, three-sphered human reality not able to be content with oppressive socialities, fractured and alienated relations, and imperiled subjectivity. Idealities (justice, reconciliation, wonder, etc.) preside over these spheres. But I am anti-foundationalist in my refusal to think that the determinacy of the Hebraic and Christian paradigms for redemption are derivable from the foundational element and in my inability to discover anonymous versions of Christian redemption in other faiths. I do think there is something like being-founded in Islam, Hinduism, and Buddhism, but I would rather be open to their own articulations. Mutual recognitions rather than logical claims would be the way this would be confirmed.

I am not sure whether John Cobb and I have a genuine disagreement. He acknowledges the validity of analyses of intermediate levels between universal metaphysics and particularity. As committed to universal metaphysics, he presumably thinks that what is descriptive of all entities also describes all peoples, traditions, times, and faiths. But he senses something inappropriate about *intermediate* levels of analysis applying to peoples, faiths, etc. One can apply Whitehead's but not Heidegger's concepts to various peoples. I am not sure why. As a Whiteheadian he would argue that all entities (including Buddhists and Christians) prehend ideal objects. And he can argue this in spite of the fact that there may be little or no thematization of this in particular Buddhist or Christian traditions. When one moves to a more intermediate level, one may find that both Buddhists and Christians, in spite of their very different ways of understanding "consciousness," are temporal not just in the general way of any entity but in ways that result from linguisticality. This notion seems to be no more a violation of the particularity of these traditions than that of prehension, etc. It is what I have called the principle of positivity that urges caution on all generic and intermediate hermeneutics. That is, all general, universal, or quasi-universal features of things undergo modification in their particular instanciation. Hence, I would surely distort Buddhism if I assumed that there was no specifically Buddhist modification of the temporality of *Dasein*. In other words I see the intermediate level of analysis as a more determinate level of formal analysis. Hence, Part One of *Good and Evil* would not apply directly to all cultures, but could be used as an exploratory device. There surely are Eskimo, Chinese, and tribal forms of institutionality (e.g., gender roles, ancestor-related rites), interhuman relation (mutual recrimination), and agency (particular anxieties, attitudes toward language, dreaming).

I do think that Cobb and I are on different tracks in the way he and I understand my notions of three spheres. He sees these as occurring in a "sharp distinction," "radically distinct," as "independent realities" involving a separation of the social and interhuman. He also sees the three as Western, even a university way of dividing up the world. I see the three quite differently. I see them as no more separated from each other than a Whiteheadian would see creativity, actual entities, and eternal objects as separate or independent. I distinguish them and emphasize the distinction because most current analyses (except twentieth-century Jewish philosophers) have no place at all for relation or the interhuman. If there is a Western or university view, it seems to be a duality of agency and sociality. I find no thematization at all of the interhuman in the world of universities. This absence has in fact distorted both the way sociality and the individual are interpreted. But I must acknowledge that the three spheres are abstractions, and at the level of particularity, they are deeply interconnected. Further, I see these spheres as spheres of a *condition,* not separable parts of some entity. As to Cobb's statement that regional ontologies neglect historicity, I entirely agree. And as to his comments on the neglect of global crisis in my writings, I also agree, though I disagree that this has something to do with a European, continental, or phenomenological tradition. I see virtually all philosophies and theologies, including process thought, as only just now turning to this problem.

The most difficult essay for me to respond to is Charles Scott's. This is only partly due to my philosophical innocence (thus the retaining of commonsense attitudes, the participation in Hellenic traditions, the discourse of the "real") and Scott's Nietzschean loss of innocence. It is difficult because on most issues I sense basic agreements between us. Thus, Scott does not simply repudiate "reflective ontology," accepts in some sense "skeletal thinking," uncovers distortion in all presentation, and even makes ordinary state-of-affairs claims. Accordingly, I must work very hard to uncover our differences.

Whether we differ depends on how one construes what Scott is (philosophically) up to, and here I see two quite different possibilities. On the one hand Scott may be a *dialectical* deconstructionist. He thus is constantly taking away with his left hand what his right hand has accomplished. He can direct thinking in a penetrating way to particular events and contents (compare Heidegger's call to think the being of technology) to be followed by genealogical analysis that shows the paradigmatic nature of the thinking and that destabilizes the direct claims. But here there is at least a right hand, or, one might say, an Apollonian element. Philosophy, like Job's God, both giveth and taketh away. The other way to construe Scott's critique is that there is only the left hand. Philosophy means simply destabilizing, taking away, de-presenting, a "de-organizing flow." Here there is no Apollonian element, and Hellenic philosophy is simply something to displace or surpass. If continental philosophy really is reduced to genealogy, it has ironically united with analytic philosophy's agenda of discourse correction. If the second way is the true Scott, then there is significant difference between us.

If I participated as deeply as Scott in the course continental philosophy has taken, I probably would not use terms like "reality" and "presence" in such a facile way. Yet I cannot give up the right hand, the Apollonian task, for this reason. Scott sees thinking that discloses patterns, enduring meanings, and the like as inevitably distortive. I agree.

What I do not hear from him is that such thinking is itself also a correction of a distortion. Under a commonsense agenda and the pragmatic attitudes that dominate the everyday world, human beings distort by simplification. Under rigorous cognitive agendas, sciences distort by focusing on abstract aspects of that with which they have to do. For me whatever is actual is complex, processive, dense, eventful, relational, mysterious, and multilayered. This is the case with anything we would think, a human individual, technology, a work of art, human evil, etc. In their concreteness these things call for a thinking of their complexity, which means thinking of how their potentially abstractable aspects are together. Pattern, metaphor, concept, is the result. Of course actual things are never simply presenting themselves but are de-presenting themselves; thus the thinking of their complexity into pattern calls for constant de-stabilization. Accordingly, to simply replace the Apollonian task of philosophy is to accede to the fragmenting distortions of the practical attitude of everyday life and of the sciences.

On this matter I traverse a route from Husserl to Heidegger. At first sight Husserl's description of the intentional object (*noema*) seems to be a search for an essence. But as he attempted to do justice to the ever-changing internal and external horizons of the intentional relation, with centers, margins, and contents constantly displacing each other, he opened up not the essence but the concrete. Heidegger's terms *das Wesen* and *die Lichtung* and his journey toward the poetical is a natural outcome of the Husserlian philosophy of intentionality. For me there are concrete things that do become illuminated and that illumination in part at least shows the being-together of their complexity. This is the right hand of philosophy, and the very occurrence of things at all, the coming together of fragments into manifestation, was the fascination of Hellenic philosophy. Accordingly, I cannot presume that this fascination and its various articulations are now simply displaced. I must acknowledge that fascination with pattern (*logos*) dominates my own thinking over genealogy and deconstruction. Hence, my thinking, such as there is, quite properly calls for what Scott is doing. But I must ask him whether thinking for him is simply de-presenting. I cannot think so because the de-presenting, the deconstruction, he brought to my work carried with it an *interpretation* of my work that synthesized texts and looked at multiple aspects as they come together. I think even for Scott Nietzsche has not completely accomplished a logocide.

II. History

Two of the essays (Duke and Forstman) react to a particularly vulnerable aspect of my work, historical interpretation. This means both my specific historical claims and my way of interweaving the historical into the theological. Forstman and Duke are related as professor to student. I recall interrupting one of their tutoring sessions by shouting Henry Ford's dictum through the door, "history is bunk." They both make the point that history in my writings is not a rigorous and persuasive accomplishment, a point with which I wholeheartedly agree. They make this point almost from opposite perspectives. Where Duke senses in the texts a way of conceiving and carrying out historical theology, Forstman is troubled by specific problems. Duke's essay is a highly nuanced account of theology discovering its own historicality and the way that impacts back on any subsequent history of that historicality. His initial move is a phenomenological one. Since the human condition itself is always already structured by historicality, the faith world as an actual and determinate instance of that condition is a thick, dense, multilayered world that belief itself and even surface kinds of historical awareness suppress. One step toward understanding the historical character of the faith world as it is set in the Christian movement arose with the Enlightenment. Here is born a critique of the faith world not unlike Kant's critique of naive objectivism. Here theology is awakened to the historical character of both itself and the contents (pieties, Scriptures, traditions, authorities, gospel) with which it deals. While this sounds like the Enlightenment gave rise to a new discipline in theological encyclopedia, the destiny of that discipline was fragmentation. That is, "historical theology" either meant the bird's eye view survey of Christianity (e.g., Harnack, Pelikan) or an aggregate of specific historical projects. Diversity and complexification simply overwhelmed history insofar as it served theological ends. Duke is convinced that such history does justice neither to the thick complexification of the faith world nor to the peculiar character of that world, viewed as something in some sense truth-bearing. It is at this point he engages, with appropriate tongue in cheek, some proposals of mine. He sees the concept of ecclesial existence as pertaining to the faith world, thus not eliminating that world in advance. He further argues that such a notion (and historical phenomenon) can combine both corrupted and ideal aspects and thus concern a historical movement and community that has a characteristic entelechy, a kind of ideal typification, that thematically unifies its diversity and serves as a criterion for its self-corruption. Second, he sees some possibility in the metaphor of portraiture — Wheeler and Kelsey propose radiography as a better metaphor — to get beyond historical studies in isolation and essence-of-Christianity and totalizing histories. Something like these concepts is needed, he argues, if we are to have a history that does justice both to the historicality and radical diversity of the Christian movement and also uncovers its continuities and its relation to an actual community of redemption.

I wish there were space to deal with Jack Forstman's queries and criticisms in an extensive way. I shall limit my reply to two issues: the "ugly ditch" problem, the unbridgeable gulf between faith and a historical redeemer, and historical theology and "Christian faith." According to Forstman's formulation, it would seem that there are two utterly different things: faith with whatever content it can have, and history with its historically established content. Faith cannot settle any factual question of the past. History cannot deal with theological or faith categories, for instance, with Jesus as redeemer. In this way Forstman can maintain history's critical principle and not fudge things with appeals to faith. Here I am in Forstman's court. But something about this stark duality troubles me. A similar duality can for the same reasons apply to faith and all cognitive endeavors, for instance, faith and cosmology. As in historical factualities, so with cosmological factualities, faith cannot settle such matters as the age of the cosmos, the number of galaxies, or questions of entropy. At the same time it is not accurate to say that cognitive sciences (history, cosmology, geology, etc.) are the sole mediators of history and cosmos and prior to the emergence of these sciences human beings had no historical or empirical awarenesses. Here we move to Duke's historicity. A kind of historical sense, a sense of the past, attends the corporate memory of human communities. Human beings are not totally cut off from the past, even the corporate past, in their everyday life, which past is delivered to them if they read the historians. A historical orientation is minimal in ancient peoples whose relation to the past and present is by way of ritual re-enactment of primordial powers of creation. It is much stronger in the Israelite community and the religious faiths it spawned. This is really all I had in mind by the appresentation of Jesus in the ecclesial community. I agree that a historical rather than mythical way of recollecting Jesus settles no question about what teachings are authentic or whether Jesus was betrayed by Judas. But neither do I think that this way of recollecting is utterly and totally dependent on the mediations of historical scholarship. In other words the ugly ditch is in some sense traversed in the religious community at the level of the way the past functions to structure its corporate memory, but this traversing is ever subject to the corrections, supplements, and dismantlings of historical scholarship. Neither faith nor its historical orientations come and go with these dismantlings.

I am not sure Forstman and I really disagree on the first issue. We do seem to have a disagreement about the second, the apparent unmediable relation between history's demand for particularity and theology's residence in and thus depiction of a certain *type* and strand of history. At stake here may be whether there is such a thing as *historical theology*. One set of Forstman's criticisms I can only accede to, his exposure of the non-rigorous character of my historical assertions. Have I really made the case for the elements of kerygma shared by various New Testament authors? Surely not. Before the critical and rigorous historians, my "historical" account of ecclesial existence is hardly a beginning. But Forstman presses a deeper question. Is it even possible? On this issue Forstman and Duke are in opposite courts.

In my view a certain type of religious community, quite different from others of its time, did arise in history, which we can call Hebraism. John Cobb (*Structures of Christian Existence*) and Paul Ricoeur *(The Symbolism of Evil)* have portrayed this type of religious existence in contrast to other types. Further, I think that a distinctive type of religious faith arose in the early Christian movement whose most general feature was a universalized form of Hebraic faith. The historical movement that ensued continued to exemplify this feature throughout its many epochs, corruptions, and splinterings. If there is no such movement and no such historical type, what I have called portraiture is clearly an impossibility. There is nothing to portray.

But I am not exactly sure what Forstman's position is. On the one hand, diversity and textual particularity seem to be ultimate, so ultimate that no distinction is possible between a community's deep symbols and passing metaphors. In the first century, there is no Christian movement, no single kerygma, theology, or gospel. Difference goes all the way down. But if difference does go all the way down to the subparticle world, solipsism is inevitable. That is, each entity in the world is different from one micro-second to the next and thus every depiction, every verbal expression violates that process of differentiation. And yet Forstman would also speak about what he calls "Christian faith." If "Christian faith" is some sort of pre-given authority, then history cannot deal with it at all. But for Forstman, it can deal with it. The study of texts can yield insight into Christian faith's meaning. What is this meaning? If it is some *content* of the texts, then Christian faith seems to be an aggregate term for something historical, something delivered by historical scholarship. But what historical scholarship gives us is not meaning but meanings, not Christian faith but faiths. If this meaning is in any way the "truth" or "reality" of things, then how would the study of *texts* yield that? At the level of texts, there are only kerygmas, differences, metaphors, and even faiths. If Forstman thinks that these various kerygmas bear or express "Christian faith," then he is back in what Duke calls the faith world and what I call ecclesial existence. In the end, according to Forstman, the theologian-historian must choose, must privilege some texts over others. On the basis of what criteria? If the criteria are external, it would seem the whole textuality, the historical coming about of a type of faith, is superfluous. If they are internal, it would seem that something like ecclesial existence ("Christian faith") is being expressed in the texts. I do think Forstman as historical theologian faces the same problem I have struggled with. But his eschewal of methods that would uncover types, master narratives, deep symbols, and comprehensible myths leaves him simply with a diversity of historically discerned faiths, not "Christian faith."

III. Practice

Essays by Buttrick, Wendy Farley, Welch, Ramsay, Wheeler and Kelsey, and Fulkerson take up aspects of my work that address or have implications for praxis: thus, preaching, ethics, feminism, pastoral theology, and (theological) education. All of these essays develop issues far beyond my treatment of them, thus correcting as well as supplementing my efforts. David Buttrick's essay on the way the postmodern constitutes a new era for preaching could well launch a new homiletic, even one beyond the new homiletic he has already forged. Buttrick has unwittingly taken up a subject that I address in a forthcoming book on the postmodern threat to "deep symbols," referred to in Wendy Farley's essay. As we have come to expect from Buttrick's work, he refuses to construe the task of preaching and of homiletic theory as a problem of new techniques. Preaching and its theory are both caught up in the massive shifts of the postmodern. Neither the preacher nor the homiletician can thus assume business is as usual. Buttrick is aware how deeply sympathetic I am with his prescription for a new homiletic paradigm; thus, the break with the Bible-to-text model, the shift from individualist to interpersonal interpretations of gospel, and the attention to a genetics of religious meaning. Most of my questions about his essay concern his "glance toward the future." The developments he projects seem to me to be more ideal *desiderata* than probable outcomes. Will Kant and a "project of consciousness" be part of the new age? In one sense such a response has already taken place in New England transcendentalism and in English and continental romanticism. "Post-rationalism" and "beyond subject and object," "nature as a project of consciousness," and "logic of consciousness" could also apply to those programs. In this sense Buttrick's scenario may be as much a glance at the past as at the future. I do think it possible that these things may persist as a strand of the future, but then I also think they have never wholly disappeared. The arts, philosophies, and religious thinking of industrial (modern) and post-industrial societies of the West have long been responding to quantification and objectification along these lines. That there will be countercultural and liberation movements in the postmodern period goes without saying. These movements do have, in my view, a new problem: surviving as transformation-oriented protests in a time in which a master narrative (Lyotard) and deep symbols needed by such protests are no longer operative. For me (and probably for Buttrick) that is the setting for a new homiletic.

Buttrick's essay on the postmodern describes the setting that all the other essays in one way or other address. Three of the essays (Wendy Farley, Welch, and Fulkerson) reflect the struggles of feminist theologians to bring about real change in the institutions of a recalcitrant, patriarchal society. I cannot take up Wendy Farley's essay without calling attention to the inexpressible experience of having one's own daughter participate in a work of this sort. She senses that feminism's receptive and even celebrative relation to the postmodern as that which replaces the old oppressive patriarchalisms may deprive it of the sources of its own protest. In her view feminists must not sever seriousness about justice and seriousness about reality (truth). Reflecting Plato and engaging my *Good and Evil,* she argues that passion (eros) is the place truth, the concern for the real, and justice come together. Apart from eros, truth is rendered objective and bloodless, floating above all suffering. And apart from an eros for truth, justice (presumably concerned with suffering) is reduced to a strategy, cut off from humanizing criteria. It is eros, a passionate way of being open to the unreducible reality (and thus mystery and beauty) of the other, that connects the feminist concern for justice to actual, living, suffering persons.

To this eloquent and passionate essay, I venture a single question. The question may reveal simply that "elemental passions" (cf. *Good and Evil*) and Wendy Farley's eros are not quite the same. In the case of the elemental passions, we have an essentially ambiguous human phenomenon. The passionate life even at its deepest level of the passion for existence itself is something (in my interpretation) that can be receptive to and transformed by what I have called the dynamics of idolatry. When human beings go wrong, when fanaticism, racism, and various kinds of malice structure their very being, it is their passions that have been re-shaped. Eros in this sense has no built-in immunity against corruption. In the light of this, it is clear that Wendy Farley is using the term "eros" in a more ideal, even eschatological sense. In her view, eros is a power that has an anti-idolatry dynamics built into it. This would have to be the case if eros for the other is simply as such subject to and dominated by the other's need, reality, and beauty. Eros simply is the way human beings are related to the other in ways that do justice to that other. Comparing this to Emmanuel Levinas, eros seems to function for Wendy Farley almost as face itself. In my view face, or something like it, must intervene to draw eros out of its own circle. This is not to say that eros is itself corrupt. Rather, it is a human existential that is open to corruptive or redemptive shaping. For Wendy Farley, eros is a redemptive relation. For me it is a redemptive relation only when its possibility of corruption is undermined by something else. In her view eros simply in itself is the locus of redemptive relation. In my view face and being-founded are necessary for eros to be that locus.

In one sense both Wendy Farley and Sharon Welch address a common issue, namely, whether social change calls for certain sensibilities. Wendy Farley argues a more general point, namely, that an uncritical relativism can undermine a feminist project at its roots. Sharon Welch carries this point into the back rooms of strategic planning. An idyllic and abstract way of understanding strategic change focuses simply on recruitment. Once the troops are gathered, things proceed apace. Sharon Welch, battle scarred from years of coalition work, knows better. The serpent shows up even in a coalition's garden of innocence. Ideological differences and meta-strategic postures can burst into serious conflict even among those who are working for a specific social change. Coalitions can fail or become ineffective if they pretend that only strategic issues are important or if their participants are uncompromising in the way they hold their views. Needed then is a self-consciousness about the deep postures and, beyond that, sensibilities that enable a transcending of typified self-identities. Welch appropriates the term *habitus* to introduce this issue of sensibilities necessary to the work of coalitions. Two comments.

First, I think it is a little misleading to compare (as she does) my use of *habitus* (in the work *Theologia*) with Theophus Smith's notion of conjure. I used that term as a way to relocate *theologia* from its usual site in fields of study. As such it is not a social transformation category. More parallel to conjure (as a way of conceiving sensibilities) is the theonomous description of agential freedoms and modes of interhuman life in *Good and Evil*. Second, I wonder if Welch confuses two levels of problem when she advocates *habitus* (conjure) as an alternate to Weber and the proposal that coalitions effect change by way of a hierarchical leadership and the myth of being certain. *Habitus* certainly has to do with the sensibilities of participants that reinforce successful strategy. Welch's case is for that, and this is the heart and contribution of her essay. But the *habitus* she sets forth (de-absolutizing, respect, etc.) may or may not settle the issue of the coalition's organization or strategic rhetoric. If she does accept this distinction, her next task would be to establish a correlation between the sensibilities of *habitus* and coalition structure. Mary Fulkerson's essay likewise pursues issues of feminism, but since it is also about theological education, I shall postpone my response to it until later.

That someone in the area of pastoral theology can make use of a work like *Good and Evil* is especially gratifying to me. It breaks the usual separation between these areas and challenges those who see the social sciences as the only or primary resource for anthropology in pastoral theology. More specifically Nancy Ramsay is not content simply to identify sin and psychopathology and works hard to both distinguish and relate them by framing a particular case. I myself would probably apply the anthropology of *Good and Evil* to any particular case in a different way than she has, but that probably means that my knowledge of cases is infrequent and superficial compared to hers. That is, I would find it difficult to take a comprehensive analysis with its many moves and ideas and so press it onto a particular case that each concept finds some exemplification in that case. This presumes that an instance of psychopathology/sin necessarily contains the total dynamics. And if that is the case, it would seem that the task of pastoral diagnosis is to discover that dynamics in each and every case. This comment may, however, be unfair to Ramsay. Her case analysis may simply be her effort to show that the various dynamics of evil, etc., can apply in an actual instance. By this means she corrects methods of diagnosis that fail because they suppress the interhuman dimension or the social sphere.

Given the three spheres of human reality, one might discover that a specific case falls primarily in one of them and less in the others, or that problems stem from a certain way the interhuman interacts with aspects of human agency. Or given the various dimensions of human agents, one might discover that a specific case reflects more biological (organic depressive?) problems than the dynamics of evil, or that in fact biologically rooted aggressive tendencies have been taken up into that dynamics. My only point here is one that Nancy Ramsay knows far better than I, that each case (person) is a unique life situation with distinctive showings of feeling, behavior, and repressed structures. That being the case, a theological anthropology offers a kind of heuristic device, a set of check-points, but not a scheme of concepts all of which must be applied or discovered. I am thus suggesting that the use of any conceptuality, psychological or theological, would profit from an initial phenomenological analysis of the "life-world" of the person. I find her essay especially helpful in the way it relates the concrete dynamics of sin to tragic aspects of the person, that is, very specific victimizing events. Her essay marks the beginning of a method of discovering how elements of psychopathology and sin can merge in a specific person.

Two essays in this volume (Wheeler and Kelsey, and Welch) take up the ongoing task of a critique of theological education. No one that I know has a better grasp of the current situation and the recent literature of theological education than Barbara Wheeler and David Kelsey. Their ongoing analyses of issues have themselves had a significant influence on current theological education. Their mediating work and their own constructive proposals bestow on the literature of the last generation an enduring significance it otherwise would not have had. Their essay prompts two comments. The first has to do with the plaintive but accurate observation that in spite of the *literary* busy-ness, the books and essays, the conferences and consultations, the debates and the reviews, little has actually changed in the schools themselves. Some faculty and administrators may *talk* a little differently about theological education. Wheeler and Kelsey also observe the birth of a new, second-generation literature that (to cite Rebecca Chopp) "return[s] to the fray of concreteness and discern[s] the historical, cultural, and symbolic factors at work in present theological education" (Chopp, *Saving Work: Feminist Practices of Theological Education* [Louisville: Westminster John Knox Press, forthcoming]). I have not seen this new literature and cannot comment on it. I would like to comment on what a "return to concreteness" would involve. To "return to concreteness" must surely confront the failure of a literature and discussion to effect actual institutional change. Wheeler and Kelsey themselves suggest some reasons for this failure. In my view the failure of institutions to change is primarily a matter of the specific character of the institutions in question, what they are up against in their setting, and what resistances to change are built into them out of the past. Preservation, not creativity, is the very point of institutions. They are successful as institutions to the degree that they enable some cause, content, structure, set of associations, social function, etc., to endure over time. Present-day *educational* institutions of higher education endure over time by way of organizations of curricula that are connected with faculty specialists and with reward systems pertaining to how the specialists teach and contribute to their fields. Many other things secure these institutions toward the future: constituencies, endowments, prestige, paradigms of knowledge and teaching, complicities in larger societal patterns (e.g., patriarchalism). Accordingly, one can imagine a school made up of a majority of change-oriented *individuals* that still cannot transform itself. Concern for actual, *institutional* change calls for awareness of the distinctive character of seminaries and divinity schools as social institutions and of the distinctive kind of resistance to change they embody. I see little of this in the literature so far. Surely, serious agendas of institutional transformation will have to have some smarts about these rather unique institutions. Thus, it is my hope that some study of the institutions of theological education will be an element in the second generation of a "literature of concreteness."

Second, Wheeler and Kelsey have performed an important service in their characterization of the anthropology behind conventional theological education and of alternatives to that anthropology. The exposition of two alternative anthropologies (bodied agent and expressive subject) was simply unclear to me. I do wonder whether the feminist movement has produced an anthropology, and further, whether there are sufficient texts in the second generation to work from. Many of the expressions used to depict the "expressive subject" anthropology had a Cartesian ring. Marcel's critique of the Cartesian anthropology is precisely a claim that human beings do not *have* bodies, and "having" is not our relation to body. The Cartesian *cogito* could also be called a "center of consciousness" marked by inwardness and known as it manifests itself in an objective medium. Since it surely is the case that feminist theology does not understand itself as Cartesian, these expressions are probably misleading.

Mary Fulkerson's essay is an example of what Wheeler-Kelsey describe as the new second-generation literature on theological education. Like Wendy Farley, Sharon Welch, John Cobb, and others, she places urgent social transformation, especially as it would redress policies and structures that marginalize and oppress, at the very center of the academic enterprise. I had argued (in *Theologia*) that theological education, lay or clergy, holds off its own potential reform by allowing relatively isolated academic disciplines to constitute theology's very raison d'être. This obscured the *habitus* and wisdom character of theology itself and eliminated the *paideia*, or forming dimension, of educational process. Fulkerson takes up this critique of theological education but connects it with agendas of social liberation. Similarly, she appropriates Alasdair MacIntyre's analysis of practice (as involving agential action, narratives, and a moral tradition) and displays its formal character, omitting as it does the way racism and patriarchalism corrupt discourse and thereby make silent the faint voices of the oppressed. I think her exposure of the formalist character of my treatment of *habitus* and *paideia* and MacIntyre's interpretation of practice is right on the mark. Her substitution of a liberation *paideia* for a more general notion is surely unavoidable in any credible proposal to reform theological education. And I think she is right in her descriptions of flawed discourse, of the new set of virtues called for by liberation practice, and of the suppressed stranger at work in biblical narratives. I have only two brief questions. First, I wonder whether she treats *habitus* as habituation. If *habitus* has the virtues of dissent she says it has, virtues that orient persons toward resistance, can *habitus* itself be habituation, that is, a conformation to a sedimented tradition? Does this risk a taming of *habitus* as a liberation-oriented practice? Second, Fulkerson says that *theologia* as formation must "replace a *Wissenschaft* approach to the marginalized as a subject matter." I think this sentence expresses her criticism of any theological education that assumes that a liberation *paideia* arises by way of adding new courses or fields to the curriculum. I agree. But it does make me wonder how she would connect the *wissenschaftlich* or scholarly element with the liberation *paideia*. I think she would argue that all fields contribute in some way to that *paideia*. But that they do or how they do remains to me unclear. Does her proposal eliminate the encyclopedic (the problem of distinguishing and organizing contents of education) element altogether or does it suggest that liberation *paideia* brings with it a new encyclopedic analysis?

Bibliography

A. Books

The Transcendence of God: A Study in Contemporary Philosophical Theology.
Philadelphia: Westminster Press, 1960.

Requiem for a Lost Piety: The Contemporary Search for the Christian Life.
Philadelphia: Westminster Press, 1966.

Ecclesial Man: A Social Phenomenology of Faith and Reality. Philadelphia:
Fortress Press, 1975.

Ecclesial Reflection: An Anatomy of Theological Method. Philadelphia: Fortress
Press, 1982.

Theologia: The Fragmentation and Unity of Theological Education. Philadelphia: Fortress Press, 1983.

*The Fragility of Knowledge: Theological Education in the Church and the
University.* Philadelphia: Fortress Press, 1988.

Good and Evil: Interpreting a Human Condition. Minneapolis: Augsburg/
Fortress, 1990.

Edited with Barbara Wheeler. *Shifting Boundaries: Contextual Approaches to
the Structure of Theological Education.* Louisville: Westminster John Knox
Press, 1991.

B. Books Scheduled for Publication

Words of Power: The Fate of Deep Symbols in Postmodern Society.

The Unthinkable: An Essay in the Theology of God. Forthcoming, Fall 1996.

Co-edited with Thomas G. Long, *World, Gospel, Scripture: Preaching as
Theological Task.* Essays in Honor of David G. Buttrick.

C. Chapters in Books

"Boundedness: The Provincialist Capture of the Church of Our Lord and Savior Jesus Christ." In Theodore Gill, ed. *To God Be the Glory.* Nashville:
Abingdon Press, 1973.

"Psychopathology and Human Evil: Toward a Theory of Differentiation."
In R. Bruzina and Wilshire, eds. *Crosscurrents in Phenomenology,* Se-
lected Studies in Phenomenology and Existential Philosophy 7 The Hague:
Martinus Nijhoff, 1978.

"The Strange History of Christian Paideia." Reprinted in John H. Westerhoff
III, ed. *Who Are We? The Quest for a Religious Education.* Birmingham:
Religious Education Press, 1979.

263

"Theology and Practice outside the Clerical Paradigm." In Don S. Browning, ed. *Practical Theology: The Emerging Field in Theology, the Church and the World.* New York: Harper and Row, 1982.

Edward Farley and Peter Hodgson. "Scripture and Tradition." In Peter Hodgson and Robert King, eds. *Christian Theology: An Introduction to Its Traditions and Tasks.* Philadelphia: Fortress Press, 1982.

"Toward a Contemporary Theology of Human Being." In J. William Angell and E. Pendleton Banks, eds. *Images of Man: Studies in Religion and Anthropology.* Macon, Ga.: Mercer University Press, 1984. Chapter 4, pp. 55–78.

"Systematische Theologie in einer systemfeindliche Zeit." In Johannes B. Bauer, ed. *Entwürfe der Theologie.* Graz: Verlag Styria: 1985, 95–125.

"Interpreting Situations: An Essay in Practical Theology." Lewis Mudge and Daniel Poling, eds. *Formation and Reflection: The Promise of Practical Theology.* Minneapolis: Fortress Press, 1987, 1–26.

"Theocentric Ethics as a Generic Argument." In Harlan R. Beckley and Charles M. Swezey, eds. *James M. Gustafson's Theocentric Ethics: Interpretations and Assessments.* Macon, Ga.: Mercer University Press, 1988, 13–37.

"Praxis and Piety: Hermeneutics beyond the New Dualism." In Douglas A. Knight and Peter Paris, eds. *Justice and the Holy: Essays in Honor of Walter Harrelson.* Atlanta: Scholars Press, 1989.

"Practical Theology," and "Sin." In *The Dictionary of Pastoral Theology.* Nashville: Abingdon Press, 1989.

"Truth and the Wisdom of Enduring." In Daniel Guerrière, ed. *Phenomenology of the Truth Proper to Religion.* Albany: State University of New York Press, 1990.

"The Presbyterian Heritage as Modernism: Reaffirming a Forgotten Past in Hard Times." In Coalter, Mulder, and Weeks, eds. *The Presbyterian Predicament: Six Perspectives.* Louisville: Westminster John Knox Press, 1990.

"The Tragic Dilemma of Church Education." In P. Palmer, B. G. Wheeler, and J. W. Fowler. *Caring for the Commonweal: Education for Religious and Public Life.* Macon, Ga.: Mercer University Press, 1990.

D. Selected Articles

"Ideas We Live By," Thirteen Lessons in the Christian Roundtable, *Crossroads,* October–December 1958.

"Must the Gospel Be *Avant-Garde?*" *Christian Century* 75, no. 50 (1959): 43–44.

"Another View of Secularism," *Christianity and Crisis* 19, no. 5 (March 30, 1959): 43–44.

"The Church and the Social Crisis," *Crossroads,* April–June 1960.

"Professional and Lay Theology — A Dilemma," *Theology Today,* April 1961.

"The Grace and Sovereignty of God," *Presbyterian Life,* March 15, 1961.

"Dimensions of Death in the Life of Faith," *Perspective* 6, no. 1 (March 1965).

"Cutting the Tie," review of *The Empirical Theology of H. N. Wieman*, ed. R. W. Bretall, *Christian Century* 81, no. 24 (June 10, 1964).

"Does Christian Education Need the Holy Spirit? I. The Strange History of Christian *Paideia*," *Religious Education* 60, no. 5 (November–December 1965).

"Does Christian Education Need the Holy Spirit? II. The Work of the Holy Spirit in Christian Education," *Religious Education* 60, no. 6 (November–December 1965).

"The Implicit What" (Critic's Corner), reply to Paul Holmer, *Theology Today* 22, no. 3 (October 1965): 432–36.

" 'Rigid Instruction' versus Brahman, a Reply," *Religious Education*, May–June 1966.

"The Quest for an Authentic Piety" (twelve articles), *Crossroads*, January–March 1966.

"Jesus Christ in Historical and Non-Historical Schemes," *Perspectives* 9, no. 1 (Spring 1968).

"Can Revelation Be Formally Described?" *Journal of the American Academy of Religion* 37, no. 3 (September 1969).

"God as Dominator and Image-Giver: Divine Sovereignty and the New Anthropology," *Journal of Ecumenical Studies* 6, no. 3 (1969).

"Can the Nonconservative Seminaries Help the Church?" *Christian Century* 91, no. 5 (February 6, 1974).

Review, David Tracy's *Blessed Rage for Order*, in "Criticism" of *Christian Century*, April 14, 1976.

"Phenomenology and Pastoral Care," *Pastoral Psychology* 26, no. 2 (Winter 1977): 95–112.

Review, Langdon Gilkey's *Reaping the Whirlwind: A Christian Interpretation of History*, in *Religious Studies Review* 4, no. 4 (1979).

"Phenomenology and the Problem of Metaphysics," *Man and World* 12, no. 4 (1979).

"The Curricular Pattern and Its Rationale as an Issue in the Reform of North American Theological Education," *Ministerial Formation*, 1981.

"The Reform of Theological Education as a Theological Task," in *Theological Education*, Spring 1981, and in *Journal of Supervision and Training for Ministry*, 1981.

"Theological Education: Some Strategies for Change," *Trinity Seminary Review* 6 (June 1984): 116–22.

"Can Church Education Be Theological Education?" *Theology Today* 42, no. 2 (July 1985): 158–71.

"The Place of Theology in the Study of Religion," *Religious Studies and Theology* 5, no. 3 (September 1985): 9–29.

"Comment on David Tracy, Hermeneutics as Discourse Analysis: Sociality, History, Religion," in Marco M. Olivetti, ed., *Archivo di Filosofia* 54, nos. 1–3 (1986): 285–300.

"The Passion of Knowledge and the Sphere of Faith: A Study in Objectivity," *Theological Education* 25, no. 2 (Spring 1989): 9–29.

"The Modernist Element in Protestantism," *Theology Today* 47, no. 2 (July 1990): 131–45.

"Phenomenology," in D. Musser and Joseph L. Price, eds., *New Handbook of Christian Theology*. Nashville: Abingdon Press, 1992.

"Thinking toward the World: A Case for Philosophical Pluralism in Theology," *American Journal of Theology and Philosophy,* January 1993.

"Re-thinking the God-terms: Tradition, the God-term of Remembering," *Toronto Journal of Theology* 9, no. 1 (1993): 67–77.

"Preaching the Bible and Preaching the Gospel," *Theology Today,* Spring 1994.

"The Place of Poetics in Theological Education: A Heuristic Inquiry," and "Music and Human Existence, a Response," both in *Theological Education*, special issue on Sacred Imagination, the Arts and Theological Education, 31, no. 1 (Autumn 1994): 133–48, 175–81.

Index

The index was prepared by James O. Duke.